Binxing Fang, Yan Jia (Eds.)
Online Social Network Analysis

Also of interest

Online Social Network Analysis, Volume 1
B. Fang, Y. Jia, 2018
ISBN 978-3-11-059606-9, e-ISBN (PDF) 978-3-11-059937-4,
e-ISBN (EPUB) 978-3-11-059807-0

Online Social Network Analysis, Volume 3
B. Fang, Y. Jia, 2018
ISBN 978-3-11-059784-4, e-ISBN (PDF) 978-3-11-059943-5,
e-ISBN (EPUB) 978-3-11-059793-6

Web Applications with Javascript or Java, Volume 1
G. Wagner, M. Diaconescu, 2018
ISBN 978-3-11-049993-3, e-ISBN (PDF) 978-3-11-049995-7,
e-ISBN (EPUB) 978-3-11-049724-3

Web Applications with Javascript or Java, Volume 2
G. Wagner, M. Diaconescu, 2018
ISBN 978-3-11-050024-0, e-ISBN (PDF) 978-3-11-050032-5,
e-ISBN (EPUB) 978-3-11-049756-4

Trusted Computing
D. Feng, 2017
ISBN 978-3-11-047604-0, e-ISBN (PDF) 978-3-11-047759-7,
e-ISBN (EPUB) 978-3-11-047609-5

Online Social Network Analysis

Volume 2: Groups and Interaction

Edited by
Binxing Fang, Yan Jia

DE GRUYTER

电子工业出版社·
PUBLISHING HOUSE OF ELECTRONICS INDUSTRY
http://www.phei.com.cn

Editors
Prof. Binxing Fang
Chinese Academy of Engineering
Building A, Tri-Tower
No. 66-1 Zhongguancun East Road
100190 Beijing, Haidian District
China

Prof. Yan Jia
National University of Defense Technology
No. 109 Deya Road, Kaifu Strict
410073 Changsha, China

ISBN 978-3-11-075629-6
e-ISBN (PDF) 978-3-11-059941-1
e-ISBN (EPUB) 978-3-11-059792-9

Library of Congress Control Number: 2018954390

Bibliographic information published by the Deutsche Nationalbibliothek
The Deutsche Nationalbibliothek lists this publication in the Deutsche Nationalbibliografie; detailed
bibliographic data are available on the Internet at http://dnb.dnb.de.

Preface: Groups and Interaction

Volume 2 of the book focuses on the second core factor, namely, "groups and interaction," which consists of four chapters. Chapter 1 is about the analysis of user behaviors, Chapter 2 is about the social network sentiment analysis, Chapter 3 is about the individual influence analysis and its techniques, and Chapter 4 is about the group aggregation and influence mechanism.

The following experts and scholars who participated in the data collection, content arrangement, and achievement contribution of this volume are sincerely appreciated: Zhaoyun Ding, Xiaomeng Wang, Bin Wang, Yezheng Liu, Xiaodong Liu, Shenghong Li, Aiping Li, Lei Li, Shiyu Du, Peng Wu, Xiuzhen Chen, Wei Chen, Yang Yang, Lumin Zhang, Peng Shi, and Yuanchun Jiang.

Thanks to Associate Professor Shudong Li for the careful coordination and arrangement for writing this volume, and also to Weihong Han and Shuqiang Yang for reviewing and proofreading.

https://doi.org/10.1515/9783110599411-201

Contents

Contents

List of Contributors

Prof. Xueqi Cheng
Institute of Computing Technology
Chinese Academy of Sciences
No. 6 Zhongguancun Kexueyuan South Road
100190 Beijing, China

Prof. Binxing Fang
Chinese Academy of Engineering
Building A, Tri-Tower
No. 66-1 Zhongguancun East Road
100190 Beijing, China

Prof. Li Guo
Institute of Information Engineering
Chinese Academy of Sciences
No. 89 Linzhuang Road
100093 Beijing, China

Prof. Changjun Hu
University of Science and Technology Beijing
No. 30 Xueyuan Road
100083 Beijing, China

Prof. Yan Jia
National University of Defense Technology
No. 109 Deya Road, Kaifu District
410073 Changsha, China

Prof. Jianhua Li
Prof. Shanghai Jiaotong University
Software Building
No. 800 Dongchuan Road
200240 Shanghai, China

Prof. Xiangke Liao
National University of Defense Technology
No. 109 Deya Road, Kaifu District
410073 Changsha, China

Prof. Jiayin Qi
Shanghai University of International Business
and Economics
Room 338, Bocui Building
No. 1900 Wenxiang Road
201620 Shanghai, China

Prof. Xindong Wu
Hefei University of Technology
No. 193, Tunxi Road
230009 Hefei, China

Prof. Jin Xu
Peking University
No. 5 Yiheyuan Road
100871 Beijing, China

Prof. Shanlin Yang
Hefei University of Technology
No. 193, Tunxi Road
230009 Hefei, China

Prof. Hongli Zhang
Harbin Institute of Technology
No. 92 Xidazhi Street
150001 Harbin, China

Prof. Bin Zhou
National University of Defense Technology
No. 109 Deya Road, Kaifu District
410073 Changsha, China

https://doi.org/10.1515/9783110599411-202

Shanlin Yang

1 Analysis of user behavior

1.1 Introduction

As an emerging information technology, online social network has become an important part in everyday life. By assessing different types of social network technologies, services, and applications, people select the most suitable technology for social communication, entertainment, and information access. Social network user behavior refers to the adoption and usage of social network services based on a comprehensive assessment of user needs, social influences, and technological characteristics of social network.

User behavior is important in the research on online social network. Existing research is mainly based on the following two thoughts. The first group considers online social network as a specific information technology and researches adoption behavior, refusal behavior, and user loyalty. The second group considers online social network as a platform that provides a wide selection of services and applications and researches the characteristics and laws presented in the usage of these services and applications.

Considering online social network as a specific information technology, researchers have classified social network user behavior into several progressive levels, such as adoption, usage, and loyalty, and consider that adoption is the antecedent of the usage behavior of actual user (AU), while loyalty is the user's trust in, dependence on, and commitment to social network technology as well as the continuous usage behavior arising therefrom [2, 8, 13, 19]. Hence, researchers have employed classical behavioral research theories such as as the Technology Acceptance Model (TAM), Theory of Planned Behavior (TPB), Theory of Expectation Confirmation, and Flow Theory to explore the influence of demographic variables, personality traits, emotional factors, cognitive factors, motivation factors, as well as social environment, physical environment, and technological environment on the adoption and loyalty of online social network users.

Considering online social network as a platform that provides various services and applications, researchers have extensively studied individual usage behavior, including self-presentation, microblog posts, search, browse, and comments, as well as social interaction behavior, including relationship establishment and content selection [26, 29, 33, 45, 47]. For this research, statistical methods, econometrics methods, queuing theory, etc., have been used to analyze the distribution of social network user behavior and its temporal and spatial laws, thereby revealing the inherent mechanism of content generation behavior and content consumption behavior in online social network and extensively exploring the relationship selection laws, content selection laws, and temporal laws of social interaction in online social network.

https://doi.org/10.1515/9783110599411-001

This chapter aims to introduce the classical theories, principal methods, fundamental processes, and conclusions regarding social network user usage behavior with adoption, usage, and loyalty as the main clues; introduce the influential factors, modeling methods, and verification processes for adoption behavior and user loyalty of social network; introduce the general laws of social network usage behavior and modeling methods for social network content generation behavior and content consumption behavior; introduce the analysis methods for the relationship selection behavior, content selection behavior, and temporal laws of social interaction. The final section summarizes the findings presented in the chapter.

1.2 Online social network user adoption and loyalty

1.2.1 Online social network user adoption

Online social network adoption refers to users' adoption behavior of online social network services based on a comprehensive assessment of their needs and motivations, social influences, and technological characteristics of online social network. According to the Diffusion Theory of Innovations (DTI) proposed by Rogers, it is essential for subsequent diffusion of online social network to be adopted and tried by as many users as possible in the early stage. At present, researchers use multiple theories to study the adoption behavior mechanism of online social network users, in which TAM and TPB are the most popular.

1. Online social network user adoption models based on the technology acceptance model

TAM, proposed by Davis Fred [1], is one of the most classic models in the field of information systems. As shown in Figure 1.1, TAM assumes that users' actual adoption and usage behavior are directly and positively influenced by their use intention, which is in turn influenced by their use attitude and perceived usefulness (PU); use attitude is influenced by PU and perceived ease of use (PEOU) whereas PEOU influences PU to a certain extent. In TAM, PU refers to the degree to which a user believes the technology will increase his/her work performance and PEOU refers to the degree to which a user believes that a specific information system is effortless to

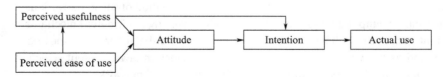

Figure 1.1: TAM proposed by Davis.

use. TAM is widely used to explain and predict user adoption and acceptance behavior of new technologies, products, and services, and yields good results. Therefore, it can be applied for researching adoption behavior in online social network.

When researching adoption behavior in online social network using TAM, it is necessary to extend the traditional TAM as it only considers influences from four internal psychological factors while neglecting those from others such as users' emotions and personality traits, as along with external social factors such as social regulations and interpersonal influence; for example., Kwon et al. [2] studied user adoption behavior in online social network based on TAM using the following process.

Step 1: Reference review and model construction. From a review and analysis of relevant reference systems of TAM, social identity (SI) theory, altruism (ALT), telepresence (TELE), etc., a research model was proposed, as shown in Figure 1.2; subsequently, the following hypotheses on relations between various variables were inferred and demonstrated: SI will have a positive effect on the PEOU/PU/PE (perceived encouragement) of a social network service (H1a, H1b, H1c); ALT will have a positive effect on the PEOU/PU/PE of a social network service (H2a, H2b, H2c); TELE will have a positive effect on the PEOU/PU/PE of a social network service (H3a, H3b, H3c); PEOU will have a positive effect on the PU of a social network service (H4); PE will have a positive effect on the PU of a social network service (H5); PEOU will have a positive effect on the AU of a social network service (H6); PU will have a positive effect on the AU of a social network service (H7); and PE will have a positive effect on the AU of a social network service. In this model, SI is defined as an individual's knowledge of belonging to a certain social group; ALT is defined as an inclination of helping others; TELE refers to an individual's feeling of being present in a virtual environment generated by media; and PE refers to the encouragement and support perceived by an individual.

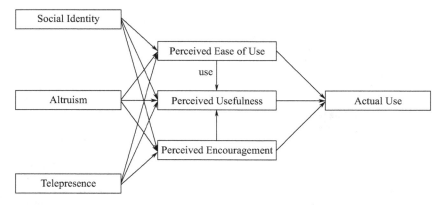

Figure 1.2: Research model of Kwon et al. (2010).

Step 2: Scale development and data acquisition. Measurement items for PEOU, PU, PE, SI, ALT, TELE, AU scales, and other variables were developed based on a related research (Table 1.1), which was used to conduct a survey on an SNS user group among employees of South Korean companies and collected 229 pieces of data for verifying the model assumptions. 53.4% of the sample comprised males and 66.2% were between the ages of 20 and 29.

Table 1.1: Measurement items used by Kwon et al. (2010).

Variable	Measurement items	Scale
PU	Using the SNS enables me to acquire more information or meet more people	1-2-3-4-5-6-7
	Using the SNS would improve my efficiency in sharing information and connecting with others	1-2-3-4-5-6-7
	The SNS is a useful service for communication	1-2-3-4-5-6-7
	The SNS is a useful service for interaction of members	1-2-3-4-5-6-7
PEOU	Learning to use the SNS is easy for me	1-2-3-4-5-6-7
	The process of using the SNS is clear and understandable	1-2-3-4-5-6-7
	I find it easy to use the SNS	1-2-3-4-5-6-7
PE	People whom I meet in the SNS tend to give me affirmative evaluation	1-2-3-4-5-6-7
	People whom I meet in the SNS tend to be satisfied with me	1-2-3-4-5-6-7
	People whom I meet in the SNS give me great encouragement	1-2-3-4-5-6-7
	People whom I meet in the SNS tend to be aware of my existence	1-2-3-4-5-6-7
SI	As a member of the community, my position is very important to me	1-2-3-4-5-6-7
	As a member of the community, I am the type of person who likes to engage in my community	1-2-3-4-5-6-7
	Activities in my community are an important part in my life	1-2-3-4-5-6-7
ALT	I tend to encourage people who are in a real crisis or need	1-2-3-4-5-6-7
	I usually help people who ask me for solution	1-2-3-4-5-6-7
	I give congratulation when people tell me good news	1-2-3-4-5-6-7
TELE	When exiting the SNS, I felt like I actually met other people	1-2-3-4-5-6-7
	I felt that the SNS creates a new world	1-2-3-4-5-6-7
	While using the SNS, I felt I was in a different society	1-2-3-4-5-6-7
	While using the SNS, the SNS world was more real or present to me compared to the "real world"	1-2-3-4-5-6-7
AU	I tend to use the SNS frequently	1-2-3-4-5-6-7
	I spend a lot of time on SNS	1-2-3-4-5-6-7
	I exerted myself to SNS	1-2-3-4-5-6-7

Note: Measurement of all variables adopts 7-level Likert scale (1, Strongly disagree; 7, Strongly agree).

Step 3: Data analysis. The research mainly used LISREL 8.7 and other software to conduct scale reliability and validity analysis and structural equation modeling (SEM) approach. Reliability and validity analysis refer to the process of verifying reliability and validity through confirmatory factor analysis (CFA), calculating Cronbach's α, among other methods. The scale has good validity as factor loads of most measurement items are larger than 0.7. As shown in Table 1.2, the scale also has good reliability as all Cronbach's α are larger than 0.7. SEM refers to the process of verifying complex models with multiple variables through partial least squares as well as other parameter evaluation methods to discover the significant relations between variables. Analysis results are as follows:

1. Despite AGFI being slightly smaller than the reference value, all remaining index values reflecting model fitness are larger than the reference value, indicating a good fit of the model (see Table 1.3).
2. Except that research hypotheses H1a, H2b, and H3b are untenable, the relation hypotheses between all remaining variables are tenable (see Table 1.4).

Table 1.2: Cronbach's α of variables used by Kwon et al. (2010).

Variables	SI	ALT	TELE	PU	PEOU	PE	AU
α	0.81	0.88	0.80	0.90	0.86	0.89	0.78

Table 1.3: Fitting degree for the model used by Kwon et al. (2010).

Index of fitting degree	χ^2/df	GFI	AGFI	NFI	NNFI	CFI	RMSEA
Index value	2.25	0.84	0.79	0.93	0.95	0.96	0.07
Reference value	≤3	≥0.9	≥0.8	≥0.9	≥0.9	≥0.9	≤0.10

Note: See *Structural Equation Modeling – Operation and Application of AMOS* written by Minglong Wu for computing formula of various indexes.

Step 4: Conclusion and discussion. According to data analysis results, TELE and ALT only influence PU indirectly through PEOU and PE, whereas SI has a significant direct effect on PEOU and PE. In addition, SNS can be viewed as a type of relationship-oriented information system with the potential to become a task-oriented information system. According to users and their orientation for SNS, information systems can be classified into four types, as shown in Figure 1.3.

In general, empirical research on adoption behavior in online social network based on TAM has been conducted by following the above steps, with the main difference being the addition of new variables when extending TAM. For example, Ernst et al. [3] constructed an SNS user adoption model by extending TAM using two variables:

Table 1.4: Estimated value for model parameter and verification results for hypothesis used by Kwon et al. (2010).

Dependent variables	Independent variables	Standardized coefficients (β)	Supported or not
PEOU ($R^2 = 0.27$)	SI	0.12	H1a (No)
	ALT	0.22**	H2a (Yes)
	TELE	0.39**	H3a (Yes)
PE ($R^2 = 0.50$)	SI	0.24**	H1c (Yes)
	ALT	0.29**	H2c (Yes)
	TELE	0.46**	H3c (Yes)
PU ($R^2 = 0.48$)	PEOU	0.44**	H4 (Yes)
	PE	0.47**	H5 (Yes)
	SI	0.01**	H1b (Yes)
	ALT	−0.11	H2b (No)
	TELE	0.01	H3b (No)
AU ($R^2 = 0.60$)	PEOU	0.39**	H6 (Yes)
	PE	0.31*	H8 (Yes)
	PU	0.21**	H7 (Yes)

Note: $* \, p < 0.05$, $** \, p < 0.01$.

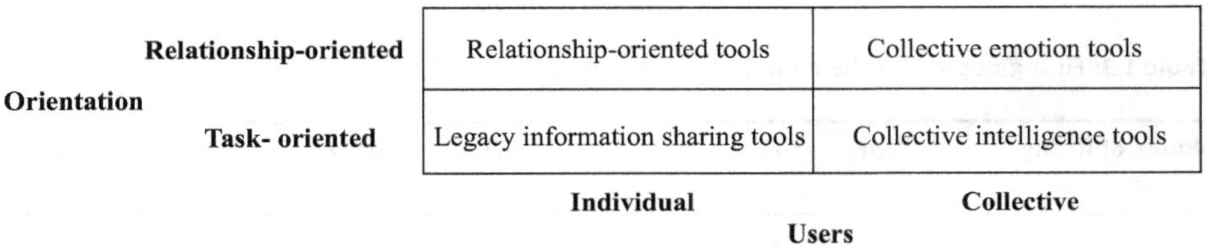

	Relationship-oriented	Relationship-oriented tools	Collective emotion tools
Orientation			
	Task-oriented	Legacy information sharing tools	Collective intelligence tools
		Individual	Collective
		Users	

Figure 1.3: Information system classification based on orientation and users.

perceived enjoyment and perceived belonging (Figure 1.4). They verified relation hypothesis among all variables in the model by empirical research. Nikou Shahrokh [4] proposed a mobile SNS user adoption model by integrating mobility, critical mass, use context, social influence, habit, and other variables into TAM (Figure 1.5). As shown in the empirical research, mobility influences use intention indirectly through PEOU; critical mass influences use intention indirectly through social influence; and social influence, PEOU, and habit have a significant direct effect on use intention. Deb Sledgianowski et al. [5] proposed a research model based on TAM by adding four variables, including perceived playfulness, perceived normative pressure, trust, and critical mass, as direct influencing factors of adoption intention. According to empirical research, they discovered that these factors have significant influence on adoption intention, with perceived playfulness having a significant direct influence on

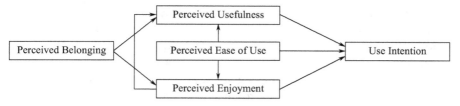

Figure 1.4: Research model used by Ernst et al. (2013).

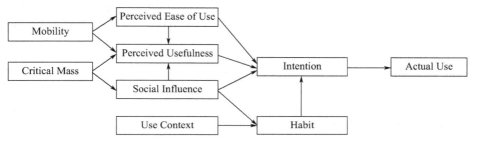

Figure 1.5: Mobile SNS user adoption model.

actual adoption. Bao et al. [6] constructed an SNS user adoption model by adding perceived popularity into TAM to reflect social influence while using perceived popularity as the reason for PU, PEOU, and use attitude. Their research verified the relation hypothesis among all variables included the model.

2. Online Social Network User Adoption Models Based on the Theory of Planned Behavior

TPB, proposed by Icek Ajzen [7], is a classic theory applied extensively to research on human behavior. As shown in Figure 1.6, TPB posits that behaviors are directly driven by behavioral intention which is determined by attitude, perceived behavioral control (PBC), and subjective norm (SN). Attitude is defined as individuals' positive or negative evaluations about performing a target behavior. PBC refers to an individual's perception of his/her resources and capacity to perform a target behavior. SN refers to an individual's perceptions of social pressure from important referents to perform or not perform the behavior.

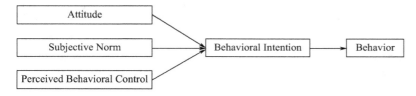

Figure 1.6: TPB proposed by Icek Ajzen.

Considering that TPB shows the effects of both individuals' internal psychological factors (attitude and PBC) and external social influence factors (SN) on behavioral intention, it may be suitable for explaining user adoption behavior in online social network. Overall, researchers usually apply TPB to study user adoption behavior in online social network using the following steps. First, new variables are integrated into the model, as shown in Figure 1.6, to construct a new research model; second, a scale is developed to investigate and obtain empirical data; third, the model is tested by using statistical methods, such as SEM approach and regression analysis; and finally, conclusions are drawn according to analysis results discussions. For example, Baker et al. [8] studied user adoption behavior in online social network on the basis of TPB using the following steps.

Step 1: Reference review and model construction. Based on the review of TPB, SI theory, self-categorization theory, and research on self-esteem in personality psychology, the authors pointed out that the factors influencing SNS user adoption behavior include attitude, PBC, SN, group norm, and self-esteem. Hence, they constructed a regression model using the above factors as independent variables and adoption intention as dependent variable. Group norm refers to behavioral principles observed by the members of a group. Group norm affects the behaviors of group members as an individual needs to observe group norm to gain the group's recognition. Self-esteem, as an important part of self-concept, refers to an overall positive or negative evaluation of the self, and has a fundamental influence on individual behavior.

Step 2: Scale development and data acquisition. The authors developed a scale for measuring model variables on the basis of a previous research. Subsequently, they conducted an investigation among Australian juniors and obtained 160 pieces of valid sample data (boys accounted for 36% of the data with an average age of 14.36 years). Attitude scale was a seven-level semantic differential response scale with five items (e.g., 1, unpleasant; 7, pleasant). SN scale was a seven-level Likert scale with two items (e.g., "Most people who are important to me want me to socialize online in the future by SNS like Facebook;" 1, strongly disagree; −7, strongly agree). PBC scale was a seven-level Likert scale with four items (e.g., "I have complete control over whether to socialize online in the future by SNS like Facebook;" 1, strongly disagree −7, strongly agree). Group norm scale was a seven-level Likert scale with four items (e.g., "Most of my friends will socialize online in the future by SNS like Facebook;" 1, strongly disagree; −7, strongly agree). Self-esteem scale, proposed by Rosenberg, included only one item (e.g., "I think that I have a number of good qualities;" 1, strongly disagree; −4, strongly agree).

Step 3: Data analysis. Descriptive statistical analysis, correlation analysis, and hierarchical regression analysis was conducted using SPSS (Table 1.5 and Table 1.6). Descriptive statistical analysis gives mean (M) and standard deviation (SD); correlation analysis gives correlation coefficient between variables and the significance level; and hierarchical regression analysis reveals the influence of various factors as independent variables on use intention for SNS as dependent variable. As shown in Table 1.5, attitude, PBC, SN, and group norm have significant positive correlation with use intention for SNS. As further shown in Table 1.6, attitude, PBC, and group norm have significant influence on use intention for SNS, with group norm having the largest influence, followed by attitude and PBC.

Table 1.5: Mean, SD, and correlation coefficient for variables used by Rosland et al. (2010).

Variables	M	SD	1	2	3	4	5	6
Attitude	4.73	1.28	1	0.47***	0.26**	0.51***	0.43***	0.00
Subjective norm	4.28	1.42		1	0.25**	0.47***	0.61***	−.05
PBC	5.35	1.32			1	0.29***	0.24**	−.18*
Intention	3.53	1.69				1	0.59***	0.11
Group norm	4.58	1.33					1	0.09
Self-esteem	2.12	0.54						1

Note: * $p < 0.05$, ** $p < 0.01$, *** $p < 0.001$.

Table 1.6: Results of hierarchical regression analysis provided by Rosland et al. (2010).

Variables	Unstandardized regression coefficients B	Standardized Error (SE)	Standardized regression coefficients β	R^2
Step 1				0.35***
Attitude	0.45	0.10	0.34***	
Subjective norm	0.33	0.09	0.28***	
PBC	0.19	0.09	0.14*	
Step 2				
Attitude	0.36	0.09	0.27***	0.45***
Subjective norm	0.10	0.10	0.08	
PBC	0.17	0.08	0.13*	
Group norm	0.49	0.10	0.38***	
Self-esteem	0.32	0.19	0.10	

Note: * $p < 0.05$, ** $p < 0.01$, *** $p < 0.001$.

Step 4: Conclusion and discussion. According to statistical analysis results, attitude and PBC have a significant influence on teenagers' use intention for SNS, thus supporting the validity of behavior prediction by TPB to a certain degree. However, SN has a nonsignificant influence on teenagers' use intention for SNS, which is not in conformity with other studies based on TPB. This variation may be because, compared with SN, the newly-added variable, group norm, can better reflect the influence of pressure from social norm on adoption behavior because the influence of SN on use intention becomes nonsignificant after group norm is added into the regression model. In addition, self-esteem has a nonsignificant direct influence on use intention for SNS, which also varies from previous studies, possibly because self-esteem needs other intermediary variables to indirectly influence behavior intention, which requires further verification by future research.

In addition to the study by Baker et al. (2010), there are other empirical studies on user adoption behavior in online social network based on TPB. They studies adopted similar procedures as Baker et al. (2010) with the main differences being added variables and statistical analysis. For instance, Pelling et al. [9] constructed a prediction model for use intention among SNS users by adding self-identity, belongingness, age, past use, and other new variables to TPB. As shown by the results of hierarchical regression analysis, attitude, SN, and self-identity have a significant positive influence on high-level use intention for SNS. Chang et al. [10] constructed a model by using five types of adoption motives as the antecedent for attitude in their research on adoption behavior of SNS users in China based on TPB. As shown by the results of SEM analysis, information, entertainment, new acquaintance, and conformity significantly influence the use attitude for SNS, and users' attitude, PBC, and SN significantly influence the adoption intention of SNS user. Leng et al. [11] also proposed an adoption model of SNS user by integrating TPB and TAM (Figure 1.7). As shown by the results of SEM analysis, PU, attitude, and PBC have a significant positive influence on adoption intention, and adoption intention significantly influences actual adoption.

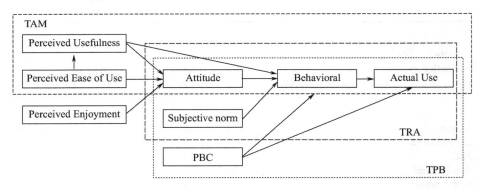

Figure 1.7: Research model used by Leng et al. (2011).

1.2.2 Online social network user loyalty

User retention is of significant importance to online social network service providers because the eventual success of social network depends on the continuance of usage rather than first-time use. However, competition pressure due to constant emergence of new network services makes it difficult to maintain online social network user loyalty. Therefore, it is very important to investigate the mechanism of online social network user loyalty. So far, multiple theories have been applied to user loyalty research, including the widely-accepted Expectation Confirmation Theory (ECT) and Flow Theory.

1. Online social network user loyalty models based on expectation confirmation theory

ECT, first proposed by Oliver (1980), is the basic theory for researching consumer satisfaction. As stated in ECT, consumers have certain expectations from products or services and they compare perceived actual performance after purchase with previous expectations to evaluate confirmation. If yes, consumers are satisfied otherwise they remain unsatisfied. Consumer satisfaction degree further influences the intention and behavior of repurchasing products or services. By combining ECT and characteristics of information system, Bhattacharjee [12] proposed expectation confirmation model of information system continuance (ECM-ISC). As shown in Figure 1.8, ECM-ISC posits that the expectation confirmation of information system users influences their intention to continue using the information system by influencing their PU and degree of satisfaction. At present, ECM-ISC is widely used in investigating user loyalty or continuous use behavior and has become one of the most popular theories in the field of information technology.

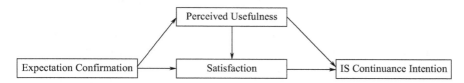

Figure 1.8: Expectation confirmation model used by Anol Bhattacherjee (2001).

For research on user loyalty in online social network based on ECT, a usual method is to add other variables to ECM-ISC, verify such a model according to the process of scale development → data acquisition → data processing, and finally, reach a conclusion based on a discussion of analysis results. Young et al. [13] researched user loyalty in online social network based on ECT according to the continuous usage behavior in Cyworld, the biggest social network in South Korea. Their research process and conclusions are discussed below.

Step 1: Reference review and model hypothesis. After reviewing the reference about ECT and combining the results of regret theory and self-image congruity, Young et al. proposed the research model, as shown in Figure 1.9, and made detailed inference and demonstration on relation hypotheses among various variables in the model, including the additional variables of regret, self-image congruity, perceived enjoyment, and past use. Regret refers to the degree to which users regret their selection of using Cyworld; self-image congruity refers to the degree to which users deem using Cyworld as congruent with their images; perceived enjoyment refers to the degree to which users

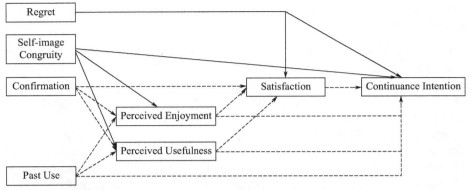

Note: --→ Path confirmed in IS studies; —→ Path in question.

Figure 1.9: Research model used by Young et al. (2009).

deem using Cyworld as an enjoyable experience; and past use refers to the situation where users used Cyworld previously. The model includes the following 13 research hypotheses: Satisfaction positively influences continuous usage intention of online social network service (H1); Confirmation of expectations positively influences satisfaction with online social network service (H2); PU positively influences satisfaction with online social network service (H3); Perceived enjoyment positively influences satisfaction with online social network service (H4); PU positively influences continuous usage intention of online social network service (H5); Perceived enjoyment positively influences continuous usage intention of online social network service (H6); Confirmation of expectations positively influences PU (H7); Confirmation of expectations positively influences perceived enjoyment (H8); Self-image congruity with online social network service positively influences continuous usage intention of online social network service (H9); Self-image congruity with online social network service positively influences PU (H10); Self-image congruity with online social network service positively influences perceived enjoyment (H11); Regret negatively influences satisfaction with online social network service use (H12); and Regret negatively influences continuous usage intention of online social network service (H13).

Step 2: Scale development and data acquisition. Based on previous research, Young et al. developed a scale for measuring various variables in the above model (Table 1.7). They conducted a field survey among Cyworld users in a university and obtained 349 pieces of valid sample data (47.9% of the data were from males, 72.8% of the users were between the ages of 20 and 29, and 81.8% of the users had over 1 year of use experience).

Step 3: Data analysis. The reliability and validity of the scale was verified by CFA and model hypothesis by SEM. The results of the descriptive statistical analysis and CFA are shown in Table 1.8. Convergent validity is acceptable as the composite reliability of all variables is higher than 0.70, and the average variance extracted (AVE) is higher

Table 1.7: Survey measurement items used by Young et al. (2009).

Variables	Items	Scale
Regret	I regret the selection of using Cyworld	Strongly disagree 1-2-3-4-5-6-7 Strongly agree
	I very much regret the selection of using Cyworld	Strongly disagree 1-2-3-4-5-6-7 Strongly agree
	I should have selected other social networks	Strongly disagree 1-2-3-4-5-6-7 Strongly agree
Self-image congruity	Visiting Cyworld helps maintain my image and character	Strongly disagree 1-2-3-4-5-6-7 Strongly agree
	Visiting Cyworld helps in reflecting who I am	Strongly disagree 1-2-3-4-5-6-7 Strongly agree
	Visiting Cyworld fits well with my image	Strongly disagree 1-2-3-4-5-6-7 Strongly agree
Confirmation	My experience with using Cyworld was better than I expected	Strongly disagree 1-2-3-4-5-6-7 Strongly agree
	The service level provided by Cyworld was better than I expected	Strongly disagree 1-2-3-4-5-6-7 Strongly agree
	Overall, most of my expectations from using Cyworld were confirmed	Strongly disagree 1-2-3-4-5-6-7 Strongly agree
Perceived enjoyment	Using Cyworld is enjoyable	Strongly disagree 1-2-3-4-5-6-7 Strongly agree
	Using Cyworld is pleasurable	Strongly disagree 1-2-3-4-5-6-7 Strongly agree
	I think it is interesting to use Cyworld	Strongly disagree 1-2-3-4-5-6-7 Strongly agree
PU	Using Cyworld improves my productivity in managing personal information	Strongly disagree 1-2-3-4-5-6-7 Strongly agree
	Using Cyworld improves my efficiency in managing my personal information	Strongly disagree 1-2-3-4-5-6-7 Strongly agree
	Overall, Cyworld is useful in managing my personal information	Strongly disagree 1-2-3-4-5-6-7 Strongly agree
Satisfaction	How do you feel about your overall experience of using Cyworld:	Very dissatisfied 1-2-3-4-5-6-7 Very satisfied Very displeased 1-2-3-4-5-6-7 Very pleased Very frustrated 1-2-3-4-5-6-7 Very contented

(continued)

Table 1.7 (continued)

Variables	Items	Scale
		Very terrible 1-2-3-4-5-6-7 Very delighted
Continuous usage intention	I intend to continue using Cyworld rather than discontinue its use	Strongly disagree 1-2-3-4-5-6-7 Strongly agree
	My intentions are to continue using Cyworld rather than use any alternative means	Strongly disagree 1-2-3-4-5-6-7 Strongly agree
	If possible, I would like to discontinue my use of Cyworld (R)	Strongly disagree 1-2-3-4-5-6-7 Strongly agree
Past use	On average, how frequently have you visited Cyworld over the past month?1 = less than once a month; 2 = once a month; 3 = a few times a month; 4 = a few times a week; 5 = about once a day; and 6 = several times a day	
	On average, how much time have you spent per day visiting Cyworld over the past month?1 = Less than 10 min; 2 = 10–20 min; 3 = 20–30 min; 4 = 30 min to 1 h; 5 = 1–2 h; 6 = 2–3 h; 7 = More than 3 h	

Table 1.8: Variable mean, SD, CR, and AVE used by Young et al. (2009).

Variable	M	SD	CR	1	2	3	4	5	6	7	8
Regret	2.61	1.20	0.92	0.89							
Self-image congruity	4.29	1.45	0.93	−0.29	0.91						
Confirmation	5.00	1.22	0.94	−0.46	0.45	0.91					
Perceived enjoyment	4.70	1.29	0.95	−0.33	0.56	0.58	0.93				
PU	5.16	1.16	0.94	−0.35	0.42	0.52	0.49	0.90			
Satisfaction	4.52	1.32	0.96	−0.20	0.30	0.34	0.43	0.33	0.94		
Continuous usage intention	5.11	1.38	0.91	−0.55	0.46	0.46	0.53	0.54	0.33	0.87	
Past use	3.69	1.68	0.87	−0.23	0.38	0.38	0.43	0.25	0.18	0.44	0.88

Note: Values on the diagonal are the square roots of AVE.

than 0.50. In addition, the square roots of all AVEs are larger than all other cross correlations, suggesting adequate discriminant validity. As shown in Table 1.9, all research hypotheses are verified, except H2 and H12.

Step 4: Conclusion and discussion. Overall, this research contributes to the online social network service continuance by demonstrating that self-image congruity and regret can be seamlessly incorporated into the ECM to explain continuous usage

Table 1.9: Estimated value for model parameter and hypothesis verification results used by Young et al. (2009).

Effects	Causes	Estimated value for model parameter	Hypothesis verification results (Supported or not?)
PU	Past use	0.018	(No)
	Confirmation	0.411***	H7 (Yes)
	Self-image congruity	0.231***	H10 (Yes)
Perceived enjoyment	Past use	0.177***	
	Confirmation	0.365***	H8 (Yes)
	Self-image congruity	0.331***	H11 (Yes)
Satisfaction	Confirmation	0.098	H2 (No)
	PU	0.131**	H3 (Yes)
	Perceived enjoyment	0.305***	H4 (Yes)
	Regret	−0.005	H12 (No)
Continuous usage intention	Past use	0.203***	
	PU	0.243***	H5 (Yes)
	Perceived enjoyment	0.140**	H6 (Yes)
	Satisfaction	0.063*	H1 (Yes)
	Self-image congruity	0.080*	H9 (Yes)
	Regret	−0.338***	H13 (Yes)

Note: $* p < 0.05$, $** p < 0.01$, $*** p < 0.001$.

behavior of online social network service. Contrary to expectation, the negative effect of regret on satisfaction is not significant, which could be partly because the impact of regret on satisfaction is significant only under negative confirmation (Taylor, 1997), but most respondents' expectations from using Cyworld in this sample were confirmed as positive (M = 5.00, SD = 1.22). In addition, the insignificant effect of confirmation on satisfaction and the weak effect of satisfaction on continuous usage intention are possibly due to behavioral habit [Kim et al. (2005), Limayem et al (2007)]. In the above research, approximately 80% of the respondents visited Cyworld a few times a week and 75% used it more than 10 min each day over the last month, indicating habitual use.

In addition to the empirical research of Young et al. (2009) on the continuous usage behavior of online social network based on ECT, there are several other similar studies. These studies adopted the same research process as that of Young et al. (2009), but used different variables when constructing a model.

For instance, Yin et al. [14] developed a model by adding perceived enjoyment, structural embeddedness, perceived privacy risk, and past use into the ECM (Figure 1.10). The results show that PU, structural embeddedness, and satisfaction have a significant positive effect on continuous usage intention. Chen et al. [15] constructed their model by integrating PEOU, perceived playfulness, and perceived switching cost into the ECM (Figure 1.11). The results show that PEOU, PU, perceived playfulness, and perceived switching cost directly influence continuous usage intention in SNS. In addition, Shin et al. [16] proposed an amended model of ECM by replacing PU with perceived characteristics of innovation, which is derived from DTI. The results show that perceived characteristics of innovation is a significant influencing factor on continuous usage intention for online social network. Li [17] proposed a model by integrating the information system success model and ECM. The results show that system quality, information quality, and perceived service accessibility significantly influence satisfaction and continuous usage intention for SNS.

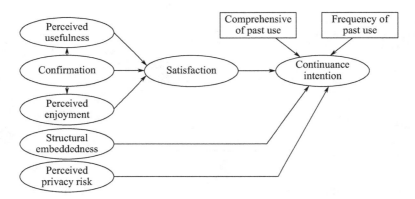

Figure 1.10: Research model used by Guopeng Yin (2010).

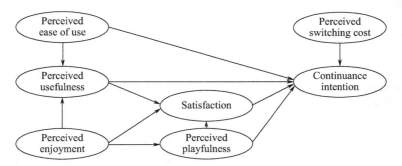

Figure 1.11: Research model used by Yao Chen (2011).

2. Online social network users' loyalty models based on flow theory

Flow theory, proposed by Csikszentmihalyi et al. [18], is important in user experience research. Flow experience refers to "the holistic experience that people feel when they act with total involvement," which is characterized by concentration on the task at hand, a loss of self-consciousness, a distorted sense of time, internal enjoyment, and so on. Flow experience is the optimal experience that may be obtained in many daily activities, and can be an autotelic experience, i.e., obtaining flow experience will become the goal of the activity, thereby motivating participants.

Some researchers investigated online social network users' loyalty based on flow theory and proposed the research model, in which flow experience was considered as an antecedent of users' satisfaction or continuous usage intention. For instance, Zhou et al. [19] researched mobile SNS users' loyalty on the basis of flow theory. The study comprised the following steps.

Step 1: Reference review and model construction. At the beginning, the authors reviewed and analyzed the theoretical basis of flow theory and trust and information system success model, and proposed a research model for mobile SNS users' loyalty (Figure 1.12). In the proposed model, information quality refers to the accuracy, comprehensiveness, and timeliness of information provided by mobile SNS service operators; and system quality refers to the reliability, response speed, and ease of use of mobile SNS platform. Flow experience, as a second-order factor, comprises three dimensions, i.e., perceived enjoyment, perceived control, and attention focus. The model considers the following hypotheses: The information quality of mobile SNS significantly influences user trust (H1); the information quality of mobile SNS significantly influences flow experience (H2); the system quality of mobile SNS significantly influences user trust (H3); the system quality of mobile SNS significantly influences flow experience (H4); user trust significantly influences flow experience (H5); user trust significantly influences his/her loyalty for mobile SNS (H6); and flow experience significantly influences user loyalty for mobile SNS (H7).

Step 2: Scale development and data acquisition. Based on the results of previous studies, Zhou et al. developed a scale for measuring various variables in the above

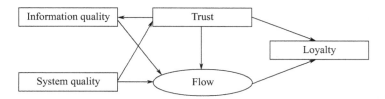

Figure 1.12: Research model used by Zhou et al. (2010).

model (Table 1.10), They conducted a survey among students in a university in eastern China and obtained 305 pieces of valid sample data (57.4% from males and 83.6% from undergraduate students).

Step 3: Data analysis. The research mainly used LISREL 8.7 and SPSS 13.0 for CFA analysis to test the reliability and validity, and SEM analysis to test the model

Table 1.10: Measurement items used by Zhou et al. (2010).

Variables	Items	Scale
Information quality	The information provided by this mobile SNS is what I need.	Strongly disagree 1-2-3-4-5-6-7 Strongly agree
	The information provided by this mobile SNS is accurate.	Strongly disagree 1-2-3-4-5-6-7 Strongly agree
	The information provided by this mobile SNS is up-to-date.	Strongly disagree 1-2-3-4-5-6-7 Strongly agree
	The information provided by this mobile SNS is comprehensive.	Strongly disagree 1-2-3-4-5-6-7 Strongly agree
System quality	This mobile SNS is reliable.	Strongly disagree 1-2-3-4-5-6-7 Strongly agree
	This mobile SNS provides fast responses to my inquiries.	Strongly disagree 1-2-3-4-5-6-7 Strongly agree
	This mobile SNS is easy to use.	Strongly disagree 1-2-3-4-5-6-7 Strongly agree
	This mobile SNS provides good navigation functions.	Strongly disagree 1-2-3-4-5-6-7 strongly agree
Perceived enjoyment	I feel that using this mobile SNS is fun.	Strongly disagree 1-2-3-4-5-6-7 Strongly agree
	I feel that using this mobile SNS is exciting.	Strongly disagree 1-2-3-4-5-6-7 Strongly agree
	I feel that using this mobile SNS is enjoyable.	Strongly disagree 1-2-3-4-5-6-7 Strongly agree
	I feel that using this mobile SNS is interesting.	Strongly disagree 1-2-3-4-5-6-7 Strongly agree
Perceived control	When using this mobile SNS, I felt calm.	Strongly disagree 1-2-3-4-5-6-7 Strongly agree
	When using this mobile SNS, I felt in control.	Strongly disagree 1-2-3-4-5-6-7 Strongly agree
	When using this mobile SNS, I felt confused.	Strongly disagree 1-2-3-4-5-6-7 Strongly agree
Attention focus	When using this mobile SNS, I was intensely absorbed in the activity.	Strongly disagree 1-2-3-4-5-6-7 Strongly agree
	When using this mobile SNS, my attention was focused on the activity.	Strongly disagree 1-2-3-4-5-6-7 Strongly agree

Table 1.10 (continued)

Variables	Items	Scale
	When using this mobile SNS, I concentrated fully on the activity.	Strongly disagree 1-2-3-4-5-6-7 Strongly agree
	When using this mobile SNS, I was deeply engrossed in the activity.	Strongly disagree 1-2-3-4-5-6-7 Strongly agree
Trust	This mobile SNS has the necessary ability to fulfil its tasks.	Strongly disagree 1-2-3-4-5-6-7 Strongly agree
	This mobile SNS will keep its promises.	Strongly disagree 1-2-3-4-5-6-7 Strongly agree
	This mobile SNS is concerned with its users' interests.	Strongly disagree 1-2-3-4-5-6-7 Strongly agree
Loyalty	I will continue using this mobile SNS.	Strongly disagree 1-2-3-4-5-6-7 Strongly agree
	I will recommend this mobile SNS to other users.	Strongly disagree 1-2-3-4-5-6-7 Strongly agree
	When using mobile SNS, I consider this mobile SNS to be my first choice.	Strongly disagree 1-2-3-4-5-6-7 Strongly agree

hypotheses. As shown in Table 1.11, all AVE values exceed 0.5 and CR values exceed 0.7, indicating good convergent validity of the scale; all Cronbach α values exceed 0.7, indicating good reliability of the scale. As shown in Table 1.12, all square roots of AVE are larger than its correlation coefficients with other variables, indicating good discriminant validity of the scale. As shown in Table 1.13, all model fitness indexes, except GFI, are larger than the reference value, indicating good fitness of the scale. As shown in Table 1.14, all estimated values for parameters were significant, indicating that all seven hypotheses are supported.

Table 1.11: AVE, CR, and Cronbach α values used by Zhou et al. (2010).

Variables	AVE	CR	α
Information quality	0.60	0.82	0.82
System quality	0.74	0.82	0.92
Perceived enjoyment	0.63	0.87	0.87
Perceived control	0.58	0.80	0.79
Attention focus	0.75	0.92	0.92
Trust	0.82	0.93	0.93
Loyalty	0.73	0.89	0.88

Step 4: Conclusion and discussion. According to the results of data analysis, both information quality and system quality significantly influence users' trust and flow

Table 1.12: Variable correlation coefficients and AVE used by Zhou et al. (2010).

	1	2	3	4	5	6	7
Information quality	0.775						
System quality	0.443	0.857					
Perceived enjoyment	0.631	0.429	0.793				
Perceived control	0.634	0.541	0.470	0.760			
Attention focus	0.377	0.466	0.279	0.686	0.864		
Trust	0.485	0.630	0.461	0.684	0.541	0.906	
Loyalty	0.426	0.436	0.485	0.652	0.578	0.616	0.853

Note: The square root of AVE is shown diagonally.

Table 1.13: Model fitness used by Zhou et al. (2010).

Fitness index	χ^2/df	GFI	AGFI	NFI	NNFI	CFI	RMSEA
Actual values	2.62	0.897	0.853	0.961	0.966	0.973	0.068
Reference values	≤3	≥0.9	≥0.8	≥0.9	≥0.9	≥0.9	≤0.08

Table 1.14: Estimated value for model parameter and hypothesis verification results used by Zhou et al. (2010).

Effects	Causes	Estimated value for model parameter	Hypothesis verification results (Supported or not?)
Trust	Information quality	0.26***	H1 (Yes)
	System quality	0.51***	H3 (Yes)
Flow experience	Information quality	0.38***	H2 (Yes)
	System quality	0.14*	H4 (Yes)
	Trust	0.45***	H5 (Yes)
Loyalty	Trust	0.20**	H6 (Yes)
	Flow experience	0.57***	H7 (Yes)

Note: $* p < 0.05$, $** p < 0.01$, $*** p < 0.001$.

experience whereas trust influences flow experience and loyalty and flow experience significantly influences user loyalty. The results also show that perceived enjoyment, perceived control, and attention focus have high loadings on the second-order factor flow experience, indicating that it is appropriate to integrate these three dimensions into a reflective second-order factor. In addition, compared with information quality, system quality has a larger influence on user trust. Therefore, mobile SNS providers need to attach importance to the reliability, response speed, navigability, and ease of use of system performance and optimize human–machine interface design of mobile terminals to improve user trust of SNS by overcoming the constraints of mobile terminals such as small screen, low resolution, and inconvenient input. On the other hand, compared with system quality, information quality has a larger influence on flow experience. Therefore, mobile service providers need to attach importance to information quality and provide the latest, most accurate, and most comprehensive information to users to promote their continuous usage behavior by improving user experience.

In addition to of the study by Zhou et al. (2010), there are other studies on online social network users' loyalty based on flow theory. For instance, Lin [20] developed a model to explain Facebook users' continuous usage by integrating the unified theory of adoption and use of technology, expectation disconfirmation theory, and flow theory. Empirical verification using 482 valid sample data was conducted using SEM technology. Results showed that flow experience not only indirectly influences continuous usage intention by satisfaction but also has significant direct influence on continuous usage intention. Chang [21] researched continuous usage behavior of SNS users in China by constructing a model based on ECM, social capital theory, and flow theory. As shown in an empirical research based on SEM, expectation conformation degree of SNS users has a significant positive influence on flow experience, which indirectly influences continuous usage intention by satisfaction; however, there was no direct influence of flow experience on continuous usage intention for SNS. In addition, Wu et al. [22] and Chang [23] also applied flow theory on the continuous usage behavior of social games and recreational application in SNS. Based on flow theory, Wu et al. (2010) proposed that perceived enjoyment is the direct antecedent for user stickiness on recreational application in SNS, whereas perceived enjoyment is influenced by design factor (e.g., internal sociability and interactivity between applications) of recreational application in SNS. Empirical research supports the above relation hypothesis. Using flow theory, Chang (2013) constructed a research model considering interactivity (human–machine interaction and social interaction), user value (tool value and entertainment value), and satisfaction as the antecedent variable of flow experience, and flow experience and satisfaction as the direct antecedent of social game. As shown by the results, relation hypothesis between various variables in the model is verified.

1.3 Individual usage behavior

1.3.1 General usage behavior

With the rapid development of forum, blog and microblog, and other online social networks, online social behavior of users shows more content and manifestation contrary to the past. Current research about user behavior in social network is mostly from surveys or interviews. For example, Tracii et al. [24] investigated Facebook usage behavior of 1,324 users, and discovered that extrovert and nervous users tend to frequently use social network and spend more time. Kelly et al. [25] researched the general behavior rules of 219 college students in Facebook, and stated that more experienced Facebook users were likely to spend more time on Facebook, post more photos, but disclose less personal information.

Along with the progress of social network applications and related technologies of data acquisition, it is possible to study online social network behavior from large-scale user behavior data. For instance, using the clickstream data in Orkut, Myspace, Hi5, LinkedIn, and other famous social network platforms, Benevenuto et al. [26] analyzed the behavioral law of 37,024 social network users, such as frequency of visiting social networks, activity types visited, and the sequences of related activities. Golder et al. [27] revealed the daily and weekly law that college students use social networks from 362 million log information posted by 4.2 million users. By analyzing behavior patterns of 1.46 million users, Maia [28] pointed out that characteristics from social interactions are more effective for user clustering than that from individual user. By analyzing the behavior of 80,000 users in Bebo, MySpace, Netlog, Tagged, and other social networks, Gyarmati et al. [29] discovered that the time that users spend on social networks follows Weibull distribution while the duration of users' online sessions follows power-law distribution.

In this book, we describe the general law of user behavior in online social networks from two aspects: user activities and time pattern. With respect to user activities, we introduce the main categories in online social network activities and the transition law between those categories; with respect to time pattern, we introduce the law that users spend time on social network and the duration of users' online sessions.

1. Behavioral law from the aspect of user activities

Activity is the basic unit of users' behavior in social networks, such as sending personal messages and browsing photos. An activity category comprises several basic units. For example, photo category contains browsing photos, uploading photos, etc. In this section, as per the research of Benevenuto et al. [26], we first introduce the method of data acquisition, followed by the eight activity categories, and finally, the transition law between activities.

1) Data acquisition

Benevenuto et al. used Social Network Aggregator to collect users' clickstream. As an account management tool, Social Network Aggregator provides access to multiple social network accounts of the same user through a common interface for the centralized management of social network accounts. Benevenuto et al.

collected clickstream data over a 12-day period from March 26 to April 6, 2009. The dataset contained all HTTP header information exchanged between the users and Social Network Aggregator, including time stamp, HTTP status, IP address of the user, etc. Data information after preprocessing is shown in Table 1.15.

Table 1.15: Summary of the clickstream data.

Online social network	Number of users	Number of sessions	Number of requests
Orkut	36,309	57,927	787,276
Hi5	515	723	14,532
MySpace	115	119	542
LinkedIn	85	91	224
Total	37,024	58,860	802,574

Benevenuto et al. obtained the main activity categories in social network by analyzing clickstream log information, and subsequently obtained the five most common activity categories in different social networks by analyzing the number of HTTP requests of each category of activity. They further analyzed the transition probability law from one activity category to another according to the sequence of user requests in clickstream.

2) Social activity category

As a user can perform multiple activities in social network, Benevenuto et al. enumerated all basic activity units of a user in social network, and then manually tagged each clickstream log entry with the appropriate activity category (e.g., friend invitation and browsing photos), and finally, lumped semantically similar activities into a category based on the webpage structure of online social network sites.

Benevenuto et al. categorized 41 identified activities into eight categories, as shown in Table 1.16. Global search enables users to capture other users' profiles, communities, and community topics in Orkut. Scrapbook shows all text messages sent to a specific user. Scrapbook is different from personal messages or emails as it is public, i.e., all users having an Orkut account can read scraps of other users. Messages are a private means of communication and are available for each user. As a commentary function to scrapbook, testimonials show messages left to a given user by all his/her friends and are viewable to any user by default. Videos and photos include activities involving shared multimedia content. Profile and friends represent all activities related to profile management or browse of other users' profiles. Any user having an Orkut account can create communities, in which members can publish topics, inform others of major events, and ask questions or play online games.

Table 1.16: Enumeration of all activities.

Category	Description of activity	Number of users	Number of requests	Number of bytes (MB)
Search	1. Global search	2383	15409	287
Scrapbook	2.* Browse scraps	17753	147249	2740113
	3. Write scraps	2307	7623	
Messages	4.* Browse personal messages	93170	3905289	645
	5. Write personal messages			
Testimonials	6.* Browse testimonials received from friends	1085	3402	57
	7. Write testimonials	911	4128	65
	8.* Browse testimonials written by oneself	540	1633	26
Videos	9.* Browse the list of favorite videos	494	2262	44
	10.* Browse a favorite video	390	862	13
Photos	11.* Browse the list of photo albums	8769	43743	871
	12.* Browse a photo album	8201	70329	2313
	13.* Browse photos	8176	122152	1147
	14.* Browse photos tagged by the user	1217	3004	47
	15.* Browse photo comments	355	842	16
	16.* Edit and organize photos	82	266	3
Profile and Friends	17.* Browse profiles	19984	149402	3534
	18.* Browse homepage	18868	92699	3866
	19.* Browse the list of friends	6364	50537	1032
	20. Manage friend invitations	1656	8517	144
	21.* Browse friend updates	1601	6644	200
	22.* Browse member communities	1455	6963	133
	23. Profile editing	1293	7054	369
	24.* Browse stars	361	1103	17
	25.* Browse user lists	126	626	9
	26. Manage user events	44	129	2
Communities	27.* Browse a community	2109	8850	164
	28.* Browse a topic in a community	926	9454	143
	29. Join or leave communities	523	3043	43
	30.* Browse members in communities	415	3639	56
	31.* Browse the list of community topics	412	2066	38
	32. Participate in a community topic	227	1680	24
	33. Community management	105	682	12
	34. Post questionnaires in communities	99	360	6
	35.* Browse the list of communities	47	337	8
	36. Manage community invitations	20	63	1
	37. Community events	19	41	1

Table 1.16 (continued)

Category	Description of activity	Number of users	Number of requests	Number of bytes (MB)
Others	38. Access applications	1092	4043	61
	39. User settings	403	2020	32
	40. Spam mail	48	150	2
	41. Account login and deletion	39	76	1
	Total	36309	787276	17.3GB

Note: Activities related to browsing behavior are marked with a (*) sign.

Table 1.16 shows users' interest in using various functions of Orkut. Browsing is the most common user behavior accounting for 92% of all user requests. For example, the number of users who browsed personal messages is 13 times larger than those who sent personal messages.

Benevenuto obtained the five most common activity categories in the above four social network sites based on the number of HTTP requests, as shown in Table 1.17. We can see from the table that Profile and Friends is the most popular activity across the four social network sites. Users are likely to browse profiles of themselves or others, friend list, etc. in social network, which reflects the "sociality" of social network.

Table 1.17: Comparison of mainstream activity categories in different social network sites.

Rank	Orkut		MySpace		LinkedIn		Hi5	
	Category	Share	Category	Share	Category	Share	Category	Share
1	Profile and Friends	41%	Profile and Friends	88%	Profile and Friends	51%	Profile and Friends	67%
2	Photos	31%	Messages	5%	Login	42%	Photos	18%
3	Scrapbook	20%	Photos	3%	Messages	4%	Comments	6%
4	Communities	4%	Login	3%	Search	2%	Login	4%
5	Search	2%	Communities	1%	Communities	<1%	Messages	3%

3) Transition law

Benevenuto et al. established a first-order Markov chain of user activities according to the sequence of user access activities. Figure 1.13 shows the transition probabilities among different activity categories. Nodes represent categories and directed edges represent the transition directions between two categories, with weight indicating transition probabilities among different activities. Edges with probabilities smaller than 4% were removed. The sum of probabilities from one vertex to remaining vertexes is 1.

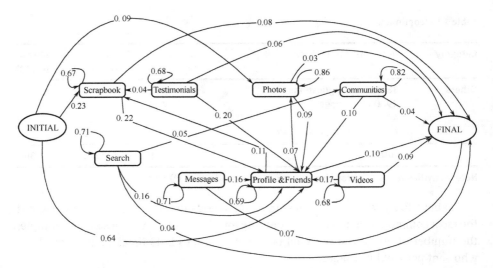

Figure 1.13: Transition law among different activity categories.

Benevenuto et al. found that most users began their sessions from Profile and Friends, Scrapbook, or Photos. This means that users first conduct these activity categories after logging in social network sites. They also found that "self-loop" was very common. For instance, when a user participates in a community activity, the probability of still taking community in next activity is 0.82. Similarly, the probability of "self-loop" in photos activities reached 0.86. Except for "self-loop," profile and friends was the next most common activity among current activities.

2. Behavioral law from the aspect of time pattern

The duration of online sessions refers to the time that users spend on browsing after logging in the sites. Session can end in two different ways: clicking the exit button or simply closing the internet browser. In this section, based on the research of Gyarmati et al. [29], we first introduce the collection method of behavior data from 80,000 users in the four social networks, present the law of time that the users spent on social network, and finally, introduce the duration law of users' online sessions in online social networks.

1) Data acquisition

As data cannot be directly obtained from the operators of online social networks, Gyarmati et al. captured the public part of users' profile pages in Bebo, MySpace, Netlog, and Tagged. More than 500 PlanetLab nodes were used to capture profile page information of more than 80,000 users from March 15 to May 2, 2009. Profile information refers to the profile of the user, status information posted, etc.

An appropriate monitoring time interval is very important as it is necessary to ceaselessly download users' profile page during data acquisition. Under limited resources (only 500 nodes), short sampling time contributes to a fine-grained dataset as more user profile pages can be downloaded; however, in this case, the number of users monitored is limited. Monitoring more users needs a larger time interval. According to practical experience, 1 min was selected as the monitoring interval. Gyarmati et al. compared the changes between all downloaded profile pages of a given user to infer the duration of being online. For instance, if the current page of a given user was different from that of 1 min ago, it implied that the user was still online. Finally, user's total online duration in 6 weeks was obtained.

2) The law of time spent on social network
Figure 1.15(a) displays the cumulative distribution function of time that users spent online during monitoring. The four social networks have similar characteristics (the figure of x axis is logarithmic), i.e., the majority of users spent no more than a few thousand minutes online or less than an hour daily during the six-week period. Gyarmati et al. performed fitting analysis and found that the measurement data and the curve of Weibull distribution overlapped, implying that the online time usage approximately follows Weibull distribution, as shown in Figure 1.14(b).

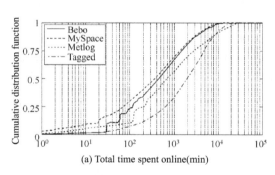
(a) Total time spent online(min)

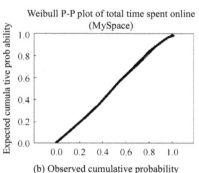
(b) Observed cumulative probability

Figure 1.14: Distribution function of usage time.

3) The duration law of online sessions
Figure 1.15 displays the session duration distribution of user behavior in Tagged and MySpace (both x and y axes are logarithmic). We can observe that the session lengths follow power-law distributions. Specifically, the figure shows the sum of two power-law distributions, and the jump is their boundary point. The change between the distributions is mainly due to the session timeout settings of the servers (both Tagged and MySpace session have a 20-min timeout period). Timeout setting means that the session remains active for some time after users end the session by simply closing the browser. Therefore, the sessions ended by clicking exit button can be shorter than

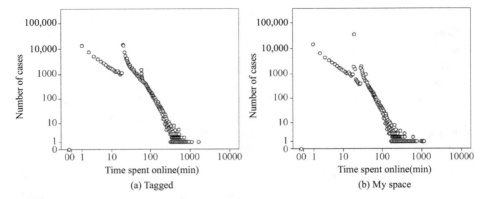

Figure 1.15: Session distribution.

those ended by closing the browser. Ending session by exiting from social network sites constitutes the first power-law distribution, while the other distribution is the sum of the two ways of exiting.

1.3.2 Behavior of content generation

With the rapid development of Web 2.0 and the rapid growth of social network applications, the interactivity and We-Media property of the internet has become increasingly prominent. Compared with Web 1.0, users in the era of Web 2.0 are more autonomous and interactive. Online users are no longer media audiences passively accepting information, but actively participate in the production, release, diffusion, and sharing of information, producing a large amount of user-generated content (UGC). For example, the cumulative number of Tweets generated per day was 250 million in October 2011. Only a few months later in March 2012, the number surprisingly reached 310 million. In the face of such large amounts of UGC, research on user generation behavior is of prime importance as companies cannot make good use of social media and develop effective social media marketing strategies without fully understanding the law of UGC.

Shriver et al. [32] found a significant causal relationship between UGC and user network structure, i.e., UGC was affected by user network structure. Furthermore, Toubia et al. [33] pointed out that the intrinsic and image-related utility influenced UGC. Depending on the motivation for creation, increase in followers can stimulate content generation and reduce users' enthusiasm for generating new content. Previous research has paid attention to the disclosure of users' personal information, including literary quality, entertainment interest, political tendency, etc. Although disclosing personal information is risky, research has shown that users are still enthusiastic about sharing their personal information. Furthermore, the disclosure preference of users (topic selection) is also widely noted. In-depth research on topic selection behavior in UGC is of great significance for personalized recommendation system. For example, Wang et al. [34] pointed out that women tended to generate more personal topics (e.g., family matters), while men discussed more public topics (e.g., politics and sports). Many scholars, especially psychology scholars, have probed the expression behavior of UGC. Yarkoni [35] analyzed the relationships between users' personality traits and 100,000 words posted by blog users and obtained meaningful conclusions. For example, users with a high sense of responsibility rarely used negative words. Qiu et al. [36] analyzed all Tweets published by 142 users, and found that their expression behaviors follow some regulations. For instance, extrovert users tend to use positive sentiment-specific words.

Based on the above analysis, we first expound the motivation for content generation and then introduce the self-presentation behavior in content generation. Furthermore, we introduce the topic preference during users' self-presentation, and finally, introduce an important form of content generation – language expression behavior.

1. Motivation for content generation

In this subsection, based on the research of Toubia et al. [33], we introduce the impact of the increase in followers on content generation behavior under different creation motivations from the aspects of intrinsic and image-related utility. Specifically, we first expound the theoretical basis, then introduce the experimental data and method, and finally, summarize the results.

1) Theoretical basis

Utility refers to a measure of consumer satisfaction obtained by consumption or enjoyment. In this book, intrinsic utility indicates that online users, for their intrinsic satisfactions rather than for other reasons, get direct utility from publishing content, i.e., users can get psychological comfort when they post content to their followers. Image-related utility assumes that users' content generation is motivated by the perceptions of others, such as pursuing prestige, but is not limited to users' appearance. Instead, image-related utility contains a sense of self-worth and social acceptance. Image-related utility is directly derived from the number of followers, and posting more content may attract more followers.

If users contribute content to Twitter for intrinsic utility, the utility function of user post behavior is concave and does not decrease with increase in the number of followers, i.e., users are likely to increase their posting activities when they have additional followers. The image-related utility is derived from the number of followers, i.e., more the followers, the higher is the utility. Posting content can increase the number of followers in the future and influence image-related utility. Contrary to intrinsic utility, the incremental image-related utility generated by posting content on a given day will be obtained in the future and depends on the number of additional followers in the future. If incremental image-related utility generated by the increase in followers decreases, users exhibit negative attitudes toward posting new content.

In summary, we can provide contrasting predictions on intrinsic utility and image-related utility according to users' response to an increase in the number of followers. If users are motivated by intrinsic utility, more followers will contribute to an increase in posting activities. However, if users' utility results from attracting more followers and they post content for gaining additional followers, the motivation to post content will decrease with the increase in the number of followers because of utility diminishing law.

2) Data and experiment method

Toubia et al. randomly selected a collection of 2,493 noncommercial Twitter users from an initial database with nearly 3 million users. They collected three variables daily for each user: the number of followers, number of users followed, and total number of Tweets since account creation. A total of 1,335 users were classified as active users based on certain criteria. The experimental period lasted 160 days, and 100 users were selected from active users as the experimental group. To investigate the influence of the number of followers, Toubia et al. gradually added 100 public followers to the users in the experimental group over a 50-day period. For example, they started by adding one follower per day to each user for 4 days, then added two followers per day for another 4 days, and so on until 100 followers were added for each user (Figure 1.16).

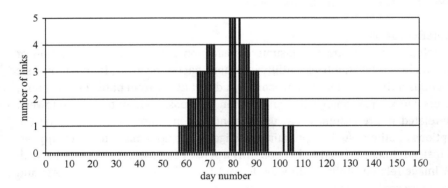

Figure 1.16: The process of adding followers.

3) Research conclusions

From the above analysis, when the number of followers increased, an increase (decrease) in posting content conformed to intrinsic utility (image-related utility). After the intervention (adding followers to selected users), users in the experimental group were more enthusiastic about posting content than that in the control group.

Specifically, 40.82% of users in the experimental group became more active compared with 34.19% of users in the control group. However, this difference was not statistically significant. Therefore, the intervention did not have a significant influence on posting activities.

Furthermore, Toubia et al. studied the influence of intervention on users' posting activities when the initial number of followers was different. There were two considerations. First, they considered intrinsic and image-related utility as the function of a user's number of followers. Therefore, the behavior of a user with few followers may be more consistent with one utility, while it may become more consistent with another utility as the number of followers increases. Second, the relative importance between image-related and intrinsic utility may be different for different users, which can be reflected by the number of followers. For example, users having more followers may be more concerned about intrinsic utility.

Figures 1.17 and 1.18 show the probabilities that users increase and decrease their posting activities before and after the intervention, respectively. The x axis refers to the log of users' initial number of followers. Toubia et al. found that selected users with few initial followers tended to post more content after the intervention. However, users with many initial followers tended to decrease their posting frequency.

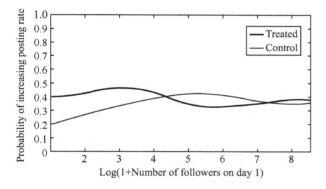

Figure 1.17: Probability of increasing posting activities before and after the intervention.

To statistically compare the influence of intervention on the posting behavior of users with different initial number of followers, Toubia et al. categorized the selected users into five subgroups, as shown in Table 1.18. Compared with the control group, users in the second experimental subgroup were more likely to increase their posting frequency. However, users in the fourth experimental subgroup acted in an opposite manner. The differences in other subgroups had no statistical significance.

In fact, it is not surprising to see the consistent performance of the first and fifth subgroups. Users in the first subgroup had few followers and seldom visited Twitter;

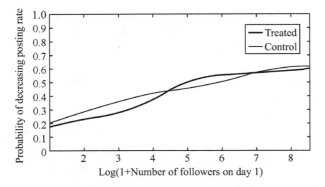

Figure 1.18: Probability of decreasing posting activities before and after the intervention.

Table 1.18: Partition of users.

Subgr-oup	Range of number of followers	Median number of followers	Average number of followers
1	0–12	7	6,499
2	13–26	19	18,941
3	27–61	39.5	40,988
4	62–245	109	125,550
5	246–18, 940	704	1,378,949

users in the fifth subgroup had many followers and were not sensitive to the addition of 100 followers over the 50-day period. Therefore, increase in the number followers had no significant influence on the first and fifth subgroups. Behavior of users in the second subgroup conformed to intrinsic utility, and, as discussed above, intrinsic utility was derived from having more followers that prompted users to post more content. The performance of users in the fourth subgroup conformed to image-related utility, and, as discussed above, the increase in the number of followers decreased the posting frequency as the image-related utility decreased with the increase in the number of followers (followers attracted by posting content). Users in the third subgroup were influenced by both intrinsic and image-related utility, which counteract each other.

2. Self-presentation behavior
In this subsection, we first introduce the general rule of self-presentation behavior, and then discuss the effect of gender on self-presentation by photos.

1) General rule of self-presentation behavior
Boyle et al. [37] found that, compared with directly listing their names on the page (59.7%), users tend to present themselves by uploading photos (75.7%), creating a

motto (74.7%), and listing personal interests (79.9%). Surveys showed that users were reluctant to create blogs (33.3%), post videos (23.9%), and upload slideshows (23.9%). Only 5% of the users posted videos of themselves or their friends and family. In comparison, MySpace users preferred to post slideshows to record their friends and family (11.6%) or their acitivities with friends (4.8%).

Users' disclosure levels of individual information differ greatly. Almost all respondents listed their relationship status (99.2%), hometown (97%), and postcode (99.2%). Most users disclosed their race (83.3%), sexual orientation (82.5%), whether they plan to have a baby (79.9%), and education (79.9%). Although 79.9% users listed personal interests, relatively few users were willing to disclose their favorite music (69.1%), movies (60.2%), television shows (59.4%), books (53.0%), or idols (57.8%). Few users were willing to reveal their income (19.1%) or groups they belong to (19%).

2) Self-presentation by photos

Based on the research of Tifferet et al. [46], we studied the influence of gender on the selection of profile and cover photos. Profile photos refer to head portraits on the homepage. Males' photos highlighted status (e.g., dress formally) and adventure (e.g., outdoor activities), while females' photos highlighted family relations (e.g., family photos) and emotional expressions (e.g., eye contact, smile intensity). Cover photos refer to the background picture at the top of the homepage. Gender had no significant influence on the selection of cover photos. The only difference is that females were more likely to show family photos on the cover.

Tifferet et al. pointed out that Facebook users prefer to present themselves with their profile photos, and nearly 60% users use their own photos as profile photos. Moreover, users used their cover photos to extend their presentation, e.g., introducing additional aspects of the self.

3. Topic preferences

In this subsection, from the research of Wang (2013), we first introduce methods for data acquisition and preprocessing, construct a topic model using latent Dirichlet allocation (LDA), and finally, discuss the relation between gender and topic selection behavior of users.

1) Data acquisition and preprocessing

Wang randomly selected one million status updates posted by American Facebook users in June 2012. For each status update, Wang analyzed metadata including posting time, number of viewers, number of comments, and likes within 3 days of posting. Wang also collected demographic information of each user, including gender, age, number of friends, and number of days after registration. The preprocessing of collected information comprised three steps. First, all status updates were tagged with OpenNLP [38]. Second, Porter stemmer was used to remove all punctuations, URLs, email addresses, and tags. Third, all updates were represented as a combination of unigrams and bigrams. For example, the sentence "I like this photo" was represented as <I, like, this, photo, I like, like this, this photo>. The first four were termed as unigrams (single word) and the last three as bigrams (word pair).

Of all the terms in one million status updates, 71% of unigrams appeared only once, and the top 500 most frequent unigrams accounted for 55% of the entire data. For instance, 10% of status updates contained "love" which was the most frequent term. High-frequent terms always co-occurred with different terms, and thus, were not useful in topic modeling. Similarly, low-frequent terms were also not useful because they almost did not co-occur with other terms. Therefore, Wang removed high (occurred in more than 0.5% of the corpus) and low (occurred in less than 0.01% of the corpus) frequent terms to reduce noise and vocabulary size. Furthermore, they excluded 500 unigrams from a stoplist, and bigrams were removed if both the words were stopwords. Nearly 50% of the updates had less than eight unigrams or bigrams after pruning those which were too short for successful topic modeling.

2) Topic modeling

Wang et al. applied LDA model to identify topics from the remaining 521,636 status updates. LDA is a statistical generative method often used to discover hidden topics and the words associated with each topic. It can analyze a large number of unlabeled documents by clustering words that frequently co-occur. Wang et al. tried to run LDA models with 10, 30, 50, 60, and 100 topics. The comparison showed that the results were the most interpretable when topic number was set to 50. Wang et al. generated a dictionary for each topic depending on the 500 terms most associated with that topic. Two experts familiar with social network content manually examined each dictionary. Through the process of removing and merging, they finally obtained 25 standard topics, as shown in Table 1.19. A status update belongs to a topic if it has at least 3 words there of.

3) Conclusions

To investigate the influence of gender and age on topics selected by users in social network, Wang et al. recalculated the popularity of each topic for men, women, boys, and girls. The popularity of a given topic refers to the percentage of updates that contains that topic. Figure 1.19 plots the differences in topic preference for women and men in the ages of 25 and above. Women prefer to discuss topics related to personal details (e.g., Father's Day, family fan, and birthday), while men prefer to discuss sports and abstract concepts (e.g., politics and deep thoughts). Despite the differences in language format and audience in social networks, this finding conforms to previous studies regarding the influence of gender on face-to-face communication and blogs.

Gender has no significant influence on teenagers' selection of topics. Figure 1.20 shows the topic selection preference [39] of girls and boys between the

Table 1.19: Overview of topic categories.

Topic	Sample term
Sleep	last night, this morning, wake up, sleep, bed
Food	lunch, cook, coffee, beer, chicken, cake, ice cream
Clothing	supermarket, line, wear, store, cloth, dress, bag
House	door, my house, cat, street, box, window, floor
Weather/Travel	road, weather, cold, city, air, town, fly, storm
Family fun	great day, time, kid, swim, cousin, evening party
Girlfriend/Boyfriend	best friend, girl, red, boyfriend, my favorite
Birthday	I love, love you, my baby, happy birthday, birthday
Father's Day	happy father, father's day, children, my dad
Topic	Sample term
Sports	beat, fan, ball, ring, Miami
Politics	national, country, the U.S., president, vote, law
Love	my heart, give, strong, love me, happy
Thankfulness	thank you, visit, my family, thankfulness, Thank God
Anticipation	wait for, celebrate, can't wait, wow, until
Asking for support/pray	My friend, worry about, help me, right now, pray, support
Medical	drop, doctor, hospital, test, blood, stress
Memorial	miss, memory, everyday, peace, grandma
Negativity about people	say, judge, waste, some people, rubbish
Complaining	hate, guess, tired, talk
Deep thoughts	idea, success, human, create, symbol, goal, universe
Christianity	God, faith, church, Christianity, spirit
Religious imagery	death, man, star, birth, earth, sun
Slang	luv, knw
Work	to work, working, boss, colleague

Note: Each expression contains two or less words.

ages of 13 and 16. Compared with adults, teenagers have no significant gender difference in topic selection. For example, complaining, girlfriend/boyfriend, and slang were the most popular topics for both teenage boys and girls.

4. Language expression behavior

Previous research on expression behavior was mainly based on Linguistic Inquiry and Word Count [40], which can extract 81 characteristics from a passage and compute the proportion of each characteristic. Many studies regarding the relationships between personality traits and language expression behavior in social networks have been conducted. Social network platforms involve blog, Facebook, Twitter, etc. The main results are shown in Table 1.20.

Some of the conclusions were consistent with each other and could be mutually confirmed, but most were different and contradictory. Therefore, the relationships between personality traits and language expression behavior need further verification. For example, Golbeck et al. [41] found that extrovert users were more likely to use words about work where Yarkoni et al. [35] obtained opposite results.

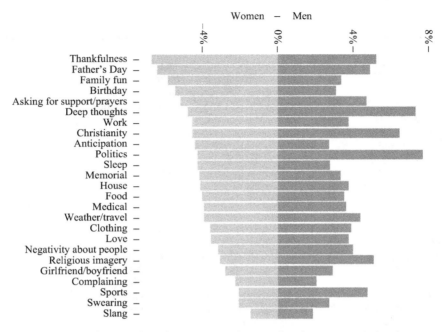

Figure 1.19: The influence of gender on topic preferences (aged 25 years and above).

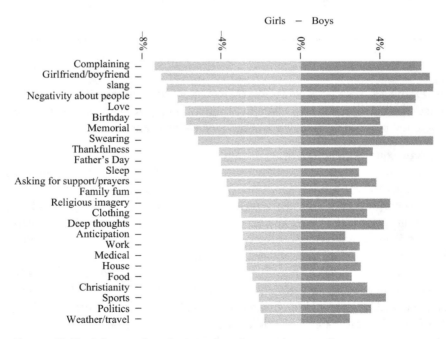

Figure 1.20: The influence of gender on topic preferences (teenagers).

Table 1.20: The relationships between personality traits and language expression behavior.

Author(s)	Platform	Extraversion	Agreeableness	Conscientiousness	Neuroticism	Openness
Golbeck et al. [41]	Facebook	Perceptual process (–), work	Emotion, positive emotion, physiological process	Bad language (–), social process, human, perceptual process (–), visual (–)	Anxiety, ingestion	Money (–)
Nguyen et al. [42]	Blog	Word consisting of 6 letters, leisure, number, money, perceptual process, bad language (–), nonfluency (–), health (–), negation (–)				
Nowson [43]	Blog	Occupation (–), achievement (–), discrepancy (–), school (–), human, social process	Discrepancy (–), word consisting of 6 letters, article, negation (–)	Death (–)	Discrepancy, work, anxiety, future tense verb, eating, human (–)	Word consisting of 6 letters, positive emotion, school (–), occupation (–), modifier, inclusive, preposition

(continued)

Table 1.20 (continued)

Author(s)	Platform	Extraversion	Agreeableness	Conscientiousness	Neuroticism	Openness
Yarkoni [35]	Blog	1st person plural pronoun, 2nd person pronoun, number (–), positive emotion, causation (–), inhibition (–), tentative (–), certainty, hearing, social process, friend, family, human, inclusive, occupation (–), work (–), achievement (–), music, religion, sexuality	Pronoun, 1st person plural pronoun, 1st person pronoun, numbers, positive emotion, negative emotion (–), anger (–),causation (–), seeing,social process, friend, family, time, past tense verb, space, inclusive, motion, leisure, home, music, money (–), death (–), sexuality, sleep, bad language (–)	Negation (–), negativeemotion (–), anger (–), sadness (–), cognitive process (–), causation (–), discrepancy (–), tentative (–), certainty (–), hearing (–), human (–), time, exclusive (–), achievement, music (–), death (–), bad language (–)	1st person singular pronoun, 2nd person pronoun (–), negation, article (–), negative emotion, anxiety, anger, cognitive process, causation, discrepancy, tentative, certainty, friend (–), space (–), exclusive, sleep, bad language	Pronoun (–), 1st person singular pronoun (–), 1st person plural pronoun (–), 1st person pronoun (–), 2nd person pronoun (–), negation (–), assent (–), article, preposition, number (–), affect (–), positive emotion (–), cognitive process (–), discrepancy (–), social process (–), family (–), human (–), time (–), past tense verb (–), present tense verb (–), future tense verb

1.3.3 Behavior of content consumption

Tens of thousands of users visit social networks (e.g., Flickr and Facebook) every day to share their photos, videos, mood, etc., while others satisfy their requirements by searching, viewing, or commenting on such information. Benevenuto et al. [26] found that browsing behavior accounted for 92% of all user activities by analyzing users' clickstream, such as browsing other profile pages, watching videos shared by others, or browsing other photo albums. By analyzing such "silent" user behavior, we can obtain a more accurate and comprehensive view of the online social network workload. Most user behavior is passive, i.e., consuming content created by others. A large number of scholars focused on this topic from all aspects and obtained meaningful results. For example, we can determine, from the side aspect, the users' consumption preferences by analyzing the question type asked on social networks.

From the access logs on Flickr, a site based on photo sharing, Van Zwol et al. [45] analyzed users' browsing behavior from temporal, social, and spatial dimensions and answered the time, reason, and location their browsing behavior. They found that users were able to browse new photos within hours after being uploaded, and most browse behaviors occur within the first 2 days. With the continuous development of social networks and the explosive growth of information, social networks have become an increasingly important information repository. For example, Facebook launched a social graph search tool called Graph Search in July 2013, which focuses on helping users' search content using relational network compared with the traditional network research featuring keywords and phrases. Since then, users have used social networks to obtain information in addition to entertainment. There are two typical ways to obtain information. One is the passive consumption behavior and the other is active consumption behavior, which refers to the phenomenon of people asking questions by social network status messages instead of traditional search engines (e.g., Google). A large number of scholars have started to pay close attention to this area. By analyzing 624 users in social network, Ringel et al. [44] found that more than half of the users had asked questions through social networks, and there were significant differences between the question type and the manner of asking.

Based on the above discussion, we intend to introduce the behavior of content consumption in social network from two aspects: passive and active consumption. We introduce the browsing behavior law from the passive aspect and information acquisition behavior law from the active aspect.

1. Passive consumption: Browsing behavior
Based on the research of Roelof et al. [45], we first introduce the data acquisition and processing, and then research the browsing behavior from temporal and spatial dimensions where temporal dimension focuses on tracking the change of browsing

behavior over time and spatial dimension aims to investigate the geographic distribution of browsing behavior.

1) Data acquisition and processing

Roelof et al. tracked the number of views of 1.83 million photos for a duration of 60 days. The observation window was a 50-day period. Hence, if a photo was uploaded on day 3, then the authors took the number of views for that photo into account up to day 53. The authors only considered page views that were explicitly oriented on viewing a single photo. Using Yahoo!'s IP address to geographic location conversion service, the authors could study the origin of the photo view request. Figure 1.21 shows the log–log distribution of photo views. The X axis refers to the 1.83 million photos ranked by the number of views, and the Y axis represents the total number of views per photo. This distribution could be fitted accurately by power-law distribution. The distribution of the photo views had a high slope, i.e., a small fraction of photos received the most views.

Based on the number of views, Roelof et al. classified all photos into ten groups with equal number of photos and computed the total views for each group. As shown in Table 1.21, the first group (0–10%) contained the most frequently browsed photos, while the groups of 50% and above contained the photos that were only viewed once.

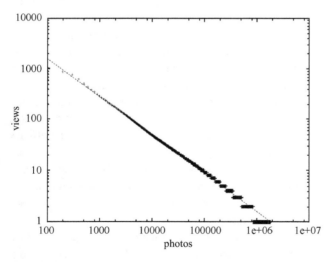

Figure 1.21: Distribution of photo views.

2) Temporal dimension

Figure 1.22 shows the total number of photo views after the photos were discovered. The number of views for the first group after 3 hours approximated that for the second group after 50 days. Moreover, popular photos had 45% of

Table 1.21: Photo classification.

Group	Number of views	Group	Number of views
0%–10%	3,802,875	50%–60%	182,856
10%–20%	812,131	60%–70%	182,857
20%–30%	515,532	70%–80%	182,856
30%–40%	365,712	80%–90%	182,857
40%–50%	312,270	90%–100%	182,857

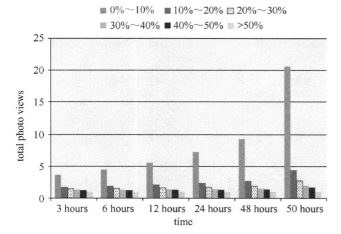

Figure 1.22: Change law of photo views.

their total views within the first 48 hours. Detailed information about Figure 1.22 is presented in Table 1.22, which lists the mean and standard deviation of total views over time. The standard deviation of the first group grew significantly over time whereas the second group showed little change.

3) Spatial dimension

Table 1.23 shows the top five most frequently viewed groups and we took only 10% of photos for each group. The second column of the table shows the average geographic diffusion of photo views in a group. The decreasing mean indicated that the geographic diffusion generally focused on a specific geographic location when the popularity of a photo decreased. The third column indicates the standard deviation of the geographic diffusion with the smallest standard deviation for the first group and relatively larger values for the other groups. One explanation for this browsing behavior was that, in the groups >20%, the location where users browse photos were near to the uploading

Table 1.22: Change law of photo views.

Group	3 hours		6 hours		12 hours	
	Mean	Standard deviation	Mean	Standard deviation	Mean	Standard deviation
0%–10%	3.63	8.25	4.44	12.51	5.55	18.66
10%–20%	1.77	0.97	1.92	1.05	2.11	1.12
20%–30%	1.47	0.67	1.54	0.7	1.62	0.73
30%–40%	1.3	0.46	1.33	0.47	1.36	0.48
40%–50%	1.25	0.43	1.27	0.44	1.3	0.46
>50%	1	0	1	0	1	0

Group	24 hours		48 hours		50 hours	
	Mean	Standard deviation	Mean	Standard deviation	Mean	Standard deviation
0%–10%	7.24	26.5	9.28	37.6	20.6	87.7
10%–20%	2.43	1.22	2.75	1.28	4.4	0.7
20%–30%	1.77	0.77	1.92	0.79	2.8	0.4
30%–40%	1.44	0.5	1.52	0.5	2	0
40%–50%	1.35	0.48	1.39	0.49	1.7	0.45
>50%	1	0	1	0	1	0

Table 1.23: User's interest related to space.

Group	Mean	Standard deviation	Location
0%–10%	28.61	10.44	740.2
10%–20%	18.84	19.29	26.4
20%–30%	13.23	19.83	5.28
30%–40%	9.54	19.57	2
40%–50%	9.03	15.99	1.69

location, i.e., users preferred to browse the photos near their locations. The fourth column shows mean views of each photo in each group.

2. Active consumption: Information acquisition behavior

For active user information acquisition behavior, we first compare the differences in information acquisition between the search engine and online social network, and then introduce the consumption preference when users acquire information from social networks.

1) Comparison of information acquisition behavior between search engine and social network

We compared the differences between social and nonsocial search based on the research of Ringel et al. [47]. Social search implied that users obtained information by asking questions through status updates of social networks (e.g., Facebook) and waited for their friends to provide answers. Nonsocial search implied obtaining answers through traditional search engines.

Ringel et al. compared the difference in solving complex information acquisition task between social and nonsocial search through a laboratory study. Twelve participants (4 females), who were all Microsoft employees and aged between 23 and 42 years (mean age = 31.9), participated in this experiment. Five participants called themselves expert searchers, while the remaining were average. All participants were asked to have at least 50 friends on Facebook to ensure that their social network was large enough to provide answers to their questions. Network size ranged from 50 to 743 (mean size = 260.3).

All questions (e.g., shopping and travel) were prepared by participants before the experiment. When the experiment began, the participants posted a question through status update on social network, and then independently searched for answers using search engines.

Participants could end the search by themselves when they felt satisfied with what they had found, and each query, URL, and corresponding timestamp were saved by a client plug-in. When participants finished the search task using search engines, Ringel et al. asked them to check their social network and capture a screenshot of all responses and timestamps to their questions. Three days later, the participants again checked their social network and captured a screenshot of new responses.

As shown in Table 1.24, Ringel et al. compared social and nonsocial search using nonparametric Wilcoxon tests. Participants spent an average of 30.3 minutes on the Web to search answers. On average, they submitted 6.5 queries and browsed 35.4 pages from 12.3 distinct, nonsearch sites. Through social search, they received an average of 1.4 responses while five participants did not get any responses. In the following 3 days, participants received an average of 4.1 responses. The number of responses received by each user ranged from 0 to 20 with two participants not getting any responses. Of the ten participants, the minimum time for receiving the first response was 5 minutes. Time to first response was negatively associated with the number of friends.

After comparing answers from social search and nonsocial search, 11 participants (91.7%) were more satisfied with the answers from search engine, and its performance seemed to better meet users' expectations. An important reason that participants preferred search engine was that they could get answers more quickly. Nevertheless, the benefits of social search were apparent. Eight participants (66.7%) had asked questions through social network before and thought that their friends may provide more customized answers as they knew additional background information (e.g., personality, preferences) of the participants.

Table 1.24: Overview of social search results.

Task	Network size	Initial responses	Total responses	Time to first response (minute)	Search time (minute)
I want buy a new phone… Any suggestions?	466	3	20	15	38
Any tips for tiling a kitchen backsplash?	231	3	7	8	29
Does anyone know how to stop an in-car nav system from constantly rebooting?	275	2	2	19	46
Does anyone know how to train for half marathon?					
Does anyone know any good vegetarian recipes?	50	0	0	N/A	21
So…after getting the PMP, what else can I do to keep up their development?	401	1	10	36	36
Should I buy iPod as a gift?	104	1	3	7	32
I want to move away from LiveSpace for storing and sharing photos… Any recommendations?	206	0	5	184	12
Can I flee from Seattle winter by taking a trip to New Zealand?	240	0	5	77	31
Any recommendations on restaurants and activities in Cancun	143	2	2	5	49
What are the must see attractions in Disneyland?	743	5	10	8	22
Any recommendations on a good terminal or high end TV?	169	0	0	N/A	34

2) Consumption preference

When acquiring information, social search had other obvious superiorities despite its slower search speed than that of search engine, i.e., social network can provide customized answers based on users' preference. Therefore, it is important to study social search. Based on the research of Ringel et al. [44], this subsection introduces the consumption preferences of content in social network using a survey method.

Six hundred and twenty-four participants (1/4 female) participated in the surveys. As social networks were heavily used by college students, a majority of participants (72.2%) were full-time employees while the remaining were summer interns. This partition made the samples more representative. To eliminate the intervention of age, 28% of the participants were aged 18–24 years, 40.1% aged 26–35 years, 25.5% aged 36–45 years, and only 6.1% aged 46 years and above. In addition to basic information, all participants were asked to report a series of questions related to asking questions and answering behaviors. For example, whether participants have ever used social networks to ask questions. If they had done so, they were further asked about a set of questions regarding the frequency of such behavior, as well as the type and the topic of the questions.

The authors also conducted nonparametric tests to detect the significance of differences in the distribution of question topic and type according to gender and age. They first explored the question type, which referred to the nature of the question. For example, whether the question belonged to recommendation or invitation. Table 1.25 lists the main categories and popularity of the different question types. We can see that the most prevalent question types were for recommendation and opinion. Both the question types asked friends to provide subjective information. An opinion question usually asked for a rating of a specific item, while a recommendation question was an open-ended request for suggestions. For example, a user may hope that their friends can suggest or recommend a cheap and fine mobile phone.

Second, in addition to question type, they also introduced the popular question topics. Topic (e.g., technology, music) referred to the subject matter of the question. Table 1.26 shows the categories and popularity of question topics, illustrating each topic using an example. The most popular topic was technology, including computer hardware, software, programming, mobile phones, etc. Entertainment questions were also popular, including movies, television, arts, music, etc.

Ringel et al. explored how the participants' demographics and social network use correlated to the types and topics of questions. The details are presented in Table 1.27. There was no significant gender differences in the types of questions asked. However, gender had a larger impact on question topic. More specifically, men asked a higher proportion of technology questions, while women preferred to ask family-related questions. Age was correlated with the type of questions asked. Compared with older people, younger participants preferred to ask invitation questions. In contrast, older participants preferred to be recommended by others. Age had no significant impact on the topic of questions asked. Furthermore, they found that the participants were

Table 1.25: Question types and the corresponding popularity.

Question Type	Percent	Example
Recommendation	29%	Building a new playlist... any ideas for good running songs?
Opinion	22%	I am wondering if I should buy the ice cream maker?
Factual knowledge	17%	Anyone know a way to put Excel charts into LaTeX?
Rhetorical	14%	Is there anything in life you're afraid you won't achieve?
Invitation	9%	Who wants to go to Navya Lounge this evening?
Favor	4%	Does anyone need a babysitter tonight?
Social connection	3%	I am hiring in my team. Do you know anyone who would be interested?
Offer	1%	Could any of my friends use boys size 4 jeans?

Table 1.26: Question topics and the corresponding popularity.

Question Topic	Percent	Example
Technology	29%	Anyone know whether WoW works on Windows 7?
Entertainment	17%	Was seeing Up in the theater worth the money?
Home and family	12%	So what's the going rate for the tooth fairy?
Professional	11%	Which university is better for Masters? Cornell or Georgia Tech?
Places	8%	Planning a trip to Whistler in the offseason. Recommendation on sites to see?
Restaurant	6%	Hanging in Ballard tonight. Dinner recs?
Current events	5%	What is your opinion on the recent proposition that was passed in California?
Shopping	5%	What's a good Mother's Day gift?
Ethics and philosophy	2%	What would you do if you had a week to live?

more likely to ask technology questions on Twitter, while they were more likely to ask questions about entertainment and home and family on Facebook. Participants who infrequently updated their status were more likely to ask questions associated with rare events or special occurrences such as travel and health.

1.4 Group interaction behavior

1.4.1 Relationship selection of group interaction

Mass online social networks are conducive to the spread of ideas and information, which has attracted the attention of scholars, advertisers, and social activists. Existing research results focus on explaining the structure of online social networks.

Table 1.27: The impact of participants' demographics and social network use on the type and topic of questions.

		Gender		Age				Network size		Frequency of Use	
		Male	Female	18–25	26–35	36–45	46–55	Facebook	Twitter	Infrequent	Frequent
Total		157	77	51	93	71	15	126	49	205	29
Question Type	Opinion	23.6%	22.1%	21.6%	18.3%	28.2%	33.3%	18.3%	30.6%	20.7%	23.4%
	Recommendation	31.2%	29.9%	13.7%	35.5%	38.0%	26.7%	31.0%	28.6%	24.1%	31.7%
	Factual knowledge	15.3%	13.0%	9.8%	22.6%	9.9%	6.7%	11.1%	26.5%	13.8%	14.7%
	Rhetorical	8.9%	16.9%	19.6%	6.5%	11.3%	20.0%	14.3%	6.1%	13.8%	11.2%
	Invitation	10.8%	10.4%	23.5%	10.8%	2.8%	0.0%	15.1%	4.1%	24.1%	8.8%
Question Topic	Technology	35.0%	22.1%	33.3%	26.9%	32.4%	40.0%	15.9%	61.2%	24.1%	31.7%
	Entertainment	17.8%	19.5%	19.6%	24.7%	11.3%	6.7%	24.6%	6.1%	24.1%	17.6%
	Home and family	8.3%	19.5%	7.8%	14.0%	14.1%	6.7%	19.0%	0.0%	13.8%	11.7%
	Professional	10.8%	9.1%	7.8%	9.7%	11.3%	6.7%	7.9%	10.2%	3.4%	11.2%
	Places	8.9%	5.2%	15.7%	5.4%	5.6%	6.7%	7.9%	6.1%	13.8%	6.8%
	Restaurants	5.7%	7.8%	0.0%	8.6%	7.0%	13.3%	7.9%	2.0%	6.9%	6.3%
	Current events	6.4%	2.6%	0.0%	8.6%	5.6%	0.0%	5.6%	10.2%	3.4%	5.4%
	Shopping	3.2%	7.8%	5.9%	2.2%	7.0%	6.7%	4.8%	4.1%	3.4%	4.9%

Some scholars analyzed interactive behavior law from the perspective of the relationship between users. The strength of a relationship can make people think about how online social activities can be distributed on different types of connections, especially on different strength of connections. In this section, We first introduce how to identify the relationship among users in online social networks, then describe the relationship selection indexes based on the strength of the relationship between users, and finally, analyze an actual case.

1. Relationship identification in online social networks

Most traditional social networks are undirected. For example, in QQ or MSN, I am your friend, you are my friend. A relationship can only be established through mutual recognition. With the development of social media, the forms of social networks have become abundant. For example, Marlow et al. [48] took Facebook as a research object and defined three types of connections based on a month's use record for users.

(1) Bidirectional connection: A user not only sends messages to his/her friend but also receives information from his/her friend.

(2) Unidirectional connection: A user only sends one or more messages to his/her friend without considering whether his/her friend replied to his message.

(3) Maintain connection: A user only cares about whether there is a friend on the other end without considering whether there is actual information exchange. "Attention to the other side information" is indicated here either by Facebook's news alert service or at least two times to visit his friend.

Huberman et al [49] also conducted a similar research on Twitter. Twitter has the characteristics of a social network and can distinguish between strong and weak relationship. Each user can specify a set of users he/she wants to follow (to view the information they send), or send messages directly to a particular person (the message is still open but labeled as sent to a particular person). The first type of interaction is a weak relationship, which causes the user to easily follow a lot of people without directly talking with them. The second type of interaction corresponds to a strong relationship, in particular, for the user sending multiple messages directly to another user.

2. Relationship selection indexes under the perspective of strong and weak relationships

In graph theory, the definition of strong and weak relationships are as follows: strong relationships refer to close and frequent social contacts, and tend to be embedded in dense areas of the network; weak relations refer to casual and less social contact and tend to cross the border of communities. At present, in online social network environment, relationship selection index based on strong and weak relationships are mainly CN (common neighbors) index, AA (Adamic-Adar) index, etc.

CN index is the most simple similarity index based on local information, i.e., the possibility of the interaction between two nodes is larger if they have a lot of common friend nodes. CN index is defined as follows: v_x denotes a node in online social network, $\Gamma(x)$ denotes the set of v_x neighbor nodes. The possibility that two nodes v_x and v_y are connected is defined as the number of their common neighbor:

$$S_{xy} = |\Gamma(x) \cap \Gamma(y)| \tag{1.1}$$

Considering the impact of the node degree at both ends based on common neighbors, five possibility indexes that two nodes are connected are generated from different aspects.

- Salton index, also known as the cosine similarity:

$$S_{xy} = \frac{|\Gamma(x) \cap \Gamma(y)|}{|\sqrt{k_x k_y}|} \tag{1.2}$$

where k_x or k_y denote the degree of node v_x or v_y, respectively.
- Jaccard index proposed by Jaccard 100 years ago:

$$S_{xy} = \frac{|\Gamma(x) \cap \Gamma(y)|}{|\Gamma(x) \cup \Gamma(y)|} \tag{1.3}$$

- Sørenson index:

$$S_{xy} = \frac{2 \times |\Gamma(x) \cap \Gamma(y)|}{|k_x + k_y|} \tag{1.4}$$

- Hub promoted index (HPI):

$$S_{xy} = \frac{|\Gamma(x) \cap \Gamma(y)|}{|\min\{k_x, k_y\}|} \tag{1.5}$$

Because the denominator is determined by the node that has smaller degree, hub nodes are easier to form adjacencies with other nodes.
- Hub depressed Index (HDI)

$$S_{xy} = \frac{|\Gamma(x) \cap \Gamma(y)|}{|\max\{k_x, k_y\}|} \tag{1.6}$$

When measuring the possibility of a connection between two nodes using CN index, the degree of common neighbor node is ignored. It is not appropriate to calculate the relationship strength between online social network nodes, which is easy to understand. For example, people who have many followers on microblogs are often stars or celebrities in one field; however if users choose such nodes to establish a connection, the effect is often not obvious. In contrast, if a node follows another user who has a small number of followers, while the third user also follows this user, the probability of establishing an interactive relationship between the second and third user will be significantly improved. Based on this idea, Lada Adamic proposed AA index [65], defined as:

$$S_{xy} = \sum_{z \in \Gamma(x) \cap \Gamma(y)} \frac{1}{\log k_z} \tag{1.7}$$

The AA index assigns a weight value to each node according to the degree of its CN node, which is equal to the reciprocal of the logarithm of the degree. Based on the AA index, inspired by network resource allocation, Zhou et al. [53] proposed the RA index, defined as:

$$S_{xy} = \sum_{z \in \Gamma(x) \cap \Gamma(y)} \frac{1}{k_z} \tag{1.8}$$

The biggest difference between RA and AA index is how to assign the weight of the CN nodes. Experimental results show that, when the average degree of the network is relatively small, the difference between RA and AA index is little, but when the average degree of the network is large, the RA index is superior to AA index.

The AA index and RA index, respectively, measure the weight of CN nodes by the reciprocal of the logarithm of its degree or the reciprocal of its degree. Because these indexes have lower complexity, they is available for large-scale online social networks. However, for high precision request on small social network, RA index and AA index have some limitations. For this kind of problem, these indexes have local path index [66], Katz index [67], LHN-II index [68], global random walk [69], local random walk [70], etc. It is worth noting that these algorithms have higher complexity and longer operation time despite their high accuracy, especially for global and local random walk. We do not discuss these indexes here in detail, interested readers can refer to the corresponding references.

3. Case analysis

Marlow et al. [48] investigated group interaction on Facebook using the above theory according to the following steps:

1. Calculate the number of followers of an account;
2. Calculate the number of accounts interacting with an account; and
3. Calculate all the accounts based on the above steps.

The study draws the following conclusions: First, on Facebook, even if the number of friends that a user claimed in his/her own data pages is large (about 500 people), the total number of friends with actual contact ranges from 10 to 40. Second, the authors believe that Facebook can promote passive engagement, i.e., people keep in touch by reading news of their friends without communicating with each other. Huberman et al. [49] came to the same conclusion on studying Twitter by a method similar to that of Marlow et al. As shown in Figure 1.23, even if a user has a large number of followers, the number of friends is limited to 45. The establishment of friend relationship here is based on the relationship selection behavior on group interaction.

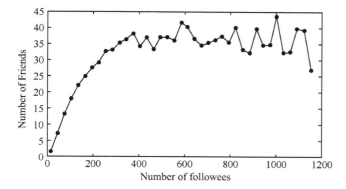

Figure 1.23: Relation graph of the number of strong relations and followers of online social network users.

Marlow et al. [48] and Huberman [49] et al. only conducted a qualitative research on the relationship selection of group interaction. Ball et al. [51] conducted a quantitative analysis on the relationship selection of group interaction using the reciprocity theory of social network. The results are shown in Figure 1.24.
Specific experimental steps included:
(1) Using LeaderRank algorithm to estimate the social status of each node in online social network; and
(2) Using the maximum likelihood model to calculate the connection probability of any two nodes under a given social status gap.

As shown in the research, nonreciprocal edges are mostly from individuals with low social status to individuals with high social status, whereas reciprocal edges are usually generated between individuals with similar social status. Social status here refers to the status of node granted by certain sorting algorithms (e.g., LeaderRank) in a given network environment, and high social status implies more followers and larger influences.

Figure 1.24(a) represents the relationship between the social status gap z of any two nodes and the connection probability from node v_x to node v_y. The probability of reciprocal connection presents a spike when $z = 0$, implying that any two nodes with the same status are more likely to generate reciprocal connection. Figure 1.24(b)

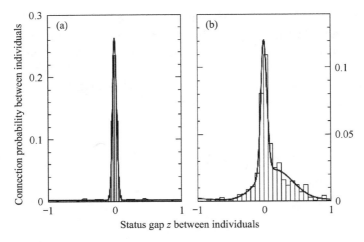

Figure 1.24: Relation graph of status gap between individuals and interaction establishment during group interaction.

corresponds to the probability of nonreciprocal connections. It is clear that any two nodes with social status gap in the range of 0 to 1 are more likely to generate reciprocal connection, implying that unidirectional edge in online social network is usually from the nodes with low social status to the nodes with high social status. It is very prominent in microblogging social network platforms in China. For example, we follow a celebrity in certain fields in microblog, but it is hard to be followed by the celebrity, making it impossible to create an interactive relationship. However, it is of high probability that celebrities follow each other, which shows that the conclusions of Ball et al. are universal and applicable.

1.4.2 Content selection of group interaction

The connection relationship among users in online social network is influenced not only by the relationship selection mechanism but also by content during interactive process. Crandall et al. [54] investigated the influence on similarity of two Wikipedia editors' behavior by their social behavior, and termed the relationship selection mechanism as relationship influence and the content during interactive process as social influence. The results show that the similarity between content used by two Wikipedia editors had significant differences before and after the interaction. Based on the data of Live Journal, a blog site, Backstrom et al. [55] used friendship between individuals and network communities with obvious characteristics that individuals participated in to build a bipartite graph. Based on the membership closure theory in the triadic closure, they found that the number of individuals in a community (as the independent variable) and the probability that individuals tend to join a community (as the dependent variable) had a positive correlation. Brzozowski et al. [56] applied the bipartite graph theory to Watercooler, a social network, and built social relation network graph based on the behavior of group user interaction and community relationship graph based on individual user label information. They found that the recommendation effect based on community relationship diagram is worse than that of the social relation network. In Watercooler, users can follow friends similar to Twitter and demonstrate themselves on a platform similar to Facebook. Hence, online social networks allow users to track or comment on some content, thus effectively focusing on relevant topics. Moreover, users can establish social relations corresponding to the content they follow or track. Therefore, the selection of group interaction is inseparable to social relations established in online social networks. In this subsection, we first introduce the theoretical basis for researching the content selection of group interaction, followed by concrete experimental procedure, and finally, a case analysis.

Theoretical basis for the research concerning content selection of group interaction is triadic closure theory and bipartite graph. The triadic closure theory solves the connection probability between two individuals having the same friend, whereas the bipartite graph solves the probability that two individuals with similar social relationships are interested in a particular content. We need to apply the theory of community closure and membership closure based on the triadic closure theory. The theory of community closure solves the connection probability between two individuals, which is a function of the number of communities they both participate in. For example, in microblog, if user A and user B participate in the entertainment and food topic activities and user A and user C participate in the entertainment topic activities, then how this difference affects the relationship between individual users. The theory of membership closure puts forward another question from opposite different direction, i.e., what is the probability of a person joining a particular community (as the function of the number of his/her friends who have participated in the community)? Again, in microblog, if user A has a friend who participates in the food topic activity and user B has two friends who participate in the food topic activity, then how big is the difference between probabilities that user A and user B are participating in the food topic activity.

The experimental procedures for researching content selection in group interaction are as follows.

(1) Select different network snapshot at equal time interval;
(2) Build the bipartite graph for each network snapshot and count the number of topics that each individual and two individuals participate in; and
(3) According to statistical data and taking time as the axis, analyze the influence of community closure and membership closure on user's relationship.

Case study of content selection of group interaction: using triadic closure theory and membership closure theory and combining them with the above steps, Crandall et al. [54] and Backstrom et al. [55], respectively, researched Live Journal, a blog site, and Wikipedia. The results are shown in Figure 1.25.

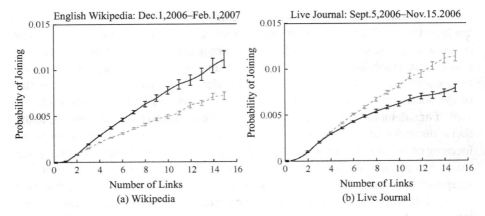

Figure 1.25: Member closure graph in online social network.

Figure 1.25 (b) shows the relationship between the number of a person's friends who joined a community and the probability that persons join this community. Figure 1.25 (a) is a similar analysis using Wikipedia. The nodes in bipartite graph denote the user's account and user's statement homepage. If one editor leaves a comment on the homepage of another editor, an edge forms between the two editors. Each article of Wikipedia is a "community." Two experiments have come to the same conclusion, i.e., the probability that an individual joins the community increases with the increase in the number of CN.

Using the same method on Watercooler, Brzozowski et al. analyzed the influence of group interaction content on recommendation effect from the perspective of evaluating recommended schemes [56]. There are three kinds of recommended schemes in the research:

(1) Based on user behavior, i.e., individual A frequently interacts with individual B, indicating that individual A is interested in B;
(2) Based on network structure, including two research methods, i.e., collaborative percolation recommendation and recommendation based on the structural hole theory;
(3) Based on user tag similarity, Watercooler allows users to label themselves with interest tags, which reflect their individual characteristics to some extent.

An interesting conclusion from the research is that the recommendation effect based on user's tag similarity is not as good as that of network structure. The authors concluded that user's content label only indicates that he/she wants to become the person with such properties, but not "id." Network structure is the mapping of real social structure as it forms by the interaction behavior between real individuals. Therefore, compared with the former, it has better authenticity and better recommendation effect.

1.4.3 The time law of group interaction

In this subsection, we first introduce the time law of group interaction in online social network, and then discuss two kinds of classical interpretation models for the time law.

The analyses of temporal characteristics of human behavior in online social networks mainly focus on the time interval distribution. For large-scale online social datasets, the dynamic mechanism of human behavior based on the time interval distribution of behavior is helpful to understand many socioeconomic phenomena, such as resource allocation, traffic control, epidemic forecasting as well as forecasting, emergency management, and personalized recommendation in economic activities. With the development of information and network technology, social network tools (QQ, blog, forum, microblog, WeChat, etc.) are emerging, making it possible to conduct empirical research and model the time interval distribution in large-scale network for human behavior. By researching the time characteristics of online video on demand [57], online games [58], and posting microblogs [59], significant differences have been noted between the time interval distribution and the negative exponential distribution in the traditional environment. The time interval distribution shows obvious power-law distribution characteristic, i.e., "the long tail" effect. This is possibly because the behavior generation of the traditional environment research object satisfies Poisson flow, and behavior decision strategies are mainly first come first served (FCFS), such as research on traffic [60] and busy line in communication [61]. However, two general characteristics of the research object in the network environment make its behavior generation to no longer satisfy Poisson flow. First, because of user interaction behavior in network environment, the network social relations formed therein make the behavior generation in nonoverlapping time domains no longer independent, such as online games. Second, users' network behavior is embedded in real behavior. The behavior priority sequence based on user's individual characteristics leads to paroxysmal characteristics of the user's network behavior, i.e., high-density out and long-time waiting, such as information exchange on instant communication platforms. Decisions are no longer made by FCFS primarily. Therefore, Barabasi et al. [62] constructed a dynamic model of behavioral decision strategy, taking the highest priority first (HPF) as the main parameter and random selection as the secondary parameter. They well explained the power-law distribution mechanism of waiting time in variable task queue length scenarios. Vazquez et al. [63] further investigated the characteristics of task waiting time and proposed two universal class views with power exponent of 1 and 1.5 for variable and immutable queue length situation, respectively. According to the change law over time of individuals' interest in participating in activities, Han et al. [64] proposed a model of human behavior time law in online social networks based on interest and motivation, showing that the time law follows power law distribution.

1. Queuing model based on the highest priority

The theoretical hypothesis of Barabasi et al. based on the highest priority model is as follows: an individual generates priority-based task queue sequence according to the importance of L tasks to be performed, performing the task with the highest priority within each time step. The task with the highest priority disappears from the queue thereafter, and a new task is added to the queue with priority x_i. Given the randomness of individuals' performance of tasks, the authors introduced variable y ($0 \leq y \leq \infty$) when creating the model. $y = \infty$ indicates that the user performs tasks exactly according to the priorities of tasks, and $y = 0$ indicates that the user performs tasks exactly by random selection. On the basis of this hypothesis, assuming the probability for performing a task within unit time is $\Pi(x) \sim x^y$ and the probability of performing the task with priority x at waiting time t is:

$$f(x, t) = (1 - \Pi(x))^{t-1}\Pi(x) \tag{1.9}$$

Thus, the average waiting time $\tau(x)$ for the task with priority x is:

$$\tau(x) = \sum_{t=1}^{\infty} tf(x, t) = \frac{1}{\Pi(x)} \sim \frac{1}{x^y} \tag{1.10}$$

$$P(\tau) \sim \frac{\rho(\tau^{-1/y})}{\tau^{1+1/y}} \tag{1.11}$$

where $P(\tau) \sim \tau^{-1}$ when $y \rightarrow \infty$ and $P(\tau)$ converge in exponential distribution when $y \rightarrow 0$.

2. Time law model of human online activity based on interest-driven

The above models are the first quantitative analysis of time distribution of the online social network activity, which inspired other researchers. Han et al. created a model of the time law of human online activity based on interest-driven. There are two theory points in the model:

(1) The probability of doing certain behavior changes after a person doing it. Consider the simplest case, i.e., assuming that the change rate is the same if the change trend is identical.

(2) There are two thresholds in the time interval of the event. The time interval being too small or too large changes the probability of executing behavior. That is, if the interval is too small, the probability of doing the behavior will be reduced, otherwise the probability increases.

Therefore, the rules of the model are: the probability of occurrence of an action event is $r(t)$ at time t (time discreteness); $r(t)$ will have to update with each event according to update rules of $r(t + 1) = a(t)r(t)$, where the value of $a(t)$ is as follows:

$$a(t) = \begin{cases} a_0, & \tau_i \leq T_1 \\ a_0^{-1}, & \tau_i \geq T_2 \\ a(t-1), & T_1 < \tau_i < T_2 \end{cases} \qquad (1.12)$$

where $T_1 \leq T_2$, $0 < a_0 < 1$.

According to the above rules, the situation that time interval between the adjacent two events is less than or equal to T_1 occurs mostly when $r(t)$ equals to or approaches T_1^{-1}. Therefore, the value of T_1 determines the maximum value of $r(t)$, the value of T_2 determines the minimum value of $r(t)$ in the vicinity of T_2^{-1}. If T_1 and the minimum time scale of the model increase in the same ratio, and the ratio of T_1 and T_2 remains unchanged, then the average ratio between the maximum and minimum value of $r(t)$ is unchanged; thus, the new time interval distribution is the same as that of the original, and T_1 represents the minimum effective time scale of the model. Therefore, in the following discussion, we assume $T_1 = 1$.

In numerical simulation, the initial value of $r(t)$is fixed at 1.0. Using numerical simulation, when the difference between T_1 and T_2 is over three magnitudes, it can generate the time interval distribution close to the power-law with the power exponent as −1. By reducing T_2, the distribution gradually deviates from the power-law to exponential distribution. When T_1 equals T_2, larger a_0 also causes the distribution curve to deviate from the power-law, as shown in Figure 1.26.

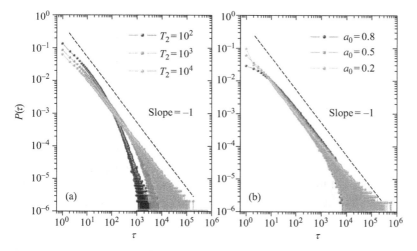

Figure 1.26: Time interval distribution generated by self-adaptive interest model.

In this model, $r(t)$ is limited to a certain range and exhibits a quasi-periodic variation because of two thresholds, as shown in Figure 1.27. Only consider the stage of $r(t)$ reduction in a cycle, $r(t) = r_m a_0^i$ where r_m denotes the initial value (also the maximum

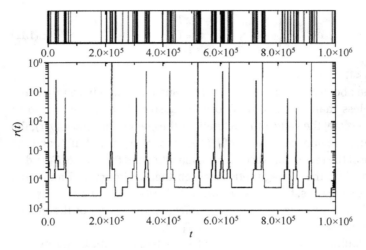

Figure 1.27: Pattern and interest change curve of events generated by self-adaptive interest model.

value) of $r(t)$ and takes value around T_1^{-1} (but with a smaller mean than T_1^{-1}) $i = 0, 1, 2, \cdots$. The time interval distribution between two adjacent events is:

$$P(\tau) = I^{-1} \sum_{i=0}^{I} (1 - r_m a_0^i)^{\tau-1} r_m a_0^i \tag{1.13}$$

The above theoretical model provides a solid theoretical basis for interpreting the power-law time distribution of human behavior in online social network environment.

1.5 Summary

As an important channel for social interaction in the Web 2.0 era, online social networks are widely used in everyday life. With online social networks, people can link with others, share information and happiness through this linkage, and interact with each other on topics of common interest. Users' social networking behavior is the external manifestation of their motivation. The characteristics and laws of users' behavior in social network can be used to analyze the internal mechanism of users' online social networking behavior, thereby providing information to online social networking service providers for innovating their business model as well as theoretical foundations to monitor the online public sentiment.

Despite theories and application results from research on social network users' behavior, we think the following issues need to be further researched and explored.

(1) For adoption and loyalty toward social network; the existing research on the adoption and loyalty behavior of online social networks focuses on comprehensive social networking platforms (e.g., Facebook), with little information regarding the vertical and mobile social networking platforms. In addition, the technical properties (e.g., interactivity) of online social networks and the influence of users' psychological experience (e.g., social presence) on adoption and loyalty behavior are also challenging issues for future studies.

(2) For individual behavior of social network users, the existing research on individual behavior in online social networks focuses on individual behavior on social network platforms such as Facebook, including information posting behavior, information search behavior, and information browsing behavior. Attracted by the rapid and efficient contact with target users by social network, in recent years, many enterprises have advertised and provided customer services through online social network platforms. Online social network platforms have gradually developed services and business functions based on information posting, entertainment, friend making, etc. Modeling individual behavior involving social and business behavior needs to be further researched.

(3) For group behavior of social network users, virtual communities in social network are usually formed by strangers with no offline connection. The formation mechanisms of virtual communities with distinct structures are still unclear. As the research on mutual influence between users in social network are usually conducted on the basis of network structure, the influence mechanism between users involving social properties needs to be further researched.

References

[1]   Davis FD: Perceived usefulness, perceived ease of use, and user acceptance of information technology. *MIS Quart* 1989, 13:319–340.

[2]   Kwon O, Wen Y: An empirical study of the factors affecting social network service use. *Comput Hum Behav* 2010, 26:254–263.

[3]   Ernst CP, Pfeiffer J, Rothlauf F: The influence of perceived belonging on social network site adoption. In Proceedings of the Nineteenth Americas Conference on Information Systems (ACIS 2013), Chicago, Illinois, USA: 1–10.

[4]   Nikou S, Bouwma H:Ubiquitous use of mobile social network services. Telemat Inform2014 31:422–433.

[5]   Sledgianowski D, Kulviwat S: Social network sites: Antecedents of user adoption and usage. In Proceedings of the 14th Americas Conference on Information Systems (AMCIS 2008), Toronto: Paper 83.

[6]   Dai B, Liu Y: Research on the usage intention of SNS based on Technology Acceptance Model and perceived popularity. Sci Tech Prog Policy 2012, 12:47–51.

[7]   Ajzen I: The theory of planned behavior. Organ Behav Hum 1991, 50:179–211.

[8] Baker RK, White KM: Predicting adolescents' use of social networking sites from an extended theory of planned behaviour perspective. Comput Hum Behav 2010, 26:1591–1597.

[9] Pelling EM, White KM: The theory of planned behavior applied to young people's use of social networking web sites. Cyberpsychol Behav 2009, 12:755–759.

[10] Chang YP, Zhu DH: Understanding social networking sites adoption in China: A comparison of pre-adoption and post-adoption. Comput Hum Behav 2011, 27:1840–1848.

[11] Leng GS, Lada S, Muhammad MZ, Ibrahim AA, Amboala T: An exploration of social networking sites (SNS) adoption in malaysia using Technology Acceptance Model (TAM), Theory of Planned Behavior (TPB) and Intrinsic Motivation. J Internet Bank Com 2011, 16:1–27.

[12] Bhattacherjee A: Understanding information systems continuance: An expectation-confirmation model. MIS Quart 2001, 25:351–370.

[13] Kang YS, Hong S, Lee H. Exploring continued online service usage behavior: The roles of self-image congruity and regret. Comput Hum Behav 2009, 25:111–122.

[14] Yin G, Bo Y: Theoretical model and empirical research of SNS user continued behavior China. J Inf Syst 2010, 4:53–64.

[15] Chen Y, Shao P: Empirical research on social web site continued usage: Based on improved expectation confirmation model. China J Inf Syst 2011, 8:23–33.

[16] Shin SI, Hall DJ: Identifying factors affecting SNS users as a temporary or persistent user: An empirical study. In Proceedings of the Seventeenth Americas Conference on Information Systems (AMCIS2011), Detroit, Michigan, USA: 316.

[17] Qian L, Bimei H: Research on the user continued usage intention of mobile social network based on DM and ECM-IT. China J Inf Syst 2013, 12:50–59.

[18] Csikszentmihalyi M. Beyond Boredom and Anxiety. San Francisco: Jossey-Bass Publishers, 1975.

[19] Zhou T, Li H, Liu Y: The effect of flow experience on mobile SNS users' loyalty. Indus Manage Data Syst 2010, 110:930–946.

[20] Hsu CL, Wu CC: Understanding users' continuance of Facebook: An integrated model with the unified theory of adoption and usage of technology, expectation disconfirmation model, and flow theory. Int J Virt Community Soc Netw 2011, 3:1–16.

[21] Chang YP, Zhu DH: The role of perceived social capital and flow experience in building users' continuous usage intention to social networking sites in China. Comput Hum Behav 2012, 28:995–1001.

[22] Wu Y, Wang Z, Chang K, Xu YJ: Why people stick to play social network site based entertainment applications: Design factors and flow theory perspective. Pacific Asia Conference on Information Systems (PACIS 2010), Taipei, Taiwan: 1041–1050.

[23] Chen CC: Examining users' intention to continue using social network games: A flow experience perspective. Telemat Inform 2013, 30:311–321.

[24] Tracii R, Xenos S: Who uses Facebook? An investigation into the relationship between the BigFive, shyness, narcissism, loneliness, and Facebook usage. Comput Hum Behav 2011, 27:1658–1664.

[25] Moore K, McElroy JC: The influence of personality on Facebook usage, wall postings, and regret. Comput Hum Behav 2012, 28:267–274.

[26] Benevenuto F, Rodrigues T, Cha M, Almeida V: Characterizing user behavior in online social networks. In Proceedings of the 9th ACM SIGCOMM Conference on Internet Measurement Conference. ACM, 2009: 49–62.

[27] Golder S, Wilkinson D, Huberman B: Rhythms of social interaction: Messaging within a massive online network. Communities and Technologies. Springer, London, 2007, 41–66.

[28] Maia M, Almeida J, Almeida V: Identifying user behavior in online social networks. In Proceedings of the 1st workshop on Social Network Systems. ACM, 2008: 1–6.

[29] Gyarmati L, Anh LT: Measuring user behavior in online social networks. IEEE Netw 2010, 24:26–31.
[30] Mediabistro: October 18, 2011. http://www.mediabistro.com/alltwitter/costolo-future-of-twitter_b14936. Source: http://blog.twitter.com/2012/03/twitter-turns-six.html, accessed October 9,2012.
[31] Shriver SK, Nair HS, Hofstetter R: Social ties and user-generated content: Evidence from an online social network. Manage Sci 2013, 59:1425–1443.
[32] Toubia O, Stephen AT: Intrinsic vs. image-related utility in social media: Why do people contribute content to twitter?. Market Sci 2013, 32:368–392.
[33] Wang YC, Burke M, Kraut R: Gender, topic, and audience response: An analysis of user-generated content on Facebook. In Proceedings of the SIGCHI Conference on Human Factors in Computing Systems. ACM, 2013: 31–34.
[34] Yarkoni T: Personality in 100,000 words: A large-scale analysis of personality and word use among bloggers. J Res Person 2010, 44:363–373.
[35] Qiu L, Lin H, Ramsay J, Yang F: You are what you tweet: Personality expression and perception on twitter. J Res Person 2012, 46:710–718.
[36] Boyle K, Johnson T: MySpace is your space? Examining self-presentation of MySpace users. Comput Hum Behav 2010, 26:1392–1399.
[37] OpenSource. (2010). OpenNLP: http://opennlp.apache.org.
[38] Blei DM, Ng AY, Jordan MI: Latent Dirichlet allocation. J Mach Learn Res 2003, 3:993–1022.
[39] Pennebaker J, Booth F: Linguistic inquiry and word count (LIWC): A computerized text analysis program. Mahwah (NJ) 2001, 7.
[40] Golbeck J, Robles C, Turner K: Predicting personality with social media. CHI' 11 Extended Abstracts on Human Factors in Computing Systems. ACM, 2011: 253–262.
[41] Nguyen T, Phung D, Brett A, Venkatesh S: Towards discovery of influence and personality traits through social link prediction. ICWSM. 2011.
[42] Nowson S: The language of weblogs: A study of genre and individual differences. Unpublished doctoral dissertation, University of Edinburgh, Edinburgh, UK., 2006.
[43] Ringel MM, Teevan J, Panovich K: What do people ask their social networks, and why?: A survey study of status message Q&A behavior. In Proceedings of the SIGCHI Conference on Human Factors in Computing Systems. ACM, 2010: 1739–1748.
[44] Roelof Z: Who is looking?. In Proceedings of the IEEE/WIC/ACM International Conference on Web Intelligence. IEEE Computer Society, 2007, 184–190.
[45] Tifferet S, Vilnai-Yavetz I: Gender differences in Facebook self-presentation: An international randomized study. Comput Hum Behav 2014, 35:388–399.
[46] Ringel MM, Teevan J, Panovich K: A comparison of information seeking using search engines and social networks. ICWSM 2010, 10:23–26.
[47] Marlow C, Byron L, Lento T, Rosenn I: Maintained relationships on Facebook. Retrieved February, 2009, 15: 2010.
[48] Huberman B, Romero D, Wu F: Social networks that matter: Twitter under the microscope. arXiv preprint arXiv: 0812. 1045, 2008.
[49] Burke M, Kraut R, Marlow C: Social capital on Facebook: Differentiating uses and users. In Social capital on Facebook: Differentiating uses and users. (ACM, 2011, edn.): 571–580.
[50] Ball B, Newman ME: Friendship networks and social status. Netw Sci 2013, 1:16–30.
[51] Zhang JF: Tipping and Residential Segregation: A Unified Schelling Model. J Region Sci 2011, 51:167–193.
[52] Zhou T, Lu L, Zhang YC: Predicting missing links via local information. Eur Phys J B 2009, 71:623–630.

[53] Crandall D, Cosley D, Huttenlocher D, Kleinberg J, Suri S: Feedback effects between similarity and social influence in online communities. In Feedback effects between similarity and social influence in online communities. (ACM, 2008, edn.): 160–168.

[54] Backstrom L, Huttenlocher D, Kleinberg J, Lan X: Group formation in large social networks: membership, growth, and evolution. In Group formation in large social networks: membership, growth, and evolution. (ACM, 2006, edn.): 44–54.

[55] Brzozowski M, Romero D: Who Should I Follow? Recommending People in Directed Social Networks. (2011, edn.).

[56] Zhou T, Kiet HA, Kim BJ, Wang BH, Holme P: Role of activity in human dynamics. EPL 2008, 82:28002.

[57] Grabowski A, Kruszewska N, Kosiński RA: Dynamic phenomena and human activity in an artificial society. Phys Rev E 2008, 78:066110.

[58] Yan Q, Wu L, Zheng L: Social network based microblog user behavior analysis. Physica A 2013, 392:1712–1723.

[59] van Lint H. Reliable travel time prediction for freeways. Netherlands TRAIL Research School, 2004.

[60] Beneš VE: Mathematical theory of connecting networks and telephone traffic. Acad Pr 1965.

[61] Barabasi AL: The origin of bursts and heavy tails in human dynamics. Nature 2005, 435:207–211.

[62] Vazquez A, Oliveira JG, Dezso Z, Goh K, Kondor I, Barabasi AL: Modeling bursts and heavy tails in human dynamics. Phys Rev E 2006, 73:036127.

[63] Han XP, Zhou T, Wang BH: Modeling human dynamics with adaptive interest. N J Phys 2008, 10:073010.

[64] Lada A, Eytan A: Friends and neighbors on the web. Soc Netw 2003, 25:211–230

[65] Spring N, Mahajan R, Wetherall D, Andcrson T: Measuring ISP topologies with rocketful. IEEE/ACM Transact Netw 2004, 12:2.

[66] Leo K: A new status index derived from sociometric index. Psychometrika 1953, 18:39–43.

[67] Leicht EA, Holme P, Newman ME: Vertex similarity in networks. Phys Rev E 2006, 73:026120.

[68] Klein DJ, Randic M: Resistance distance. J Math Chem 1993, 12:81–95.

[69] Liu W, Lu L: Link prediction based on local random walk. Europhys Lett 2010, 89:58007.

Bin Zhou and Binxing Fang
2 Social network sentiment analysis

2.1 Introduction

With the rapid development of internet, network has become a main resource for users to obtain information and post opinions. Text can be divided into two types: objective description information mainly used to provide objective description of events, products, etc. and subjective information mainly derived from user comments on people, events, products, etc. Subjective information expresses user's emotional color and orientation such as "positive," "negative," or "neutral." Sentiment analysis (opinion mining) refers to the process of analyzing, processing, and summarizing subjective information. It originates from the natural language processing domain, and mainly researches and judges the sentimental orientation of the text according to the syntactic and semantic rule. With the rise and rapid development of social network, sentiment analysis has been gradually applied to other research domains, such as text mining and web data mining, and has been extended to management science, social science, and other disciplines. At present, it is widely used in product comments, public sentiment monitoring, and information prediction.

This chapter will systematically introduce sentiment analysis techniques in social network. Section 2.2 introduces the sentiment analysis techniques for regular long text such as news and reports. Section 2.3 provides a detailed introduction of the main techniques for sentiment analysis in social network according to the short text characteristics in social network, as well as the influence of social network link structure and group interaction on user sentiments. Section 2.4 introduces the sentiment summary technique and sentiment analysis technique on the basis of transfer learning.

2.1.1 History of sentiment analysis

Sentiment analysis first originated from the analysis of words with an emotional color. For example, "nice" is usually commendatory, whereas "ugly" is derogatory. Although many researchers realized the importance of sentiment analysis, sentiment analysis techniques developed slowly before the 1990s mainly owing to a lack of available data.

With the rise of internet, network has become the major source of information. Large amounts of available data, such as news and reports, brings breakthrough for sentiment analysis techniques. Professor Jance Wiebe from the University of

https://doi.org/10.1515/9783110599411-002

Pittsburgh first analyzed author's subjective opinion in 1994 and divided sentences into objective and subjective text. Objective sentences are used to describe objective facts whereas subjective sentences are used by authors to express their views, opinions, attitudes, and so on [1]. Sentiment analysis was first proposed by Sanjiv Das and Mike Chen [2] in their research on stock market text in 2001. They researched messages on the message board of the stock market and defined sentiment as positive and negative opinions in the message. In 2003, Dave et al. [3] first used the term opinion mining, which aims to automatically extract the attributes of products (e.g., weight and feature) as well as to mine positive, neutral, and negative opinions for each attribute. Since then, sentiment analysis and opinion mining have been widely used in academic research. The main resources for sentiment analysis during that period were long texts such as news and reports whose grammar are regular enough for analysis and processing.

With the rise of Web 2.0 and social network, users can now express their views and opinions at any time, which results in massive corpus for sentiment analysis while presenting new problems and challenges. Compared with long text such as news and reports, text information in social networks has short length, irregular syntax rules, big data noise, and, in particular, lots of popular internet slang, making sentiment analysis more difficult. At the same time, group characteristics in social network as well as link and interaction characteristics among groups also leads to a new research area for traditional sentiment analysis.

In 2008, Pang Bo and Lillian Lee regarded sentiment analysis and opinion mining as a unified term [4] defining them as extracting opinion, sentiment, and subjectivity in text. In 2012, Liu Bing defined sentiment analysis (opinion mining) as analyzing opinions, sentiments, attitudes, emotions, and other subjective information contained in user text related to products, services, events, topics, and so on [5].

In this book, we also regard sentiment analysis and opinion mining as the same term.

2.1.2 Sentiment definition and classification

According to text granularity, sentiment analysis can be divided into three levels: article level, sentence level, and word level. Article-level sentiment analysis regards the whole article as a target for sentiment analysis to mine its sentiment orientation on an event or a product, generally expressed by ternary classification (positive, neutral, and negative) or numerical evaluation (e.g., 1~5). Article-level sentiment analysis aims to mine the author's overall attitude while neglecting sentiment polarity in some sentences. For example, in a sentiment analysis for a report on iPhone, it is difficult to mine some negative comments despite the overall positive attitude of the author. Sentence-level sentiment analysis regards a sentence as an independent target for sentiment analysis, which can effectively cover the above shortage. To analyze a sentence, first classify it as an objective or subjective sentence and determine the sentiment polarity of the subjective sentence. Word-level sentiment analysis aims to determine the sentiment polarity for each word, which is mainly used in constructing sentiment dictionary. However, it neglects the influence of context, thus, is not available for differentiating the sentiment polarity of the same word in different contexts. For example, the word "high" in the sentence "the price of cannon is high" is a negative word but is positive in the sentence "the iPhone's cost performance is high."

We define views and opinions to be extracted in sentiment analysis according to Bing [5].

Definition 2.1 (Opinion) is generally defined as a tetrad $\langle g, s, h, t \rangle$ where g denotes the sentiment object or target, s denotes the sentiment orientation, h denotes the opinion holder, and t denotes the time.

Sentiment orientation s (sentiment polarity) is usually expressed by ternary classification as positive, neutral, and negative.

We take a comment for iPhone in Sina Weibo as an example.

Example 2.1 User A: (1) I bought an iPhone 5 yesterday. (2) It has beautiful and fashionable appearance, high pixel camera, and good photograph quality. I like it very much. (3) However, my classmate B thinks it is too expensive despite its pretty appearance. The cost performance is low (2013-12-20).

In Example 2.1, sentence (1) is an objective sentence describing the fact that the author bought a mobile phone without any sentiment orientation. Sentence (2) is a positive comment for iPhone with opinion holder as user A. Sentence (3) is a negative comment, but the opinion holder is user B. The post time of comment represents the time that user holds such an opinion. Therefore, we can extract the following two opinions.

Example 2.2 Extract opinions in product comments in Example 2.1:

Opinion 1: $\langle g, s, h, t \rangle$=<iPhone, positive, user A, 2013–12–20>

Opinion 2: $\langle g, s, h, t \rangle$=<iPhone, negative, user B, 2013–12–20>

The goal of sentiment analysis is to extract opinions from comments. For example, extraction of Opinion 1 and Opinion 2 from comments in Example 2.1 involves comment target, sentiment orientation, opinion holder, and comment time.

We can see from Example 2.1 that, although user A and user B comment on the same product iPhone, user A is more concerned about the appearance and camera performance while user B is more concerned about the price. Therefore, they hold different sentiment tendencies. In 2004, Liu Bing introduced the concept of entity into sentiment analysis. Each entity coomprises many features or aspects to represent different attributes of the product. Example 2.1 regards iPhone as an entity with such attributes as appearance, quality, weight, battery, and price. After introduction of the entity, the target for sentiment analysis to be extracted is no longer the entity but different attributes of the entity. Therefore, we can extend Definition 2.1 as follows.

Definition 2.2 (Entity-based opinion) An opinion about the entity is a quintuple $\langle e, a, s, h, t \rangle$ where e denotes the entity, a denotes different attributes of the entity, s denotes the sentiment orientation, h denotes the opinion holder, and t denotes the time.

Entity-based sentiment analysis requires not only extracting the sentiment orientation of each entity but also conducting sentiment analysis on each attribute. Opinions in Example 6-1 can extend as follows.

Example 2.3 Extract opinion in Example 2.1 based on entity.

Opinion 1: $\langle e, a, s, h, t \rangle$=<iPhone, appearance, positive, user A, 2013-12-20>

Opinion 2: $\langle e, a, s, h, t \rangle$=<iPhone, camera, positive, user A, 2013-12-20>

Opinion 3: $\langle e, a, s, h, t \rangle$=<iPhone, price, negative, user B, 2013-12-20>

Opinion 4: $\langle e, a, s, h, t \rangle$=<iPhone, cost performance, negative, user B, 2013-12-20>

Given a document set D, sentiment analysis comprises the following tasks.

Task 1: (Entity extraction and classification) Extract all entities in D and classify or group them. Each category represents an unique entity such as the entity iPhone.

Task 2: (Attribute extraction and classification) Extract attributes of each entity and classify or group them. Each category represents a unique attribute of the entity such as the appearance, quality, and camera of iPhone.

Task 3: (Opinion holder extraction) Extract the opinion holder of each opinion in Definition 2.2.

Task 4: (Time extraction) Extract the comment time for each opinion or the time that opinion holder expresses such opinion and standardize the time. For example, relative time like "Yesterday" should be changed to the GMT format.

Task 5: (Sentiment orientation extraction) Extract the sentiment orientation for evaluation object of opinion holder expressed by ternary classification (positive, neutral, and negative) or numerical evaluation (e.g., 1~5).

Task 5 is the main task of the sentiment analysis for text. In this chapter, we mainly introduce the techniques for sentiment orientation extraction. Table 2.1 shows the common terms and relevant interpretations in this chapter without causing conflict.

Table 2.1: Common terms and relevant interpretations in this chapter.

Term	Similar term or interpretations
Sentiment analysis	Opinion mining
Sentiment orientation	Sentiment polarity
Positive	Means the sentiment orientation is positive
Negative	Means the sentiment orientation is negative
Evaluation word	Sentiment word used to express author's sentiment, such as "beautiful" and "fashionable"

2.1.3 Application of sentiment analysis

Sentiment analysis is widely used in the domains of product comment, public sentiment monitoring, and information prediction. Before users buy a product, they tend to check comments related to the product and make the final decision after comparing the product with others. As users do not have enough time and energy to browse all comments, various systems are developed for providing comments of all attributes to facilitate users in making final decisions according to statistics, conclusion, and inference. For example, Bing et al. developed the OpinionObserver system to process product comments of online customers [6] and conduct visualized comprehensive quality comparison on different kinds of products. Theresa et al. developed the OpinionFinder system to automatically identify subjective sentences and extract sentiment information therein [7].

Public sentiment monitoring is another important application domain for sentiment analysis. Because the social network is open, virtual, divergent, permeable, random, among other characteristics, more and more users are willing to express their attitudes, which makes social network the main resource for generating and propagating public sentiment. As everyone has the right to speak on the network, various topics and views related to national economy and people's livelihood can be posted at any time and subsequently spread in a "fission" manner. Opinion leaders can mobilize people with the same views, sentiments, and appeals and rapidly mobilize the masses to participate in social activities offline, thereby creating a social mobilization force. The integration of and interaction between virtual social network and real society have a large direct influence on society. Therefore, the perception and analysis of people's sentiment and attitude in the network are of great importance in maintaining national security and promoting social development.

Sentiment analysis plays an important role in information prediction. People's thoughts and actions are largely influenced by the occurrence of a new event or heated discussion over an event. Sentiment analysis can predict the development orientation of future events by analyzing and processing users' sentiment orientation in text, playing an important role in economic and political domains. For example, Ann et al. predicted future financial orientation by performing sentiment polarity recognition on financial comment text [8]. Soo-Min et al. successfully predicted the results of US presidential election in 2008 by analyzing a large number of corresponding network news comments [9].

2.2 Sentiment analysis techniques

Sentiment analysis techniques in online social network mostly derive from text sentiment analysis. The text here, different from social networks such as Sina Weibo, usually refers to "long text," such as network news, netizen blogs, and forum posts. Research methods for text sentiment analysis can be classified into semantic rule-based techniques, supervised learning-based techniques, and topic model-based sentiment techniques, which will be discussed in this section in detail.

2.2.1 Semantic rule-based sentiment analysis

From the perspective of parts of speech, noun usually represents an entity or its attribute whereas adjective and adverb are usually used for expressing sentiment views, i.e., comment words usually consist of adjective and adverb. It is easy to calculate the sentiment orientation of the author if sentiment polarity of all comment words is obtained. For example, considering the comment "iPhone has beautiful, new-fashioned, characteristic and fashionable appearance," it is easy to determine author's sentiment orientation as positive because sentiment words "beautiful, new-fashioned, characteristic and fashionable" used for expressing the author's view are positive. This method relies on the sentiment dictionary labeled with sentiment orientation and is called sentiment dictionary-based method.

Sentiment dictionary-based method can give a preliminary judgment of sentiment orientation of text but is not applicable for all conditions as no single sentiment dictionary can include all comment words and some sentiment words have different polarities in different contexts. The semantic rule-based method can achieve sentiment classification by calculating the distance between comment words and seed words in a sentiment dictionary (words indicating the degree of sentiment orientation labeled in sentiment dictionary).

Essentially, semantic rule-based sentiment analysis techniques are unsupervised learning methods. Peter Turney proposed a typical algorithm SO-PMI [10] in 2002. In the algorithm, only "excellent" and "poor" were used as benchmark words for positive and negative comments, and sentiment classification was achieved by calculating the distance between comment words and the above two reference words based on pointwise mutual information.

Algorithm 2.1 SO-PMI algorithm.

Input: Document d to be analyzed
Output: Sentiment orientation of the document d
Steps are as follows:
Step 1 Extract comment word set W from the document to be analyzed by labeling the parts of speech with mainly adjective and adverb as comment words. Note: comment words are generally used to express user orientation that varies under different contexts.
Step 2 Select "excellent" and "poor" as the benchmark words. For each sentiment word $w_i \in W$, calculate its semantic orientation based on point-wise mutual information as follows:

$$SO(w_i) = PMI(w_i, \text{excellent}) - PMI(w_i, \text{poor})$$

Point-wise mutual information:

$$PMI(\text{word}_1, \text{word}_2) = \log_2 \frac{P(\text{word}_1 \& \text{word}_2)}{P(\text{word}_1)P(\text{word}_2)}$$

where $P(\text{word}_1 \& \text{word}_2)$ denotes the probability that word_1 and word_2 appear at the same time and $P(\text{word}_i)$ denotes the probability that word_i appears alone.
Step 3 Calculate the average semantic orientation of sentence:

$$SO(W) = \frac{1}{|W|} \sum_{w_i \in W} SO(w_i)$$

If $SO(W) > 0$, the sentiment orientation is positive; if $SO(W)0$, the sentiment orientation is negative.

SO-PMI algorithm uses point-wise mutual information to measure the distance between comment words and seed words. The basic principle is that bigger PMI value between comment words and seed words has a larger probability that comment words and seed words appear at the same time, indicating more similar sentiment orientation.

We take Example 2.1 to show the text sentiment analysis steps of SO-PMI algorithm.

Example 2.4 Calculate sentiment orientation using Example 2.1.

(1) First, label the comment by parts of speech and extract the comment words as shown in Table 2.2.
(2) Second, calculate the point-wise mutual information between each comment word and reference word (i.e., "excellent" and "poor" using the formula $PMI(\text{word}_1, \text{word}_2) = \log_2 \frac{P(\text{word}_1 \& \text{word}_2)}{P(\text{word}_1)P(\text{word}_2)}$. Assume that the times of comment words and reference words in 1,000 corpora are as shown in Table 2.3.

Table 2.2: Comment words.

No.	Comment words
Sentence 2	Fashionable, new fashioned, high pixel, good quality
Sentence 3	Beautiful, high press, low-cost performance

Table 2.3: Times of comment words and reference words.

	Excellent	Poor	Times alone
Fashionable	57	3	97
New fashioned	37	1	122
High pixel	23	2	85
Good quality	28	4	76
Beautiful	46	3	97
Expensive	6	29	68
Low-cost performance	1	52	79
Times alone	137	102	

The cross terms in Table 2.3 denote the times that the two words appear, and the last column and row denote the time that a single word appears. For example, in 1,000 comments, the word "fashionable" appears 57 times with the word "excellent" but only 3 times with "poor." Meanwhile, "fashionable" appears 97 times alone, "excellent" appears 137 times alone, and "poor" appears 102 times alone. Therefore,

$$\text{PMI("fashionable," excellent)} = \log_2 \frac{P(\text{fashionable, excellent})}{P(\text{fashionable})P(\text{excellent})} = \log_2 \frac{0.057}{0.097 \times 0.137} = 2.1007$$

$$\text{PMI("fashionable," poor)} = \log_2 \frac{P(\text{fashionable, poor})}{P(\text{fashionable})P(\text{poor})} = \log_2 \frac{0.003}{0.097 \times 0.102} = -1.7216$$

Therefore,

$$\text{SO(fashionable)} = \text{PMI(fashionable,excellent)-PMI(fashionable,poor)} = 3.8223$$

Similarly, we can calculate the SO – PMI value of each comment word, as shown in Table 2.4.

(3) Calculate overall SO value. According to the length of the text, we can derive the sentiment orientation for the document, Sentence 2, and Sentence 3.

(1) Sentiment orientation of the comment:

$$\text{SO}(W) = \frac{1}{|W|} \sum_{w_i \in W} \text{SO}(w_i) = 1.2535 > 0$$

Therefore, the overall polarity of the comment is positive.

Table 2.4: Calculate SO-PMI values.

Comment word w	PMI(w, excellent)	PMI(w, poor)	SO(w)
Fashionable	2.1007	−1.7216	3.8223
New fashioned	1.1465	−3.6374	4.7839
High pixel	0.9819	−2.116	3.0979
Good quality	1.4272	−0.9546	2.3818
Beautiful	1.7914	−1.7216	3.513
High price	−0.6347	2.0639	−2.6986
Low-cost performance	−3.436	2.69	−6.126

(2) Sentiment orientation of Sentence 2:

$$SO(W_2) = \frac{1}{|W_2|} \sum_{w_i \in W_2} SO(w_i) = 3.5215 > 0$$

Therefore, Sentence 2 is positive.

(3) Sentiment orientation of Sentence 3:

$$SO(W_3) = \frac{1}{|W_3|} \sum_{w_i \in W_3} SO(w_i) = -1.7705 < 0$$

Therefore, Sentence 3 is negative.

SO-PMI was the first model to analyze text sentiment by unsupervised learning algorithm and apply it to the domains of car and movie comments. The average precision in car and movie comments is 84% and 66%, respectively. Many studies were performed based on it thereafter. For example, Xiaowen et al. proposed a whole dictionary-based opinion mining method [11] in 2008. They thought that each sentence s contained multiple features and corresponding sentiment words. The orientation of each feature can be determined according to the following formula:

$$score(f) = \sum_{w_i : w_i \in s \cap w_i \in V} \frac{w_i \cdot SO}{dis(w_i, f)}$$

where w_i denotes the sentiment word, V denotes the set of sentiment word, $dis(w_i, f)$ denotes the distance between the sentiment word w_i, and feature f, $w_i \cdot SO$ denotes the sentiment polarity of w_i with positive as 1 and negative as −1. For each feature f, $score(f) > 0$ implies that the sentiment polarity for feature f is positive, while $score(f) < 0$ implies that the sentiment polarity is negative or neutral. Meanwhile, they considered the influence of negative and adversative words on improving precision. For example, "negative word + negative = positive" and "negative + positive = negative." Adversative words, such as "but" and "whereas," always imply an opposite sentiment orientation.

In 2005, Kim Soo-Min and Eduard Hovy proposed a method to collect sentiment words from WordNet semantic distance [12]. They first collected 34 adjectives and 44 adverbs as seed words and used WordNet to extend sentiment words. The basic idea is that the synonyms and antonyms of a sentiment word are also sentiment words. For each word w, they used the following formula to decide its sentiment polarity.

$$\arg\max_c P(c|w) \cong \arg\max_c P(c|syn_1, syn_2 \ldots, syn_n)$$

where c denotes the target classification (sentiment word or nonsentiment word), w denotes the target word, and syn_i denotes the synonym or antonym of w in WordNet. According to Bayesian formula, we have:

$$\arg\max_c P(c|w) = \arg\max_c P(c)P(w|c)$$
$$= \arg\max_c P(c)P(syn_1, syn_2, syn_3, \ldots, syn_n|c)$$
$$= \arg\max_c P(c) \prod_{k=1}^{m} P(f_k|c)^{\mathrm{count}(f_k, \mathrm{synset}(w))}$$

where f_k denotes the k feature of category c and belongs to the synonym set of w and count $(f_k, \mathrm{synset}(w))$ denotes the number of times that f_k appears in the synonym set ofw. The sentiment orientation of w is decided by the results of the classification.

2.2.2 Supervised learning-based sentiment analysis

Supervised learning-based sentiment analysis first manually labels text polarity and uses it as a training dataset, and also constructs classifiers based on machine learning technique to perform sentiment classification for the target text.

Bo et al. first introduced machine learning techniques in text sentiment analysis on movie comment data in 2002. They first labeled 752 negative comments and 1,301 positive comments as a training dataset, and used Naïve Byes, maximum entropy, and support vector machines to perform sentiment classification for the target text. The results showed that machine learning techniques can effectively improve the precision of sentiment analysis.

1. Naïve Byes classification

Let $d = \{f_1, f_2, \ldots, f_n\}$ be a document where f_i denotes the feature or attribute of the document. Let c be the sentiment orientation of the document where 1 implies positive and -1 implies negative. Given a target document d, Naïve Byes method first calculates the posterior probability using a training dataset and uses the maximum probability of c as the document orientation of d, that is:

$$c = \arg\max_c P(c|d)$$

According to Naïve Bayesian conditional probability equation,

$$P(c|d) = \frac{P(c)P(d|c)}{P(d)}$$

where $P(d)$ is the probability of the document d. As $P(d)$ is independent of sentiment orientation c, it has no influence on classification results. Assume f_i, the features of d, is independent of each other, then conditional probability is:

$$P(d|c) = P(f_1, f_2 \dots f_n|c) = \prod_i P(f_i|c)$$

The Naïve Byes method first calculates the prior probability distribution $P(c)$ and the conditional probability $P(d|c)$ to obtain sentiment classification results. The algorithm is as follows:

Algorithm 2.2 Sentiment analysis based on Naïve Bayesian method.

Input: Document dataset $D = \{d_i, c_i\}$ labeled with sentiment classification where sentiment orientation of d_i is c_i with values as 1 or −1.
Output: Sentiment orientation of the target document d.
Steps of the algorithm are as follows:
Step 1 Calculate prior probability $P(c)$ and conditional probability $P(f_i|c)$:

$$P(c) = \frac{\#c}{N}$$

where $\#c$ denotes the number of documents with sentiment orientation of c in D and N denotes the number of total documents.

$$P(f_i|c) = \frac{P(f_i, c)}{P(c)}$$

Step 2 Calculate posterior probability:

$$P(c|d) \propto P(c)P(d|c) = P(c) \prod_i P(f_i|c)$$

Step 3 Choose the maximized posterior probability as the output:

$$c = \arg\max_c P(c|d)$$

We use Example 2.5 to show how Naïve Bayesian model works. In this example, the training dataset contains 15 documents, and each document contains two features, f_1 and f_2. The feature f_i can denote the comment words in a document or any other attributes showing users' sentiment orientation, and value $\{0, 1, 2\}$ denotes the number of times that f_i appears in the document. c denotes the sentiment orientation with value as $\{-1, 1\}$, where 1 denotes positive and −1 denotes negative. We only use this example to show the steps for classifying user sentiments by Naïve Bayesian algorithm. In real corpus, the number of training datasets and features are much bigger.

Example 2.5 Using the training dataset in Table 2.5 to calculate the sentiment orientation of $d = \{1, 0\}$.

Table 2.5: Training dataset.

	1	2	3	4	5	6	7	8	9	10	11	12	13	14	15
f_1	0	0	0	0	0	1	1	1	1	1	2	2	2	2	2
f_2	0	1	1	0	0	0	1	1	2	2	2	1	1	2	2
c	-1	-1	1	1	-1	-1	-1	1	1	1	1	1	1	1	-1

Solution:

Step 1 Calculate the prior probability and conditional probability as follows:

$$P(c=1) = \frac{9}{15}, \quad P(c=-1) = \frac{6}{15}$$

$$p(f_1=0 \mid c=1) = \frac{2}{9}, P(f_1=1 \mid c=1) = \frac{3}{9}, P(f_1=2 \mid c=1) = \frac{4}{9}$$

$$P(f_2=0 \mid c=1) = \frac{1}{9}, P(f_2=1 \mid c=1) = \frac{4}{9}, P(f_2=2 \mid c=1) = \frac{4}{9}$$

$$P(f_1=0 \mid c=-1) = \frac{3}{6}, P(f_1=1 \mid c=-1) = \frac{2}{6}, P(f_1=2 \mid c=-1) = \frac{1}{6}$$

$$P(f_2=0 \mid c=1) = \frac{3}{6}, P(f_2=1 \mid c=1) = \frac{2}{6}, P(f_2=2 \mid c=1) = \frac{1}{6}$$

Step 2 Calculate the posterior probability:

$$P(c=1/d) = P(c=1)P(f_1=1/c=1)P(f_2=0 \mid c=1) = \frac{9}{15} \times \frac{3}{9} \times \frac{1}{9} = \frac{1}{45}$$

$$P(c=-1/d) = P(c=-1)P(f_1=1/c=-1)P(f_2=0 \mid c=-1) = \frac{6}{15} \times \frac{2}{6} \times \frac{3}{6} = \frac{1}{15}$$

Step 3 Select the maximized probability as output:

$$P(c=-1/d) > P(c=1/d)$$

As the sentiment classification of document d is $c = -1$, document d is negative.

2. Maximum entropy model

The maximum entropy theory was first proposed by Edwin T. Jaynes in 1957 [13]. According to the theory, if we only know a part of the whole information, we should choose the probability distribution that meets those conditions but has the maximum entropy. Assuming $P(X)$ is the probability distribution of variable X, its information entropy is:

$$H(P) = -\sum_{x} P(x) \log P(x)$$

We can prove that the information entropy meets the following inequation:

$$0 \le H(P) \le \log_2 N$$

where N denotes the number of possible values of X. If and only if X meets uniform distribution, the right inequation becomes an equation, i.e., entropy has the maximum value when X meets uniform distribution.

Given some constraints of X, there are several probability distributions meeting these constraints. Each probability distribution can be regarded as a model. The maximum entropy theory is to choose the model with the maximum entropy as the output model.

Example 2.6 Calculate information entropy.

Assume the values of variable X are in $\{a, b, c, d, e, f, g, h\}$.

(1) If other information is unknown, we only have the following constraint:

$$p(a) + p(b) + p(c) + p(d) + p(e) + p(f) + p(g) + p(h) = 1$$

There are several probability distributions meeting the above constraint, and each distribution has its information entropy such as the following two probability distributions:

① If X meets uniform distribution, i.e.,

$$p(a) = p(b) = p(c) = p(d) = p(e) = p(f) = p(g) = p(h) = \frac{1}{8},$$

then the information entropy is:

$$H(P_1) = -8 \times \frac{1}{8} \log_2 \frac{1}{8} = 3$$

② If X meets probability distribution $\{\frac{1}{2}, \frac{1}{4}, \frac{1}{8}, \frac{1}{16}, \frac{1}{64}, \frac{1}{64}, \frac{1}{64}, \frac{1}{64}\}$, the the information entropy is

$$H(P_2) = -\left(\frac{1}{2} \log_2 \frac{1}{2} + \frac{1}{4} \log_2 \frac{1}{4} + \frac{1}{8} \log_2 \frac{1}{8} + \frac{1}{16} \log_2 \frac{1}{16} + \frac{1}{64} \log_2 \frac{1}{64} \right.$$
$$\left. + \frac{1}{64} \log_2 \frac{1}{64} + \frac{1}{64} \log_2 \frac{1}{64} \right) = 2$$

and we have $H(P_1) > H(P_2)$

(2) Based on constraint 1, we add another constraint:

$$p(a) + p(b) = \frac{1}{2}$$

There are also many distributions meeting the above two constraints. When X has uniform distribution on the premise of meeting these constraints, i.e., $P(X) = \{\frac{1}{4}, \frac{1}{4}, \frac{1}{12}, \frac{1}{12}, \frac{1}{12}, \frac{1}{12}, \frac{1}{12}, \frac{1}{12}\}$, the information entropy has the maximum value as follows:

$$H(P_3) = -\left(2 \times \frac{1}{4}\log_2\frac{1}{4} + 6 \times \frac{1}{12}\log_2\frac{1}{12}\right) = 2.79$$

The information entropy of other distributions are smaller than that of this distribution.

Given a training document D labeled with text polarity, we can extract a feature function from the training document as the constraints. Assume

$$F_i(d,c) = \begin{cases} 1, & \text{if } d \text{ and } c \text{ meets fact} \\ 0, & \text{otherwise} \end{cases}$$

then the maximum entropy model can transfer to an optimization problem, i.e.,

$$\max H(p(c|d)) = \max -\sum_{c,d}\tilde{p}(d)p(c|d)\log p(c|d) = \min \sum_{c,d}p(c,d)\log p(c|d)$$

then

$$\begin{cases} \sum_{c,d}p(c|d)\tilde{p}(d)F_i(d,c) = \sum_{c,d}\tilde{p}(c|d)\tilde{p}(d)F_i(d,c) \\ \sum_{c}p(c|d) = 1 \end{cases}$$

where $\tilde{p}(d)$ denotes the probability that document d appears in the training dataset D, $\tilde{p}(c|d)$ denotes the probability that document d is classified into sentiment category c.

We give the solution for the above optimization problem, i.e., the format of the maximum entropy model, as follows. Please refer to Reference [14] for the detailed inference process.

$$P_{ME}(c|d) = \frac{1}{Z(d)}\exp\left(\sum_i \lambda_{i,c}F_{i,c}(d,c)\right)$$

where

$$Z(d) = \sum_c \exp\left(\sum_i \lambda_{i,c}F_{i,c}(d,c)\right)$$

and $\lambda_{i,c}$ denotes model parameter. Iteration-based numerical methods are effective in solving the maximized model parameters. Two typical methods are generalized iterative scaling algorithm and improved iterative scaling algorithm.

3. Support vector machines method

Support vector machines (SVM) is a binary classification method with the basic model defining the linear classifier with the maximized interval in eigen space. Given eigen space, if we can find a hyperplane that can divide the entities in eigen space into different categories, with the space being linear separable. The hyperplane has the following format: $w \cdot x + b = 0$, where w denotes the normal vector and b denotes the intercept. For example, Figure 2.1 shows a linear separable space where there is a hyperplane that can divide positive and negative data into two groups.

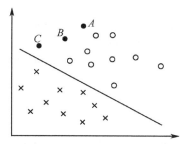

Figure 2.1: Linear separable space.

The hyperplane is not unique, and SVM tries to achieve classification by solving the optimal hyperplane using maximized interval. This problem can transfer to the following optimization problem:

$$\min \frac{1}{2} \|w\|^2$$

Then for all training datasets:

$$y_i(w \cdot x_i) + b - 1 \geq 0$$

The steps for text sentiment classification of SVM algorithm is as follows:

Algorithm 2.3 Support vector machines model.

Input: Document dataset labeled with sentiment category $D = \{d_i, c_i\}$ where c_i denotes the sentiment orientation of document d_i with values as 1 or −1.
Output: Hyperplane with the maximized interval and classification decision-making function.

Step 1 Construct and solve an optimization problem:

$$\min \frac{1}{2} \|w\|^2$$

then,

$$c_i(w \cdot d_i) + b - 1 \geq 0$$

Obtain optimal solution $w^\star$ and $b^\star$.
Step 2 Construct a hyperplane

$$w^\star \cdot x + b^\star = 0$$

and a classification decision-making function

$$f(d) = \text{sign}\left(w^\star \cdot x + b^\star\right)$$

Therefore, the sentiment orientation of a given document d can be determined by classification decision-making function $f(d)$. If $f(d) = 1$, document d is positive; if $f(d) = -1$, document d is negative.

2.2.3 Topic model-based sentiment analysis

Many scholars have introduced the emerging topic model into sentiment analysis to analyze users' sentiment or attitude towards a certain topic or event. Topic model-based models such as probabilistic latent semantic analysis (PLSA) [15] and latent Dirichlet allocation (LDA) [16] add sentiment word variable from a topic model to identify the topic of the document and author's sentiment orientation at the same time. Both PLSA and LDA models are Bayesian generative models. Please refer to "Pattern recognition and machine learning" for further understanding.

In 2010, Zhao et al. proposed a maximum entropy LDA model for sentiment analysis [17]. They improved LDA model to identify the comment target and word. The generative model is shown in Figure 2.2.

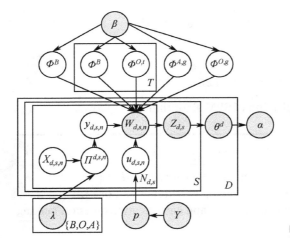

Figure 2.2: Maximum entropy LDA model.

In this model, parameter α denotes the Dirichlet prior distribution for documents over topics and β for topics over words. For each document d, topic distribution follows a Directlet distribution with parameter α, i.e., $\theta^d \sim \mathrm{Dir}(\alpha)$. For each topic, distribution is the same as that in the LDA model, which meets $z_{d,s} \sim \mathrm{Multi}(\theta^d)$ where $\mathrm{Multi}(\cdot)$ implies a multinomial distribution. The maximum entropy LDA model, according to the parameter β, generates four different target distributions: background model ϕ^B, general aspect model $\phi^{A,g}$, topic aspect model $\{\phi^{A,t}\}_{t=1}^T$, and topic aspect-specific opinion model $\{\phi^{O,t}\}_{t=1}^T$. Parameter $y_{d,s,n}$ denotes the category of the word, i.e., background word, feature word, or sentiment word. Parameter $u_{d,s,n}$ indicates whether the word is general aspect or aspect-specific. The maximum model is used to train parameters $\pi^{d,s,n}$ and $\chi^{d,s,n}$. The word distribution $w^{d,s,n}$ is as follows:

$$\omega(d,s,n) \sim \begin{cases} \text{Multi}(\phi^B), & y_{d,s,n} = 0 \\ \text{Multi}(\phi^{A,Z,d,s}), & y_{d,s,n} = 1, u_{d,s,n} = 0 \\ \text{Multi}(\phi^{Ag}), & y_{d,s,n} = 1, u_{d,s,n} = 1 \\ \text{Multi}(\phi^{O,Z,d,s}), & y_{d,s,n} = 2, u_{d,s,n} = 0 \\ \text{Multi}(\phi^{Og}), & y_{d,s,n} = 2, u_{d,s,n} = 1 \end{cases}$$

The author's sentiment orientation for comment target can be determined by previous semantic rule-based techniques according to the sentiment polarity of comment words. The major advantage of this model is that it can improve algorithm efficiency by extracting comment targets and comment words at the same time.

Moreover, there are many topic model-based methods. For example, in 2011, Sauper et al. proposed a joint topic-sentiment model to detect sentiment orientation for short documents [18], also known as hidden Markow model (HMM)-LDA model as HMM is used therein. In 2012, Mukherjee and Bing proposed a hybrid model based on semi-supervised learning that allows users to provide seed words to improve the precision of sentiment analysis [19].

2.3 Social network sentiment analysis techniques

The new feature of online social network brings new problems for the traditional long text sentiment analysis techniques and results in some sentiment analysis techniques for online social network. For example, sentiment analysis techniques for short text, sentiment analysis techniques using mutual influence between groups in social network, a series of data processing technologies for possible influence on true sentiment analysis by spam users and opinions, etc. This section introduces some studies on the above work.

2.3.1 Sentiment analysis technique for short text

With the rapid development of Twitter, Facebook, and Sina Weibo, people can post their views and opinions on the network anytime and anywhere. Different from long text, such as traditional news and reports, social network text has short length, irregular grammar, and lots of noise. Therefore, research on sentiment analysis techniques for short text in social network is of great importance.

In 2009, Go et al. tested the sentiment classification effect of supervised learning algorithm on short text on Twitter with models such as as multinomial Bayesian classification, maximum entropy, and SVM. Go et al. adopted emoticon on Twitter rather than the method of obtaining training set by manual labeling in long text to obtain positive and negative comment, thereby saving considerable manual labeling cost and significantly improving the size of the training set. Using Twitter's Application Programming Interface (API), they collected microblogs containing ":)" as positive comments and ":(" as negative comments, with pre-processing including removing username, URL, and repetitions. Single-factor model, two-factor model, and mixed model were ultimate test methods in feature selection. Their sentiment classification result was about 80%, which is close to the supervised learning method used by Pang et al [20].

Pak Alexander and Patrick Paroubek also adopted emoticons to derive the training set. They added objective information into subjective emoticons [21], thereby extending the model to three-factor classification of traditional sentiment analysis. For the sentiment classification method, they adopted Naïve Bayes classification to obtain initial results and information entropy to remove the influence of $n-gram$ for improving classification results.

Many social network media open their API for users to read content such as Twitter, Facebook, Sina Weibo, and Tencent Weibo. Users can capture data as required by the search interface provided by the social network media. Collecting data by emoticons saves manual labeling work and significantlyimproves the size of the training set. The following are examples for obtaining sentiment training set by the API of Twitter and Sina Weibo.

Example 2.7 Collecting sentiment document training set by API.

1) Twitter API (https://dev.twitter.com)
    Twitter API provides users with a series of search rules for convenient quick search. The positive document can be obtained by ":)" and the negative document can be obtained by ":(". Users can also obtain the required dataset by combining rules with text content, for example:

    movie -scary:)   Containing "movie", but not "scary", and with a positive attitude.
    flight:(Containing "flight" and with a negative attitude.

2) Sina Weibo API (https://open.weibo.com)
    Sina Weibo provides numerous emoticons and specific emoticons API for users (http:/open.weibo.com/wiki/2/emotions). In Sina Weibo, emoticons posted by users is transformed to the corresponding text. Regular expression "[**]" is used for labeling, such as [happy], [sad], and [joy]. Users can adopt multiple keywords to obtain microblog including specific emoticons.

Although the usage of emoticons saves the cost of manual labeling, it also introduces noise and reduces the accuracy of training data. In 2012, Liu et al. analyzed the influence of collecting training set by manual labeling and emoticons on sentiment analysis results [22]. Assuming the training set collected by manual labeling as *A* and the training set collected by emoticon as *B*, they adopted probabilistic model for text modeling and separately calculated the sentiment classification probability of feature keywords in *A* and *B*. The final sentiment classification results were calculated by Laplacian smoothing:

$$P_{co}(w_i|c) = aP_a(w_i|c) + (1-a)P_u(w_i|c)$$

where $p_a(w_i|c)$ denotes the sentiment classification probability of feature word *wi* in manual labeling training set, $p_u(w_i|c)$ denotes the sentiment classification probability of feature word *wi* in the emoticon training set, and *a* denotes the smoothing factor. The experimental results show that the combination of two training sets can improve the accuracy of sentiment classification.

With the emergence of microblog, the sentiment analysis for short text has become important in the field of social network sentiment analysis. At present, many conferences focus on sentiment analysis. For example, conferences such as NLP&CC and COAE regard sentiment analysis as important. Sentiment analysis is different from the traditional three-factor sentiment classification (positive, neutral, and negative) and adopts more fine-grained model. For example, NLP&CC2013 classifies user sentiment into seven categories (anger, disgust, fear, happiness, like, sadness, and surprise). Zhang et al. adopted sentiment vector model to express users' diversified sentiment in social network and built hierarchical structure of sentiment vector based on cluster [23]. The steps of the algorithm are as follows:

Algorithm 2.4 Hierarchical sentiment vector model.

Step 1 Combine with the sentiment checklist in clinical psychology to exact initial sentiment vectors that can well express sentiment.

Step 2 Monitor microblog data stream and automatically discover and absorb new cyberwords that can express sentiment from statistics according to large-scale corpus. Establish self-learning and self-update mechanism of sentiment vector to guarantee comprehensiveness.

Step 3 Use a bottom-up method to establish hierarchical structure from classification and summary. Label bottom sentiment vector and establish orientation analysis layer from orientation word.

The ultimate hierarchical sentiment model is shown Figure 2.3.

Microblog sentiment expression model based on sentiment vector can effectively express diversified sentiment. Use the method combining clinical psychology to

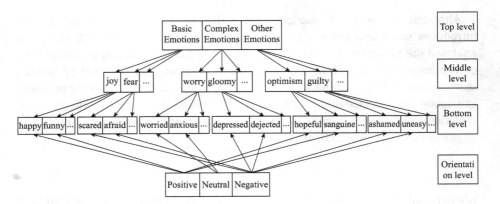

Figure 2.3: Hierarchical sentiment vector model.

construct sentiment vector and the self-update mechanism to guarantee comprehensiveness and authority. The hierarchical structure constructed using the bottom-up method can avoid sparsity.

For the sentiment analysis of topic, Wang et al. analyzed sentiment by constructing hashtag-graph at the topic layer for hashtags in Twitter [24]. Assuming $HG = \{H, E\}$ indicates hashtag-graph where $\forall h_i \in H$ denotes a hashtag and $e_k = \{h_i, h_j\} \in E$ denotes that h_i and h_j appear in the same tweet.

Example 2.8 Hashtag-graph model (See Figure 2.4).

In the hashtag-graph model, hashtags can be classified into three categories: topic tag such as #president and #healthcare; sentiment tag such as #ideal and #leader; and sentiment-topic tag such as #iloveobama. The link between two hashtags indicates that they appear in the same microblog.

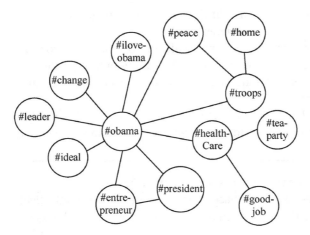

Figure 2.4: Hashtag-graph model.

Given a hashtag-graph model *HG*, the main task is to label the sentiment orientation $y_i \in \{pos, neg\}$ for each hashtag $h_i \in HG$. According to Markov assumption, the sentiment polarity of a hashtag is determined by the polarity of the microblog containing the hashtag as well as its neighbors. Therefore, this problem can be transferred to an optimization function:

$$\log(P(y|HG)) = \sum_{h_i \in H} \log(\Psi_i(y_i|h_i)) + \sum_{(h_i, h_j) \in \varepsilon} \log(\Psi_{i,j}(y_j, y_k|h_j, h_k)) - \log Z$$

where *Z* is the normalization factor and functions ϕ and Ψ are defined as follows:

$$\phi_i(y_i|h_i) = \sum_{\tau \in T_i} P_{y_i}(\tau)$$

$$\Psi_{i,j}(y_j, y_k|h_j, h_k) = \frac{\#(h_j, h_k)}{\#(h_j) + \#(h_k)} \cdot I_{y_j = y_k}$$

where $\phi_i(y_i|h_i)$ denotes the probability that hashtag h_i is the sentiment orientation y_i; $\#(h_j, h_k)$ denotes the number of times that h_j and h_k appear at the same time; $\#(h_j)$ denotes the number of time that hashtag h_j appears alone; and $I_{y_j = y_k}$ is a decision-making function taking 1 if $y_j = y_k$ and 0 otherwise. Topic hashtag can be classified according to sentiment classification results of the final hashtag.

In 2010, Bermingham and Smeaton compared the effectiveness of SVM algorithm and multinomial Bayesian algorithm of long text and short text [25]. The results showed that SVM performed better for long text dataset whereas multinomial Bayesian algorithm performed better for short documents. At the same time, the results showed that, although short text in social network like Twitter contains massive noise, it is easier to perform sentiment analysis for short text than long text.

2.3.2 Sentiment analysis based on collective intelligence

In social networks, users can express their views and opinions at will but are unconsciously influenced by other nodes based on the link structure. Interaction function provided by social network enhances sentiment interaction between users and enables sentiment information to diffuse with the structure of social networks.

Thelwall Mike performed sentiment analysis on friend relationship network in Myspace and found that linked users are more likely to have the same sentiment orientation [26]. Bollen et al. researched the homogenesis phenomenon of happiness in social network from massive data from Twitter in 2011 and found that users are more likely to select friends with the same happiness exponent [27]. They constructed the graph from mutual follow relationship and used Jaccard similarity to calculate the weight of edges as follows:

$$w_{ij} = \frac{\|C_i \cap C_j\|}{\|C_i \cup C_j\|}$$

Then, from document dataset and corpus dataset they quantified users' happiness exponent and used Peason index to calculate the correlation between vectors $S(S)$ and $S(T)$, which are constructed by grouping SWB value of the starting point and end point of all edges.

Tan et al. researched user-level sentiment analysis techniques in Twitter [28]. For each topic, they constructed a heterogenous graph model based on linked structure and content information, as shown in Figure 2.5.

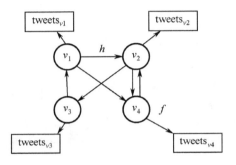

Figure 2.5: Heterogenous graph model based on linked structure and content information.

Where v_i denotes the user node and tweets$_{vi}$ denotes the content of microblog posted by user. h denotes the link structure between users and f is the link structure between user and their microblogs. For each user v_i, the sentiment label y_i denotes the sentiment orientation. Based on Markov assumption, the sentiment label of a user is determined by the sentiment in his/her microblogs and of his/her neighbors. Therefore, the model function is as follows:

$$\log P(Y) = \left(\sum_{v_i \in V} \left[\sum_{t \in \text{tweets}_{v_i}, k, l} \mu_{k,l} f_{k,l}(y_{v_i}, \hat{y}_t) + \sum_{v_j \in \text{Neighbors}_{v_i}, k^l} \lambda_{k,l} h_{k,l}(y_{v_i}, y_{v_j}) \right] - \log Z \right)$$

where $u_{k,z}$ and $\lambda_{k,l}$ are the weight factors. Function f denotes user-microblog factor and h denotes user–user factor with the following definitions:

$$f_{k,l}(y_{v_i}, \hat{y}_t) = \begin{cases} \frac{\omega_{\text{labeled}}}{|\text{tweets}_{v_i}|}, & y_{v_i} = k, \hat{y}_t = l, v_i \text{ labeled} \\ \frac{\omega_{\text{labeled}}}{|\text{tweets}_{v_i}|}, & y_{v_i} = k, \hat{y}_t = l, v_i \text{ unlabeled} \\ 0, & \text{otherwise} \end{cases}$$

$$h_{k,l}(y_{v_i}, y_{v_j}) = \begin{cases} \frac{\omega_{\text{relation}}}{|\text{Neighbors}_{v_i}|}, & y_{v_i} = k, y_{v_j} = l \\ 0, & \text{otherwise} \end{cases}$$

As not all users in social network contain labels, the authors adopted a semi-supervised learning algorithm and used labeled dataset to perform label estimation from the following four relationship networks.
(1) Follow relationship network;
(2) Bi-follow relationship network;
(3) Mention relationship network;
(4) Bi-mention relationship network.

The results showed that, compared with sentiment analysis only by text content, reasonable use of link structure information in social network can effectively improve the accuracy of sentiment analysis.

Moreover, Reza et al. systematically researched the sentiment influence between users in Live Journal [29]. Assume $\wedge_s$ as the user set, $m(u, t)$ as the sentiment of user u at time t, and $m(U, t)$ as the sentiment of a user group U at time t, the sentiment diffusion in social networks can be defined as given user group U at time t_i (U has the same sentiment), and user group U at t_j influences target user u at time t_j if

$$\left| m(U, t_i) - m(u, t_j) \right| \le \left| m(\wedge_s, t_i) - m(u, t_j) \right| + b_1$$

and

$$\left| m(U, t_i) - m(u, t_j) \right| \le \left| m(U, t_i) - m(u, t_i) \right| + b_2$$

The authors used <excellent, poor> and <happy, sad> as the sentiment reference words and used Google distance to determine the polarity for each feature word. They found that users posting relatively few microblogs are more likely to be influenced by others.

2.3.3 Mining techniques on spam opinions in social network

In social network, spam users and internet marketers publish a lot of false information to increase product sales or make an event popular. Therefore, detection and analysis of spam opinions is significant for extracting factual information.

Jindal and Liu proposed the concept of spam comment detection [30] for products based on sentiment analysis, which regarded spam comment detection as two-factor classification problem; they also used logistic regression mode to classify user comments into spam comments and nonspam comments from Amazon's 5.8 million product comments and their overlapping ratio. Further, they conducted a detailed analysis on spam comments in 2008, and regarded content, authors, and objective of comments as basic characteristics to effectively mine spam comments as false information from a mass of comments.

For product rating behaviors (e.g., product quality divided into 1~5 levels), Lim et al. found that spam users often comment on specific-concerned products and their comment results have considerable deviation from normal comments. Further, they proposed a detection method of spam users based on comment objectives [31] and deviation. For spam users detection method based on rating objectives, comment function based on rating behaviors is as follows:

$$C_{p,e}(u_i) = \frac{s_i}{\text{Max}_{u'_i \in U^{s'_i}}}$$

where u_i denotes user, p denotes products, and s_i denotes nonstandardized spam users comment function. The definition is as follows:

$$s_i = \sum_{e_{ij} \in E_{ij}, |E_{ij}| > 1} |E_{ij}| \cdot \text{sim}(E_{ij})$$

where E_{ij} denotes a comment set of user i on product j and sim() denotes similarity function defined according to comment set.

Comment function for defining spam users on the basis of comments is as follows:

$$C_{p,v}(u_i) = \frac{s'_i}{\text{Max}_{u'_i \in U^{s'_{i'}}}}$$

where

$$s'_i = \sum_{v_{i,j} \in V_{ij}, |V_{ij}| < 1} |V_{ij}| \cdot \text{sim}(V_{ij})$$

From the two comment functions mentioned above, the comment function for defining spam users is as follows:

$$C_p(u_i) = \frac{1}{2}(C_{p,e}(u_i) + C_{p,v}(u_i))$$

For spam users detection method based on deviation, spam users usually speak highly of concerned products and poorly about other products to promote the sales volume. Therefore, the basis deviation of user comment is as follows:

$$d_{ij} = e_{ij} - \underset{e \in E_{*j}}{\text{Avg}} \, e$$

where e_{ij} denotes the comment of user i on product j and $\underset{e \in E_{*j}}{\text{Avg}} \, e$ denotes the average comment of all users on product j. Therefore, the final comment function for defining the average deviation of all comment behaviors of users is as follows:

$$c_d(u_i) = \underset{e_{ij} \in E_{i*}}{\text{Avg}} \ |d_{ij}|$$

Use the above two user behavior characteristics to detect spam comments.

2.4 Extension and transformation of sentiment analysis technique

In social network, there are numerous extensions and transformations related to sentiment analysis. This section will briefly introduce sentiment summary technique and sentiment analysis of interdisciplinary transfer learning. Please refer to references for further reading on the development of sentiment analysis.

2.4.1 Sentiment summary technique

Sentiment summary technique aims at automatically analyzing and concluding the results of sentiment analysis for numerous theme sentiment documents, thus saving the time that users spend in reading relevant documents. There is a large difference between sentiment summary techniques and traditional multi-document summary techniques. The main purpose of traditional multi-document summary is to extract the topics and their main contents from multiple documents whereas sentiment summary technique is based on sentiment comment object and aims at concluding sentiment information for a certain topic or product and has obvious quantitative characteristics. For example, for a product, 80% documents are positive while 20% are negative.

In 2005, Liu proposed the sentiment summary technique [6] and discussed different product attributes in a structured manner. Users can compare the features of different products horizontally to make a final decision depending on demand. For a product set $P = \{P_1, P_2, \ldots, P_n\}$, P_i denotes a kind of product. For each product P_i, $R_i = \{r_1, r_2, \ldots, r_k\}$ denotes the corresponding comment set. For each feature f, if r_i contains the feature f, then f is termed the explicit feature. If r_i does not contain feature f directly but implicitly, then f is termed the implicit characteristics. For each feature f, P_{set} denotes the positive comment set, and N_{set} denotes the negative comment set. Therefore, sentiment summary tasks can be defined as follows: For each kind of product P_i and its comment set R_i, mine the explicit and implicit features from comments and extract positive and negative comments of each feature f.

Example 2.9 Sentiment summary visualization.

This method of sentiment summary visualization rates different attributes of product and generates different sentiment summaries for different attributes. In Figure 2.6,

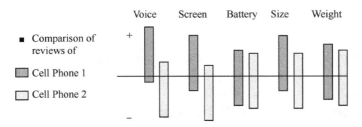

Figure 2.6: Sentiment summary structural display.

phones provides several factors, such as sound, screen, battery, size, and weight. According to user comments, mine the sentiment orientation degree of different attributes and make a standard display.

In extraction technique of sentiment summary, Liu Bing extracted product features based on supervised association rule mining. For this, first, training set of feature was labeled manually, followed by mining of frequent terms mined in the dataset based on the method of association rule mining and further manual processing was done to improve the accuracy of feature selection. In this process, the implicit features are mapped to the explicit features. Finally, synonymous features are combined based on Wordnet semantics to generate the final feature set. For each feature, the proportions of positive and negative information are displayed according to statistical data.

Lu et al. proposed a sentiment summary method [32] based on online ontology for topics and different facets. They assumed that online ontology contained topic features focussing on solving two questions: how to choose effective features from several features and how to sort features for helping users to read them. For selecting features, they proposed the method based on the size of the set, the method based on opinion coverage, and the method based on conditional entropy. They sorted features according to the appearing order of topic features in the article. Defining feature set to be sorted as $A' = \{A_i\}$ where each feature A_i corresponds to a series of associating subjective sentences $S_i = \{S_{i1}, S_{i2}, ...\}$. The coherent order of feature A_i, A_j was defined as:

$$Co(A_i, A_j) = \frac{\sum_{S_{i,k} \in S_i, S_{j,t} \in S_j} Co(S_{i,k}, S_{j,t})}{|S_i||S_j|}$$

where $Co(S_{i,k}, S_{j,k})$ was set as 1 if $S_{i,k}$ appears in the article prior to $S_{j,i}$ otherwise as 0. $|S_i|$ denotes the number of words in a sentence. Therefore, for a feature set A', optimal coherent degree can be defined as:

$$\hat{\pi}(A') = \underset{\pi(A')}{\arg\max} \sum_{A_i, A_j \in A', A_i < A_j} Co(A_i, A_j)$$

where $A_i < A_j$ denotes that feature A_i is prior to feature A_j. As it is a NP-hard problem, greedy algorithm can be used to obtain the local optimal sorting of features.

2.4.2 Sentiment analysis technology based on the mechanism of transfer learning

Text sentiment analysis algorithm has a strong correlation between the domains, with the same word having different sentiment orientations in different domains. Therefore, it is necessary to study interdisciplinary sentiment classification using transfer learning.

Transfer learning divides the data source into source domain and target domain. The source domain usually has a large number of labeled dataset, and the target domain usually does not have or only has a small amount of labeled samples. Transfer learning aims to directly apply feature representations or models learnt from the source domain to the target domain through feature association between source and target domains. Transfer learning does not need training data and test data to follow the same distribution, such that information can be effectively shared and transferred between similar domains or tasks, which is different from the traditional machine learning methods.

Features can be divided into two categories: domain-dependent feature word and domain-independent feature word. If the feature ranks high in both the source and target domains (such as word frequency), the domains have nothing to do with the feature word, which is termed domain-independent feature word. If the feature is strongly representative in the source domain but weakly representative in the target domain, the feature word is domain dependent. In 2006, Yang et al. realized interdisciplinary sentiment analysis task [33] based on the simple strategy of transfer learning depending on feature selection in TREC task. The technique selected the words that rank high in both product and film comment and successfully classified the sentiment for product comment domain from 2,041 comments and 2,217 negative movie comments.

Blitzer et al. studied domain sentiment analysis techniques [34] based on different product categories (book, DVD, electronic products, and kitchen utensils) of Amazon in 2007. They not only improved the accuracy of sentiment analysis based on transfer learning methods but also researched the dependency between the source and target domains, i.e., how to obtain the best transfer learning effect on a given target domain by selecting the source domain.

For feature selection, Blitzer et al. proposed structural correspondence learning [35] in 2006. First, they selected m central features from the source and target domains, with each of them having strong representation in both the domains, i.e., domain-independent feature. Subsequently, they trained the mapping θ from initial feature space to shared feature space based on these central features. In the mapping feature space, bigger inner product of vectors indicates higher similarity. Blitzer et al. proposed the SCL-MI algorithm to improve the above algorithm in 2007. For feature selection, they considered not only high-frequency domain-independent feature words but also mutual information of feature words and labels in the source domain to enhance the effectiveness of feature selection and the accuracy of sentiment analysis in the target domain. They used A-distance based on SCL mapping to measure the applicability of source domain in the target domain, and only considered those feature words that lead to different classification results while ignoring other differences between the source and target domain. A-distance of two probability distributions was defined as:

$$d_A\ (D, D') = 2 \sup_{A \in A} |Pr_D[A] - Pr_{D'}[A]|$$

where sup denotes the upper bounding function.

2.5 Summary

With the rapid development of internet technology, online social network is becoming main medium for users to express their views and disseminate information. In this chapter, we provided an overview of sentiment analysis and opinion mining in online social network, and systematically introduced sentiment analysis technique for long text, such as news report, as well as the influence of link structure and group interaction features of social networking on sentiment analysis. Sentiment analysis for social network has great value for applications and will play increasingly important roles in financial, political, economic, and other fields.

At present, sentiment analysis technique for text is still under development and a unified and mature theoretical system has not formed. Moreover, sentiment analysis technique for social network is still in its exploratory phase, especially for sentiment analysis method for short text such as Twitter. Online social network greatly enriches the corpus of sentiment analysis while presenting further issues and challenges. We think the following issues in sentiment analysis technique for social network need to be further researched and explored.

(1) Sentiment model. Traditional text sentiment analysis uses three-factor model (positive, negative, and neutral) to describe user sentiments. However, in a social network, user sentiment is often diversified and much more complex, especially on emergencies in social network. The traditional three-factor model is not sufficient for representing user sentiment in social network. We need to establish sentiment model with higher granular degree in sentiment analysis for social network to accurately represent the user sentiment. Although there are related

research (e.g., Reference [23]) and conferences (e.g., NLP&CC and COAT), it is necessary to further establish general and authoritative models.

(2) Sentiment analysis and group interaction. In social network, user sentiment is influenced by both its subjective consciousness and neighbor nodes. The emergence of online social network allows users to perform more frequent interaction and more common affective exchange. Because existing work mainly focuses on analyzing the text sentiment orientation, it is necessary to further perform sentiment analysis work combined with social network features, such as researching diffusion and diffusion model of sentiment in social networks, mining evolution law of opposed sentiment in groups, and mining sentiment communities.

References

[1]   Wiebe JM: Tracking point of view in narrative. *Comput Linguist* 1994, 20:223–287.
[2]   Das S, Chen M: Yahoo! for Amazon: Extracting market sentiment from stock message boards. In Proceedings of the Asia Pacific Finance Association Annual Conference (APFA) 2001.
[3]   Dave K, Lawrence S, Pennock DM: Mining the peanut gallery: Opinion extraction and semantic classification of product reviews. In Proceedings of WWW 2003, 519–528.
[4]   Pang B, Lee L: Opinion mining and sentiment analysis. *Founds Trends Inf Ret* 2008, 2:1–35.
[5]   Liu B: Sentiment analysis and opinion mining. *Syn Lect Hum Lang Tech* 2012, 5:1–67.
[6]   Liu B, Hu M, Cheng J: Opinion observer: Analyzing and comparing opinions on the web. In Proceedings of the 14th international conference on World Wide Web, ACM 2005, 342–351.
[7]   Wilson T, Hoffmann P, Somasundaran S, Kessler J, Wiebe J, Choi Y, Cardie C, Riloff E, Patwardhan S: OpinionFinder: A system for subjectivity analysis. In Proceedings of hlt/emnlp on interactive demonstrations, Association for Computational Linguistics 2005, 34–35.
[8]   Devitt A, Ahmad K: Sentiment polarity identification in financial news: A cohesion-based approach. In Proceedings of the 45th Annual Meeting of the Association for Computational Linguistics 2007, 45:984.
[9]   Kim SM, Hovy EH: Crystal: Analyzing predictive opinions on the Web. In Proceedings of the 2007 Joint Conference on Empirical Methods in Natural Language Processing and Computational Natural Language Learning (EMNLP-CoNLL) 2007, 1056–1064.
[10]   Turney PD: Thumbs up or thumbs down?: Semantic orientation applied to unsupervised classification of reviews. In Proceedings of the 40th Annual Meeting on Association for Computational Linguistics 2002.
[11]   Ding B, Liu B, Yu PS: Aholistic lexicon-based approach to opinion mining. In Proceedings of the 2008 Conference on Web Search and Data mining (WSDM-2008) 2008.
[12]   Kim SM, Hovy E: Automatic detection of opinion bearing words and sentences In Companion Volume to the Proceedings of the International Joint Conference on Natural Language Processing (IJCNLP) 2005, 61–66.
[13]   Jaynes ET: Information theory and statistical mechanics. *Phys Rev* 1957, 106:620.
[14]   Li H: Statistical learning method. Beijing: TsingHua Press 2012.
[15]   Hofmann T: Probabilistic latent semantic indexing. In Proceedings of the Fifteenth Conference on Uncertainty in Artificial Intelligence 1999.
[16]   Blei DM, Ng AY, Jordan MI: Latent dirichlet allocation. *J Mach Learn Res* 2003, 3:993–1022.

[17] Zhao WX, Jiang J, Yan H, Li X: Jointly modeling aspects and opinions with a MaxEnt-LDA hybrid. In Proceedings of the 2010 Conference on Empirical Methods in Natural Language Processing, Association for Computational Linguistics 2010 56–65.

[18] Sauper C, Haghighi A, Barzilay R: Content models with attitude. In Proceedings of the 49th Annual Meeting of the Association for Computational Linguistics 2011.

[19] Mukherjee A, Liu B: Aspect extraction through semi-supervised modeling. In Proceedings of 50th Annual Meeting of Association for Computational Linguistics 2012.

[20] Pang B, Lee L, Vaithyanathan S. Thumbs up?: Sentiment classification using machine learning techniques. In Proceedings of the ACL-02 Conference on Empirical Methods in Natural Language Processing-Volume 10 2002.

[21] Pak A, Paroubek P: Twitter as a corpus for sentiment analysis and opinion mining. In LREC 2010.

[22] Liu KL, Li WJ, Guo M: Emoticon smoothed language models for Twitter sentiment analysis. In AAAI 2012.

[23] Zhang L, Jia Y, Zhou B, Han Y: Microblogging sentiment analysis using emotional vector. IEEE International Conference on Cloud and Green Computing 2012, 430–433.

[24] Wang X, Wei F, Liu X, Zhou M, Zhang M: Topic sentiment analysis in twitter: A graph-based hashtag sentiment classification approach. In Proceedings of the 20th ACM International Conference on Information and Knowledge Management, ACM 2011, 1031–1040.

[25] Bermingham A, Smeaton AF: Classifying sentiment in microblogs: Is brevity an advantage?. In Proceedings of the 19th ACM International Conference on Information and Knowledge Management, ACM 2010.

[26] Thelwall M: Emotion homophily in social network site messages. *First Monday* 2004, 15.

[27] Bollen J, Gonçalves B, Ruan G, Mao H: Happiness is assortative in online social networks. *Artif Life* 2011, 17:237–251.

[28] Tan C, Lee L, Tang J, Jiang L, Zhou M, Li P: User-level sentiment analysis incorporating social networks. In Proceedings of the 17th ACM SIGKDD International Conference on Knowledge Discovery and Data Mining, ACM 2011, 1397–1405.

[29] Reza Z, Cole WD, Liu H: Sentiment propagation in social networks: A case study in livejournal. *Adv Soc Comput* 2010, 413–420.

[30] Jindal N, Liu B: Mining comparative sentences and relations. In Proceedings of National Conference on Artificial Intelligence 2006.

[31] Lim EP, Nguyen VA, Jindal N, Liu B, Lauw HW: Detecting product review spam users using rating behaviors. In Proceedings of ACM International Conference on Information and Knowledge Management (CIKM-2010) 2010.

[32] Lu Y, Duan H, Wang H, Zhai C: Exploiting structured ontology to organize scattered online opinions. In Proceedings of International Conference on Computational Linguistics 2010.

[33] Yang H, Luo S, Callan J: Knowledge transfer and opinion detection in the TREC 2006 blog track. In Proceedings of TREC 2006.

[34] Blitzer J, Mark D, Pereira F: Biographies, bollywood, boom-boxes and blenders: Domain adaptation for sentiment classification. In Proceedings of Annual Meeting of the Association for Computational Linguistics 2007.

[35] Blitzer J, McDonald R, Pereira F: Domain adaptation with structural correspondence learning. Proceedings of the 2006 Conference on Empirical Methods in Natural Language Processing. Association for Computational Linguistics 2006.

[36] Zhou L, He Y, Wang J: Overview on sentiment analysis research. *Comput Appl* 2008, 28:2725–2728.

[37] He Y, Lin C, Alani H: Automatically extracting polarity-bearing topics for crossdomain sentiment classification. In Proceedings of the 49th Annual Meeting of the Association for Computational Linguistics 2011.

[38] Go A, Huang L, Bhayani R: Twitter sentiment classification using distant supervision. *Entropy* 2009, 17:252.

[39] Zhao Y, Bing Q, Liu T: Text sentiment analysis. *J Software* 2008, 21:1834–1848.

[40] Wang G, Xie S, Bing L, Philip SY: Identify online store review spam users via social review graph. *ACM T on Intel Syst Tech* 2011.

[41] Bishop CM: Pattern recognition and machine learning. New York: Springer 2006

Yan Jia and Binxing Fang
3 Influence Analysis and Its Technologies

The influence of individuals in social networks, which plays an important role in guiding public opinions and social operations, has been extensively studied by researchers from various fields such as social psychology, telecommunications, marketing, and computer science.. With the emergence of a large number of online social network services and the participation of users, researches on the influence of individuals in social networks have attracted the attention of many scholars both at home and abroad. In the era of online social networking, social networks have had a significant impact on our daily life and behavior patterns. A small number of malicious users and opinion leaders fabricate and disseminate public opinions by taking advantage of social networking services. By expressing their opinions on current events and interacting with the media and internet users, opinion leaders are often very powerful in influencing the minds of their fans and the direction of public opinions. In recent years, while opinion leaders have played an important role in guiding public opinions on events such as "Cracking Down on the Abduction of Women and Children through Weibo," and offering "free lunch" for children in poor areas, other incidents such as demolition, petition, accidents and disasters, they have also played role in the generating, fermenting, propagating, and sensationalizing such events. Analysis of individual influence has been widely used in a number of fields, such as recommendation systems, social network information dissemination, link prediction, viral marketing, public health, expert discovery, incident detection, and advertising. Therefore, the analysis of individual influence in social networks has great theoretical value and practical significance.

Identifying users of high influence in a heterogeneous, multi-attribute social network and analyzing the strength of influence among users in social networks are key issues in information related decision-making in this fast-changing age of the internet.

This chapter is arranged as follows: Section 3.2 introduces the methods for analyzing and calculating the strength of influence between users, including the network structure-based, behavior-based, and topic-based strength calculation methods; Section 3.3 describes the methods for identifying influencers, which involves the network structure-based individual influence calculation, PageRank algorithm, behavior-based individual influence calculation, the topic-based individual influence calculation.

https://doi.org/10.1515/9783110599411-003

3.1 Introduction

The technologies for analyzing individual influence in social networks are mainly classified into two types: one is based on analyzing the strength of influence among users and the other is based on identifying the influencers.

1. Influence strength among users

The strength of influence among individuals in a social network depends on many factors such as the network distance and temporal action pattern. Simply put, the strength of influence is the quantitative size of the edge of a social network. For example, in Figure 3.1, the strength of influence between v1 and v2 is 0.33, and the strength of influence between v2 and v4 is 0.5.

2. Identification of influencers

To identify influencers in a social network, individual influence ranking technology is applied. The influence of an individual depends on several factors such as the network structure and behavior pattern of users in the social network. The influence of an individual is the quantitative size of the node in a social network. For example, in Figure 3.1, the influence of v1 is quantified as 0.025, and the influence of v2 is 0.0259.

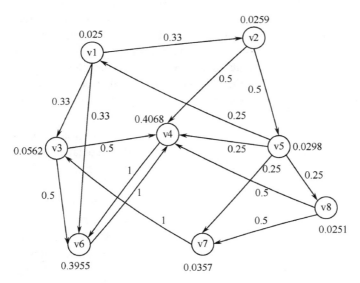

Figure 3.1: Analysis of individual influence in social networks.

The concepts involving individual influence analysis technology employed in social network studies first appeared in sociology, which were then explored in information science.

At first, researchers in the field of sociology explored the inequality of individual influences and discovered the diversity of individual influences. In 1955, Professor Elihu Katz [1] proposed the two-level communication theory based on a study of voters' intention to vote during the US presidential election. He discovered the difference in individual influences and found that a small part of opinion leaders or influencers held the power to influence over the majority of ordinary people.

Later in 1962, Everett Rogers [2] defined the term "influential" or "influencer" as an individual who is able to change the idea of other individuals to a certain degree. Influencers usually have three characteristics: inclined to convey their own ideas to others; representing the views of most common people; holding novel ideas; they are also known as opinion leaders, innovators, hubs, connectors, mavens, etc.

Early works in this field focused on exploring and analyzing the performance and related factors of influence in social activities, where the function model and the generation mechanism of social influence were studied in detail. Many social phenomena associated with influence and the underlying principles were discovered. However, due to the limited sample size at that time, the data attainable was limited, while objective data support and verification was needed.

With the rapid development of the Web 2.0 technology and the rise of online social networks, for the first time researchers have the opportunity to analyze and study the complex relationships among the mass of interactive information and large-scale social networks. Influence research turns to the rich data generated by online social networks for support to establish various influence analysis models and make extensive use of different quantitative techniques; researchers have also conducted research and explored the influences of users themselves, the mutual influence of users during online interactions, the interaction between users and their societies, and the evolution of influence over time. These studies have not only validated and expanded several early assumptions and theoretical models but also observed noted phenomena and rules. In addition, a large number of scientific issues and application scenarios associated with social influence have been discovered in this new research environment.

In 2006, Noah Friedki [3] defined "social influence," and pointed out that the existing social networking will change the (variable) characteristics of people.

Finally, to quantitatively measure the ability of social influence, we defined influence strength as the quantitative social influence, indicating the degree of interaction between individuals on social networks, which is also known as the strength of relationship, relationship strength, or tie strength.

Definition 3.1 (influence strength): Given two user nodes u *and* v in the network $G = (N, E)$, we denote $I_u(v) \in R$ as the influence strength of user v on user u. Furthermore, if $e_{uv} = 1$, we call $I_u(v)$ the direct influence of user v on u; if $e_{uv} = 0$, we call $I_u(v)$ the indirect influence of user v on u. The influence strength satisfies the anisotropy, i.e., $I_v(u) \neq I_u(v)$.

Overall, online social influence analysis mainly involves two aspects: first, the influence strength measurement. Based on the qualitative identification of social influence, considering complex social relations, to design and choose a measurement method that not only has certain universality but can also fully explore the characteristics of social networks is one of the core issues in the field. Second, identifying influential individuals. Based on the quantitative calculation of social influence, to accurately calculate the individual's influence and identify influentials based on ranking is of significant value for the analysis of social network evolution, social behavior, and information transmission mode.

3.2 Influence strength calculation

Early researches on the influence strength of individuals in social networks only considered the network structure and simply used the overlap of common neighbors, the edge betweenness, the frequency of forwarding, among other factors to measure influence strength. Later, to address the problem of limited use of information on user behaviors and interactions based on the method of network topology, some researchers proposed a method for calculating influence strength based on individual behaviors. Considering the difference in users' influence strength in different topics, some researchers studied the topic-based influence strength calculation.

3.2.1 Influence strength calculation based on network structure

1. Influence strength calculation based on the overlap of neighborhoods

In 1973, Mark S. Granovetter [4] proposed a method for measuring the influence strength between two nodes based on the overlap of neighborhoods. In general, if the overlap of neighborhoods between A and B is large, we consider A and B to have a strong influence strength, otherwise the influence strength is low. We formally define the strength $S(A, B)$ in terms of the Jaccard coefficient:

$$S(A, B) = \frac{|n_A \cap n_B|}{|n_A \cup n_B|} \tag{3.1}$$

Here, n_A and n_B denotes the sets of neighbors of A and B, respectively. If the overlap of neighborhoods between A and B is large, we consider A and B to have a strong tie. Otherwise, they are considered to have a weak tie. Similar to Jaccard coefficient, the social influence in the network is measured by overlapping similarity and cosine distance.

2. Influence strength calculation based on edge betweenness
In 1977, Linton C. Freeman [5] proposed the concept of betweenness to measure the importance of an edge in a network, assuming that the information flows between node s and t are evenly distributed on the shortest paths. That is, if there is only one shortest path between them, such a path is given a weight of unity. The betweenness of an edge e is calculated by summarizing the total "weights" of all shortest paths going through it. We defined the influence strength as follows:

$$E^{\text{BET}}(e_{ij}) = \sum_{s<t} \left| g_{st}^{ij} \right| \tag{3.2}$$

Here, $\left| g_{st}^{ij} \right|$ denotes the number of shortest paths between s and t simultaneously passing i and j (through the edge e_{ij}). The betweenness of an edge is calculated by summarizing the total number of all shortest paths going through the edge e_{ij}.

3. Influence strength calculation based on forwarding frequency
In 2006, when the propagation of the influence of blogs was analyzed, directed multigraph was used to represent the influence between nodes. Directed graph with edge weights indicated how much influence a particular source node had on its destination; the direction of the arc represented the source of influence and the weight represented the intensity of the influence. When $c_{u,v}$ indicates the number of arcs from u to v and $\deg^{\text{in}}(v)$ denotes the in-degree of v the formula becomes:

$$w_{u,v} = \frac{c_{u,v}}{\deg^{\text{out}}(v)} \tag{3.3}$$

How to use the above formula to calculate the influence of individuals in blog post networks is elaborated in Figure 3.2.

3.2.2 Behaviour-based influence strength calculation

Influence calculation based on network topology has some inherent limitations. First, the social network topology that researchers achieved is static, equivalent to a snapshot of the original network, on which all explicit social relations

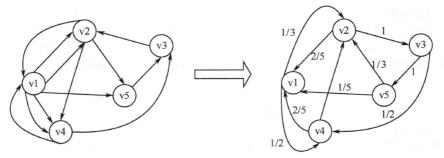

Figure 3.2: Influence strength calculation based on forwarding frequency.

before the acquisition are recorded; thus, all connections established 10 years ago and even 1 second ago are collected at the same time. A connection that received just one notice and a connection of intimate communications between two friends are treated equally in the calculation model. Second, in such a network topology, the weights of all connections are equal or identically distributed, implying that the connected users have the same influence on each other or that the influence among the users in the social network satisfies a simple probability function. The above situation is obviously inconsistent with the reality, and the fundamental reason is possibly the limited use of information on users' behaviors and their interactions in the calculation method based on network topology, leading to the deviation of results of this method from the actual scenario.

User behaviors in online social network include information release, shopping, commenting on topics, forwarding information, establishing friendships, etc. Analyzing the distribution rules and causality of such behaviors will help to not only evaluate the influence between the initiator of the behavior and the disseminator but also predict the behavior of people in social networks and deepen our understanding of human social behavior.

In general, online social networks record a large amount of information arising from interactive activities of people, which include all types of user behavior data. By analyzing these data, we can not only measure the influence between users and the way and scope of its diffusion but also establish the social relations between users. Goya et al. [7] studied the influence of both users and their behaviors based on logs:

$$\text{infl}(u) = \frac{|\{a|\exists v, \Delta t : \text{prop}(a, v, u, \Delta t) \wedge 0 \le \Delta t \le \tau_{v,u}\}|}{A_u} \tag{3.4}$$

$$\text{infl}(a) = \frac{|\{u|\exists v, \Delta t : \text{prop}(a, v, u, \Delta t) \wedge 0 \le \Delta t \le \tau_{v,u}\}|}{U(a)} \tag{3.5}$$

where u and v denote users; a denotes action; Δt represents the time interval of actions; $\tau_{v,u}$ is a time constant; $\text{prop}(a, v, u, \Delta t)$ denotes the transmission of actions between users; A_u represents the number of actions of user u; and $U(a)$ denotes the number of users executing actions. Different from the network topology-based influence strength calculation method, the above model uses the frequency of action transmission as the indicator for measuring influence strength, and the execution scope of the action is used to measure the influence of the action itself. To calculate the influence of users on their neighbors, the authors designed the static probability model, continuous time model, and discrete time model. The relative parameters were estimated by machine learning method, and the influence coefficient among Flickr users was calculated.

Figure 3.3 shows a schematic diagram of the method for calculating influence strength based on behavior.

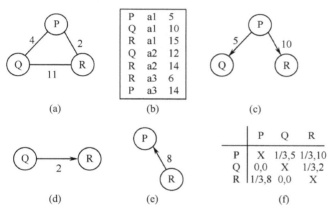

Figure 3.3: Influence strength based on the behavior.

3.2.3 Topic-based influence strength calculation

In social activities, information is often generated and transmitted in the form of topics. Studies have found that users' influence strength varies with different topics. Therefore, measuring influence strength using topics as the basic object is conducive to depicting influence among users from many different perspectives. In establishing an influence strength model, it is possible to construct the relationship between a user and a topic by directly resorting to the content of the topic and the degree of the user's participation in the topic, without having to refer to the social network topology established based on user behaviors, such as as applying for a friend relation or following someone as the model input. The influence strength resulting from analysis based on the former method is termed "implicit influence," whereas that from the latter is termed "explicit influence."

Entities in online social networks include users, text, and multimedia information, which internally and mutually form a heterogeneous network structure more complex than homogeneous networks.

Tang et al. [8] proposed a Topical Factor Graph (TFG) model to formulate the topic-level social influence analysis into a unified graphical model. The goal of this model is to simultaneously capture information related to topics, such as topical distributions, similarity between users' topics, and network structure. Factor graph model was based on object likelihood function:

$$P(v, Y) = \frac{1}{Z} \prod_{k=1}^{N} \prod_{z=1}^{T} h(y_1, ..., y_N, k, z) \prod_{i=1}^{N} \prod_{z=1}^{T} g(v_i, y_i, z) \prod_{e_{kl} \in E} \prod_{z=1}^{T} f(y_k, y_l, z) \qquad (3.6)$$

where $v = [v_1, ..., v_N]$ denotes a set of observed variables; $Y = [y_1, ..., y_N]$ denotes a set of latent variables; g and f, respectively, represent feature functions of nodes and edges; h denotes global feature functions; and Z represents normalized factors.

Figure 3.4 shows a schematic diagram of the factor graph model in which $g(\cdot)$ represents a feature function defined on a node; $f(\cdot)$ represents a feature function defined on an edge; and $h(\cdot)$ represents a global feature function defined for each node indicating forwarding frequency among other factors; the latent vector y_i models the topic-level influence from other nodes to node v_i.

Liu et al. [9] proposed a generative graphical model which leveraged both heterogeneous link information and textual content associated with each user in the network to mine the implicit influence between users and predict user behavior

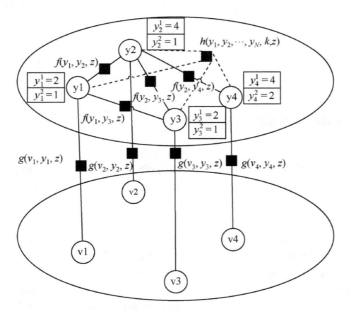

Figure 3.4: Schematic diagram of the factor graph model.

by using the similarity of textual content. The generative probabilistic model is shown in Figure 3.5.

Using Gibbs sampling and iterative learning, the influence strength $\gamma_d(c)$ on d from c due to its citation of c is:

$$\gamma_d(c) = \frac{1}{K}\sum_{k=1}^{K}\frac{C_{d,c,s}(d,c,0)^{(k)}+\alpha_\gamma}{C_{d,s}(d,0)^{(k)}+|L(d)|\cdot\alpha_\gamma} \tag{3.7}$$

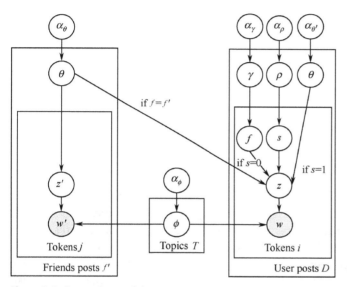

Figure 3.5: Generative model.

For random variables var_1, var_2...var_n, the notation $C_{\text{var}_1,\,\text{var}_2,\,...,\,\text{var}_n}(\text{val}_1,\text{val}_2,...,\text{val}_n) = |\{\forall i : \text{var}_{1,i} = \text{val}_1 \wedge \text{var}_{2,i} = \text{val}_2 \wedge ... \wedge \text{var}_{n,i} = \text{val}_n\}|$ counts occurrences of a configuration $\text{val}_1, \text{val}_2,..., \text{val}_n$. For example, $C_{d,c,s}(1,2,0)$ denotes the number of tokens in document 1 assigned to citation 2 where the coin result of Bernoulli distribution is 0. α_γ represents the superparameter (Bernoulli distribution parameter); K represents the number of iterations; and $|L(d)|$ indicates the length of the document. As shown in Figure 3.6, the "Bryant" vocabulary of user A comes from its friends B and C, and according to the probability-generating model, it is possible to calculate the probability of "Bryant" of user A from its friends B and C.

This method integrates the information from user interaction in the social network structure. Moreover, by analyzing the relationship between topic information and users, it can measure both the generation and change process of user influence more accurately.

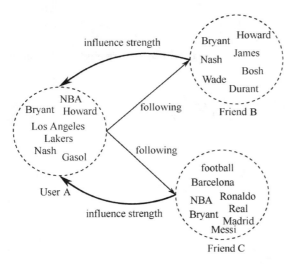

Figure 3.6: Influence strength based on generative model.

3.3 Identification of influentials

The identification of influentials is mainly realized using the technology of ranking the influence of individuals. The influence of individuals depends on many factors such as the structure of networks and the behavior patterns of users in social networks.

The early methods of individual influence calculation were mainly based on concepts such as "degree centrality," "closeness," and "betweenness." Later, some methods based on random walk, such as HITS [10] and PageRank [11], were proposed to identify influentials. In recent years, with the increasing complexity of individual behavior and the diversity of topics in social networks, researchers have studied individual identification methods based on individual behaviors and topic levels.

3.3.1 Individual influence calculation-based network structure

Degree centrality: degree centrality refers to the number of nodes in a social network; that is, the number of nodes directly connected to a specific node which measures the average influence of a node to its neighbors. Let A be the adjacency matrix of a network and $\deg(i)$ be the degree of node i. The degree centrality of node i c_i^{DEG}, i.e., the degree of the node is:

$$c_i{}^{\text{DEG}} = \deg(i) \tag{3.8}$$

For example, in Figure 3.1, the in-degree of node v_1 is 1 and the in-degree of node v_4 is 5.

Cha et al. [12] calculated the degree centralities of the following, forwarding, and referring networks to measure the individual influence on Twitter. They used Spearman's rank correlation coefficient as a measure of the strength of the association between two rank sets.

$$\rho = 1 - \frac{6 \sum (x_i - y_i)^2}{N^3 - N} \tag{3.9}$$

where x_i and y_i are the ranks of users based on two different influence measures in a dataset of N users. The Spearman rank correlation coefficient is used to determine the degree of closeness between the two sets of rankings; and the calculation is based on the rankings. The higher the consistency of the two groups, the higher the Spearman rank correlation coefficient. When the group variable is exactly the same, the Spearman rank correlation coefficient is 1.

Closeness: closeness is the sum of short distances (shortest paths) between an individual and all other nodes in a social network. Closeness centrality can be used to measure a node's indirect influence to other nodes or the distance from a node to others. It can also be used to measure the strength of a user's social ties. The higher the closeness centrality of a user, the shorter the distance between it and other users, and the faster its influence will be spread to other users. The most popular centrality measure in this group is the Freeman's closeness centrality. The closeness centrality c_i^{CLO} of node i is defined as follows:

$$c_i^{CLO} = e_i^T S \mathbf{1} \tag{3.10}$$

where S is a matrix whose $(i,j)th$ element contains the length of the shortest path from node i to j and $\mathbf{1}$ is the all-one vector.

The averages of the shortest distances to all other nodes are computed, and the computational load is relatively heavy. The advantage is that it can measure the indirect influence of a node.

Betweenness: betweenness refers to the ability of a node to be on the shortest path to other nodes in a social network. It is used to analyze the influence of a node on the diffusion of information; that is, the extent to which an individual is between others and whether it plays the role of an "intermediary." The betweenness centrality c_i^{BET} of node i is defined as follows:

$$c_i^{BET} = \sum_{j,k} \frac{b_{jik}}{b_{jk}} \tag{3.11}$$

where b_{jk} is the number of shortest paths from node j to k, and b_{jik} is the number of shortest paths from node j to k that pass through node i. The naive algorithm for computing the betweenness involves all-pair shortest paths. This requires $O(n^3)$ time overhead and $O(n^2)$ space overhead. Ulrik [13] designed a faster algorithm using single-source-shortest-path algorithms which requires $O(n+m)$ space overhead and runs in $O(nm)$ and $O(nm+n^2\log n)$ time overhead, where n is the number of nodes and m is the number of edges.

The disadvantage of betweenness centrality is that the computational load is relatively heavy, whereas the advantage is that this method can span structural holes in a social network.

HITS: also called as Hypertext Induced Topic Search, this method was proposed by Kleinberg [10]. HITS was first used in search engines where the importance of pages was measured by Hub and Authority. For a given node v_i in a network, the authority is defined as $a(v_i)$ and the hub is defined as $h(v_i)$. Hub and Authority are measured as follows:

$$a^{(k+1)}(v_i) = \sum_{v_j\in\text{inlink}[v_i]} h^{(k)}(v_j), \quad h^{(k+1)}(v_i) = \sum_{v_j\in\text{outlink}[v_i]} a^{(k+1)}(v_j) \qquad (3.12)$$

Authority page: when a webpage is often cited, it may be very important; even though a webpage is not cited often but is cited by important webpages, it is possible that it is also important. The importance of a webpage is evenly passed to the citing of webpages. Such a web page is called an "authoritative" page.

Hub page: A webpage that provides a link to an authoritative webpage, which itself may not be important, or there are not many pages linking to it, but provides a collection of links to a site which is critical for a topic; for example, the list of references on the home page of a course.

In HITS algorithm, shown below, both the authority and the hub are measured for each page.

---

initialize authority and hub weights, a0 and h0
  while (not converged)
  for each vertex i

$$a^{(k+1)}(v_i) = \sum_{v_j\in\text{inlink}[v_i]} h^{(k)}(v_j)$$

$$h^{(k+1)}(v_i) = \sum_{v_j\in\text{outlink}[v_i]} a^{(k+1)}(v_j)$$

    end
  end

Figure 3.7 is a schematic diagram of HITS. The authority of node $v1$ is measured by the hub of $v2$, $v3$, $v4$. The hub of $v1$ is measured by the authority of $v5$, $v6$, $v7$, $v8$.

$$a(v_1) = h(v_2) + h(v_3) + h(v_4)$$

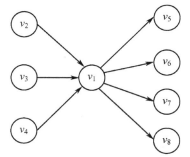

Figure 3.7: HITS.

$$h(v_1) = a(v_5) + a(v_6) + a(v_7) + a(v_8)$$

Romero et al. [14] devised a general model for analyzing influence in Twitter using the concept of passivity in a social network and developed an efficient algorithm similar to the HITS algorithm, called Influence-Passivity (IP) algorithm. For every arc $e = (i, j) \in E$, they defined the acceptance rate $u_{ij} = \dfrac{w_{ij}}{\sum\limits_{k:(k,j)\in E} w_{kj}}$. The acceptance rate can be considered as the dedication or loyalty user j has to user i. On the other hand, for every $e = (j, i) \in E$, the authors defined rejection rate by $v_{ji} = \dfrac{1 - w_{ji}}{\sum\limits_{k:(j,k)\in E}(1 - w_{jk})}$.

The algorithm is based on the following operations:

$$I_i \leftarrow \sum_{j:(i,j)} u_{ij} P_j$$
$$P_i \leftarrow \sum_{j:(j,i)} v_{ji} I_j \tag{3.13}$$

For example, Figure 3.8 illustrates the IP algorithm. A user's influence score depends on:

(1) the passivity score of its influence.
(2) friends' rate of acceptance to its influence in relation to other users.

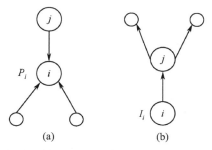

(a)   (b)   **Figure 3.8:** IP.

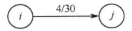

Figure 3.9: Weight calculation.

A user's passivity score depends on:
(1) the influence score of its neighbors.
(2) friends' rate of rejection against its influence in relation to other users.

The acceptance rate and the rejection rate are computed using the above methods. The calculation of weights is critical. The weight of edge (i, j) is defined as the ratio of user i forwarding the posts of user j. Figure 3.9 gives an example of weight calculation.

3.3.2 PageRank

The authority and the hub, whose values were computed by the iterative process, were considered in HITS algorithm. However, the repartition of influence was neglected.

PageRank was proposed by Larry Page [11], which was considered in search engine. The influence of a page in PageRank was measured by values of linked-in pages, where the network structure was considered. The rating of a page is determined by the importance of all the links to it. Later, PageRank was applied to social networks by some researchers where the influence of each node in social networks was measured. The Markov Model-based random walk concept was adopted to simulate the behavior of browsing webpages. If π is the score of influence and $\boldsymbol{P}$ is the transfer matrix of a social network, then PageRank is defined as follows:

$$\pi = \alpha P^T \pi + (1-\alpha)\frac{1}{n}e, e = (1, 1, \cdots, 1)^T \tag{3.14}$$

where α is a jump factor, $\frac{1}{n}e$ is a restart vector assuming that each node is visited randomly by other nodes with equal probability. Let $i \rightarrow j$ be a direction from node i to node j. The adjacency matrix M of the social network G is defined as follows:

$$M(i,j) = \begin{cases} 1, & i \rightarrow j \\ 0, & \text{otherwise} \end{cases} \tag{3.15}$$

The transfer matrix $P = \{p_{ij}\}$ of a social network G is defined as follows:

$$p_{ij} = \begin{cases} \dfrac{M(i,j)}{\sum_{v_k \in \text{outlink}[v_i]} M(i,k)} & , \text{outlink}[v_i] \neq 0 \\ M(i,j) = 0, \text{otherwise} \end{cases} \tag{3.16}$$

where outlink$[v_i]$ represents the link-out nodes of node v_i. The transfer matrix P indicates that the node passes its authority equally to the nodes it links out to.

Thus, the traditional PageRank included two main characteristics:
(1) The node passes its authority equally to the nodes it links out to; and
(2) Each node is visited by other nodes at the same probability $1/n$.

The specific algorithm is as follows:

---

initialize ranks $\pi\, 0$
while (not converged)
    for each vertex i
        $\pi = \alpha P^T \pi + (1-\alpha)\frac{1}{n}e, e = (1, 1, \cdots, 1)^T$
    end
  end

For example, the adjacency matrix town in Figure 3.10 is as follows:

$$M = \begin{bmatrix} 0 & 1 & 1 & 0 & 0 & 1 & 0 & 0 \\ 0 & 0 & 0 & 1 & 1 & 0 & 0 & 0 \\ 0 & 0 & 0 & 1 & 0 & 1 & 0 & 0 \\ 0 & 0 & 0 & 0 & 0 & 1 & 0 & 0 \\ 1 & 0 & 0 & 1 & 0 & 0 & 1 & 1 \\ 0 & 0 & 0 & 1 & 0 & 0 & 0 & 0 \\ 0 & 0 & 1 & 0 & 0 & 0 & 0 & 0 \\ 0 & 0 & 0 & 1 & 0 & 0 & 1 & 0 \end{bmatrix}$$

The above adjacency matrix is then converted into the transfer matrix.

$$P = \begin{bmatrix} 0 & 1/3 & 1/3 & 0 & 0 & 1/3 & 0 & 0 \\ 0 & 0 & 0 & 1/2 & 1/2 & 0 & 0 & 0 \\ 0 & 0 & 0 & 1/2 & 0 & 1/2 & 0 & 0 \\ 0 & 0 & 0 & 0 & 0 & 1 & 0 & 0 \\ 1/4 & 0 & 0 & 1/4 & 0 & 0 & 1/4 & 1/4 \\ 0 & 0 & 0 & 1 & 0 & 0 & 0 & 0 \\ 0 & 0 & 1 & 0 & 0 & 0 & 0 & 0 \\ 0 & 0 & 0 & 1/2 & 0 & 0 & 1/2 & 0 \end{bmatrix}$$

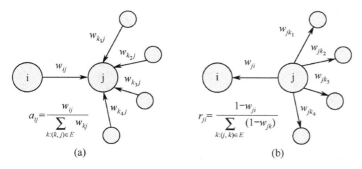

Figure 3.10: Acceptance and rejection rate calculations.

Finally, repeated iteration is carried out using the PageRank algorithm to calculate the influence scores of each node (Table 3.1).

The personalized PageRank was proposed by Haveliwala et al. [15] based on PageRank, as shown in the following equation. For example, element r_i indicates the degree of an individual's preference to the topic, the degree of novelty, and sensitivity of the information released by an individual, etc.

$$\pi = \alpha P^T \pi + (1 - \alpha) r \tag{3.17}$$

In the personalized PageRank, vector $\frac{1}{n} e$ is replaced by the personalized vector r.

Table 3.1: Influence scores.

ID	PR	Inlink	Outlink
1	0.0250	v_5	v_2, v_3, v_6
2	0.0259	v_1	v_4, v_5
3	0.0562	v_1, v_7	v_4, v_6
4	0.4068	v_2, v_3, v_5, v_6, v_8	v_6
5	0.0298	v_2	v_1, v_4, v_7, v_8
6	0.3955	v_1, v_3, v_4	v_4
7	0.0357	v_5, v_8	v_3
8	0.0251	v_5	v_4, v_7

Figure 3.11 shows the influence scores of two different types of personalized vectors in line with the case in Figure 3.11.

ID	π	r
1	0.0250	0.125
2	0.0259	0.125
3	0.0562	0.125
4	0.4068	0.125
5	0.0298	0.125
6	**0.3955**	**0.125**
7	0.0357	0.125
8	0.0251	0.125

ID	π	r
1	0.1024	0.65
2	0.0365	0.05
3	0.0515	0.05
4	0.3774	0.05
5	0.0230	0.05
6	0.3792	0.05
7	0.0177	0.05
8	0.0124	0.05

ID	π	r
1	0.0100	0.05
2	0.0103	0.05
3	0.0225	0.05
4	0.4384	0.05
5	0.0119	0.05
6	**0.4825**	**0.65**
7	0.0143	0.05
8	0.0100	0.05

uniform vector   bias on v_1 bias on v_6

Figure 3.11: Personalized PageRank algorithm calculations.

The traditional PageRank is only suitable for directed graph. For weighted directed graph [11], scholars studied the weighted PageRank algorithm. Figure 3.12 shows a weighted graph.

$$M = \begin{bmatrix} 0 & 1 & 1 & 0 & 0 & 1 & 0 & 0 \\ 0 & 0 & 0 & 1 & 1 & 0 & 0 & 0 \\ 0 & 0 & 0 & 1 & 0 & 1 & 0 & 0 \\ 0 & 0 & 0 & 0 & 0 & 1 & 0 & 0 \\ 1 & 0 & 0 & 1 & 0 & 0 & 1 & 1 \\ 0 & 0 & 0 & 1 & 0 & 0 & 0 & 0 \\ 0 & 0 & 1 & 0 & 0 & 0 & 0 & 0 \\ 0 & 0 & 0 & 1 & 0 & 0 & 1 & 0 \end{bmatrix} \Longrightarrow M = \begin{bmatrix} 0 & 2 & 1 & 0 & 0 & 3 & 0 & 0 \\ 0 & 0 & 0 & 1 & 2 & 0 & 0 & 0 \\ 0 & 0 & 0 & 4 & 0 & 1 & 0 & 0 \\ 0 & 0 & 0 & 0 & 0 & 3 & 0 & 0 \\ 2 & 0 & 0 & 3 & 0 & 0 & 5 & 1 \\ 0 & 0 & 0 & 1 & 0 & 0 & 0 & 0 \\ 0 & 0 & 4 & 0 & 0 & 0 & 0 & 0 \\ 0 & 0 & 0 & 2 & 0 & 0 & 1 & 0 \end{bmatrix}$$

Adjacent Matrix   Weighted Adjacent Matrix

Figure 3.12: Weighted adjacency matrix.

PageRank value of the weighted adjacency matrix is measured as follows.

Tunkelang et al. constructed an algorithm similar to PageRank targeted at the followed–following relationship in Twitter to measure the influence of individuals in Twitter, which uses the influences of fans to measure the influence of an individual.

ID	π	r		ID	π	r
1	**0.0250**	0.125		1	0.0239	0.125
2	0.0259	0.125		2	0.0255	0.125
3	0.0562	0.125		3	0.0541	0.125
4	0.4068	0.125		4	0.4142	0.125
5	0.0298	0.125		5	0.0332	0.125
6	0.3955	0.125		6	0.3902	0.125
7	0.0357	0.125		7	0.0376	0.125
8	0.0251	0.125		8	**0.0213**	0.125

↑   ↑
Un-weighted   Weighted

Figure 3.13: Weighted PageRank values.

The higher the influence of the fans and the smaller the number of other users being followed by these fans, the greater their contribution to individual's influence. The model is constructed as follows:

1. Influence(X) = expected number of people who will read a microblog that X tweets, including all reposts of that microblog.
2. If X is a member of Followers (Y), then there is a $1/\|\text{Following}(X)\|$ probability that X will read a microblog posted by Y, where Following(X) is the set of people that X follows.
3. If X reads a microblog from Y, there is a constant probability p that X will repost it.

From this model, it is easy to measure someone's influence recursively assuming that we know the constant repost probability p:

$$\text{Influence}(X) = \sum_{Y \in \text{Followers}(X)} (1 + p \cdot \text{Influence}(Y)) / \|\text{Following}(Y)\| \qquad (3.18)$$

3.3.3 Individual influence calculation based on behavior

In social networks, especially in Twitter, a user's influence is subject to its behavioral characteristics; the influence of a user is measured by four relationships: repost, reply, reintroduce (copy), and read [16].

Some studies [16] have taken into account a variety of network relationships in microblogs to fully measure a user's influence in the topic level, as shown in Figure 3.14 (a), where the influence of user A by user B is represented in four types:

(1) User A reposts the microblogs of user B by using an informal convention such as "RT @user" or "via @user";
(2) User A replies to the microblogs of user B by using an informal convention such as "@user";
(3) User A reintroduces the microblogs which are similar to those previously posted by user B but without acknowledgement of the source from user B; and
(4) User A reads the message tweeted by user B.

Therefore, it is clear that the influence network is a multi-relational network. Romero et al. defined the following four types of networking relationships: Repost's Network,

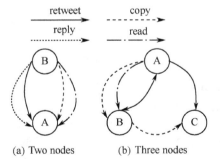

(a) Two nodes   (b) Three nodes   **Figure 3.14:** Multi-relation network.

Reply's Network, Copy's Network, and Read's Network. For example, in Figure 3.14, the multi-relational influence network consists of three users and four relationships.

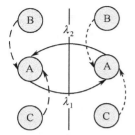

Figure 3.15: Inter-network and intra-network transition probability.

The random walk process in the repost network graph $G_a^i = (V_a^i, E_{\text{Retweet}}^i, W(E_{\text{Retweet}}^i))$ is constructed as follows: user i reposts microblogs of his/her "friends" in the i-th topic space at a certain transition probability under the influence of his friend. The random walk process in the repost network graph simulates the reposting behavior of users in Weibo. The transition matrix for the topic i, denoted as P_a^i, is defined as follows:

$$P_a^i(u_t^i | u_s^i) = \frac{w_a(u_s^i, u_t^i)}{\sum\limits_{u^i \in \text{out}(u_s^i)} w_a(u_s^i, u^i)} \tag{3.19}$$

where $w_a(u_s^i, u_t^i)$ is the frequency of user u_s^i reposting user u_t^i in the i-th topic space. $\sum\limits_{u^i \in \text{out}(u_s^i)} w_a(u_s^i, u^i)$ sums up the number of reposts by user u_s^i of the microblogs from all his/her friends.

The random walk process in the reply network graph $G_b^i = (V_b^i, E_{\text{Reply}}^i, W(E_{\text{Reply}}^i))$ is constructed as follows: user i replies to the microblogs of his/her "friends" in the i-th topic space at certain transition probability under the influence of his friend. The random walk process in the reposting network graph simulates the reply behavior of users in microblog. The transition matrix for the topic i, denoted as P_b^i, is defined as follows:

$$P_b^i(u_t^i | u_s^i) = \frac{w_b(u_s^i, u_t^i)}{\sum\limits_{u^i \in \text{out}(u_s^i)} w_b(u_s^i, u^i)} \tag{3.20}$$

where $w_b(u_s^i, u_t^i)$ is the frequency of user u_s^i replying user u_t^i in the i-th topic space. $\sum\limits_{u^i \text{out}(u_s^i)} w_b(u_s^i, u^i)$ sums up the number of replies by user u_s^i to microblogs from all his/her friends.

The "copy" behavior in microblog is a "repost" behavior, except that the "RT @B" or "via @B" tags are not explicitly used.

If two microblogs in a "copy" relationship are defined as a tuple $<p_t, p_s>$, then all the microblog pairs in the "copy" relationship between the two friends is a binary set U. It can be deduced that the copy network graph $G_c^i = (V_c^i, E_{Copy}^i)$ is a weighted directed graph, and the weight $w_c(u_s^i, u_t^i)$ between user u_s^i and u_t^i is defined as follows:

$$w_c(u_s^i, u_t^i) = \sum_{\langle p_t^i, p_s^i \rangle \in U_{s,t}^i} \text{sim}(p_s^i, p_t^i) \times f\left(\Delta t_{p_s^i, p_t^i}\right) \qquad (3.21)$$

$U_{s,t}^i$ is the binary set of the microblog pairs that are in the "copy" relationship between user u_s^i and u_t^i in the i-th topic space. The probability distributions of similarity and the time difference between the two microblogs are taken into account in the weight calculation. The higher the similarity between the two microblogs, the less the time difference between them, indicating that the probability of "copy" is higher.

The random walk process in the copy network $G_c^i = (V_c^i, E_{Copy}^i, W(E_{Copy}^i))$ is constructed as follows: the user is influenced by his/her friend in the i-th topic space and will copy his/her friend's microblog with a certain probability of transition. The random walk process in the copy network graph simulates the copy behavior of the user in Weibo. Assuming the transition probability matrix in the copy network in the i-th topic space is P_c^i, then the transition probability between users is defined below.

In the copy network in the i-topic space, the transition probability of user u_s^i's random copy of user's u_t^i microblogs is defined as:

$$P_c^i(u_t^i | u_s^i) = \frac{w_c(u_s^i, u_t^i)}{\sum\limits_{u^i \in out(u_s^i)} w_c(u_s^i, u^i)} \qquad (3.22)$$

where $w_c(u_s^i, u_t^i)$ represents the weight of the "copy" relationship between user u_s^i and u_t^i; and $\sum\limits_{u^i \in out(u_s^i)} w_c(u_s^i, u^i)$ represents the sum of the weights of user u_s^i's "copy" relationship with all his/her friends in the i-th topic space.

The inference of the probability of a read relationship between users is related to the following three factors:

(1) Users read with a higher probability the microblogs posted by friends who excel in quantity of posts

(2) Users read with a higher probability the microblogs with a higher similarity of topics;

(3) Users read with a higher probability the microblogs posted by friends with high similarity in the time series pattern of posting.

Therefore, the probability of user u_s reading the posts of his/her friend u_t is defined as follows:

$$P_{\text{read}}(u_s, u_t) = \frac{\tau_t \times \text{sim}(u_s, u_t) \times \text{simSeries}(u_s, u_t)}{\sum\limits_{u \in \text{out}(u_s)} \tau_u \times \text{sim}(u_s, u) \times \text{simSeries}(u_s, u)} \tag{3.23}$$

where τ indicates the number of posts published by user u in the dataset (not including the posts that are already in the repost, reply, and copy relationship). $\text{simSeries}(u_s, u_t)$ represents the time series similarity between user u_s and his/her friend u_t, and $\text{out}(u_s)$ represents the friend's set followed by user u_s.

Users' influence from their friends is expressed as the random walk process in four types of influence networks, which will jump to another type of influence network at a certain probability. If the probabilities of a user staying in the repost network, reply network, copy network, and read network are respectively λ_1, λ_2, λ_3, and λ_4 and $\lambda_1 + \lambda_2 + \lambda_3 + \lambda_4 = 1$ is satisfied, then the user will jump to other networks from the repost network at a probability of $1 - \lambda_1$, from the reply network at a probability of $1 - \lambda_2$, from the copy network at a probability of $1 - \lambda_3$, and from the read network at a probability of $1 - \lambda_4$.

According to the PageRank algorithm, the user not only travels along the network randomly but also randomly jumps to other nodes at certain probabilities. Therefore, considering the inter-node jump probability β, the inter-network jump probability λ, and the transition probability matrix to be B, the transition probabilities in the four networks in the i-th topic space is defined as follows:

(1) repost network:

$$B_a^i(u_t^i | u_s^i) = \lambda_1 \times (1 - \beta) \times \frac{w_a(u_s^i, u_t^i)}{\sum\limits_{u^i \in \text{out}(u_s^i)} w_a(u_s^i, u^i)} + \frac{\beta}{n} \tag{3.24}$$

(2) reply network:

$$B_b^i(u_t^i | u_s^i) = \lambda_2 \times (1 - \beta) \times \frac{w_b(u_s^i, u_t^i)}{\sum\limits_{u^i \in \text{out}(u_s^i)} w_b(u_s^i, u^i)} + \frac{\beta}{n} \tag{3.25}$$

(3) copy network:

$$B_c^i(u_t^i | u_s^i) = \lambda_3 \times (1 - \beta) \times \frac{w_c(u_s^i, u_t^i)}{\sum\limits_{u^i \in \text{out}(u_s^i)} w_c(u_s^i, u^i)} + \frac{\beta}{n} \tag{3.26}$$

(4) read network:

$$B_d^i(u_t^i | u_s^i) = \lambda_4 \times (1 - \beta) \times \frac{w_d(u_s^i, u_t^i)}{\sum\limits_{u^i \in \text{out}(u_s^i)} w_d(u_s^i, u^i)} + \frac{\beta}{n} \tag{3.27}$$

Let $r^i(u)$ be user u's ranking in the i-th topic space; taking into account the random walk of the user in the four network, user u's ranking in the i-th topic space is defined as follows:

$$r^i(u) = \sum_{(u^i_t,u) \in E^i_{\text{Retweet}}} \mathbf{B}^i_a(u|u^i_t)r^i(u^i_t) + \sum_{(u^i_t,u) \in E^i_{\text{Reply}}} \mathbf{B}^i_b(u|u^i_t)r^i(u^i_t)$$
$$+ \sum_{(u^i_t,u) \in E^i_{\text{Copy}}} \mathbf{B}^i_c(u|u^i_t)r^i(u^i_t) + \sum_{(u^i_t,u) \in E^i_{\text{Read}}} \mathbf{B}^i_d(u|u^i_t)r^i(u^i_t) \tag{3.28}$$

Therefore, the ranking of a user is mainly determined by the probability of its followers' random jump to the user.

3.3.4 Individual influence calculation based on topics

In social networks, the influence of an individual varies with different topics. Weng et al. [17] measured the influence of an individual on each topic taking into account both the topical similarity between users and the link structure in the Twitter dataset. Given a topic t, each element of matrix P_t, i.e., the transition probability of the random surfer from follower s_i to friend s_j, is defined as:

$$P_t(i,j) = \frac{|T_j|}{\sum\limits_{a\,:\,s_i \text{ follows } s_a} |T_a|} \times \text{sim}_t(i,j) \tag{3.29}$$

$|T_j|$ is the number of tweets published by sj, and $\sum\limits_{a\,:\,s_i \text{ follows } s_a} |T_a|$ sums up the number of tweets published by all of si, s friends.

Topical difference between two Twitter users si and sj can be calculated as: $\text{dist}(i,j) = \sqrt{2D_{JS}(i,j)}$.

$D_{JS}(i,j)$ is the Jensen–Shannon divergence [18] between the two probability distributions $DT'_{i.}$ and $DT'_{j.}$ defined as:

$$D_{JS}(i,j) = \frac{1}{2}(D_{KL}(D'_{i.}||M) + D_{KL}(D'_{j.}||M)) \tag{3.30}$$

M is the average of the two probability distributions, i.e., $M = \frac{1}{2}(D'_{i.} + D'_{j.})$. D_{KL} is the Kullback–Leibler divergence which defines the divergence from distributions Q to P as: $D_{KL}(P||Q) = \sum\limits_i P(i) \log \frac{P(i)}{Q(i)}$.

Thus, the similarity of the two topics is defined as follows:

$$\text{sim}_t(i,j) = 1 - |DT'_{it} - DT'_{jt}| \tag{3.31}$$

Figure 3.16 gives an example of TwitterRank.

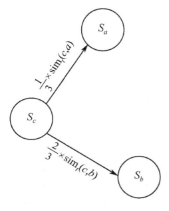

Figure 3.16: Schematic diagram of TwitterRank.

3.4 Summary

With the rapid development of online social networks and the rapid growth of online users, social networks have become an ideal platform for people to share information, sell goods, express opinions, and develop personal influences. Influence analysis and modeling online social networks constitutes an important part of social network analysis. Analyzing the influence modes and the ways of influence diffusion will not only deepen our understanding of people's social behaviors from a sociological viewpoint but also provide a theoretical basis for public decision-making and public opinion guidance. Furthermore it can also promote the communication and dissemination of information in political, economic, cultural, and other fields, and can have important social significance and applications.

Although fruitful results have been achieved in the field of influence analysis in social networks, we believe that the following questions require further investigation and exploration:

(1) Due to the large number of social networking users and the very complex relationships between users, qualitative analysis of social influence is subject to many factors and interferences. Although many researches have attempted to objectively and accurately clarify the relationship between influence and other factors, they have not yet solved this problem effectively. Such a situation is associated with both the complicated generation and diffusion mechanisms of social influence and the definition of influence itself. The existing concept of influence is nothing more than a description of the effect of influence, which, in essence, does not explain the problem as to "what is influence," resulting in the enormous social influence models, with the lack of benchmark comparison models and methods. Perhaps we cannot precisely define the concept of social influence, but as far as the specific environment of online social network is concerned, it is necessary to study the indicators of evaluating social influence to provide directional

guidance for designing new models so that they can describe the complexities of online social networks more accurately.

(2) At present, the social influence modeling methods can be divided into two categories: empirical methods and inference methods. The empirical method summarizes mathematical models that comply with samples based on the observation and analysis of experimental data, and then identify parameter values in the models by fitting with the actual data. The inference method directly derives influence models according to the relevant theory, while also determining parameter values in the models by learning and fitting. Both methods have their own advantages and successful applications; however, neither can universally and accurately depict the influence in social networks. To change such a situation, breakthroughs are needed in the fields of definition of influence, relationship between social information and influence, and so on. It is also necessary to seek improvements in the modeling methods. We can use information such as social network topology, user interaction data, and action records to analyze the generation and dissemination of user influence in social networks globally from multiple perspectives. For high real-time requirements, we can also consider using incremental models to reduce the amount of computation.

References

[1] Katz E: Personal influence: The part played by people in the flow of mass communications. Glencoe, Illinois, 1955.
[2] Everett R: Diffusion of innovations. Simon and Schuster, 1962.
[3] Friedkin N: A structural theory of social influence, Cambridge University Press, 2006.
[4] Granovetter M: The strength of weak ties. *Am J Sociol* 1973, 78:l.
[5] Freeman L: A set of measures of centrality based on betweenness. *Sociometry* 1977, 35–41.
[6] Java A, Kolari P, Finin T, Oates T: Modeling the spread of influence on the blogosphere. In Proceedings of the 15th International World Wide Web Conference, 2006.
[7] Goya A, Bonchi F, Lakshamanan LV: Learning influence probabilities in social networks. In Proceedings of the Third ACM International Conference on Web Search and Data mining, ACM, 2010.
[8] Tang J, Sun J, Wang C, Yang Z: Social influence analysis in large-scale networks. In Proceedings of the 15th ACM SIGKDD International Conference on Knowledge Discovery and Data Mining, ACM, 2009.
[9] Liu L, Tang J, Han J, Jiang M, Yang S: Mining topic-level influence in heterogeneous networks. In Proceedings of the 19th ACM International Conference on Information and Knowledge Management, ACM, 2010.
[10] Kleinberg J: Authoritative sources in a hyperlinked environment. *JACM* 1999, 46:604–632.
[11] Page L, Sergey B: The PageRank citation ranking: Bringing order to the web, 1999.
[12] Cha M, Haddadi H, Benevenuto F, Gummadi PK: Measuring user influence in Twitter: The million follower fallacy. *ICWSM* 2010, 10:10–17.
[13] Ulrik B: A faster algorithm for betweenness centrality. *J Math Sociol* 2001, 25:163–177.
[14] Romero DM, Galuba W, Asur S, Huberman BA: Influence and passivity in social media. Machine learning and knowledge discovery in databases, Springer, 2011: 18–33.

[15] Haveliwala T. Kamvar S, Jeh G: An analytical comparison of approaches to personalizing PageRank, 2003.

[16] Ding Z, Jia Y, Zhou B, Han Y: Mining topical influencers based on the multi-relational network in micro-blogging sites. *China Commun* 2013, 10:93–104.

[17] Weng J, Lim EP, Jiang J, He Q: TwitterRank: Finding topic-sensitive influential twitterers. In the 3rd ACM International Conference on Web Search and Data Mining (WSDM'10). New York, USA, 2010: 261–270.

[18] Fuglede B: Jensen-Shannon divergence and Hilbert space embedding. International Symposium on Information Theory, 2004. ISIT 2004. Proceedings. p. 30. doi:10.1109/ISIT.2004. 1365067.

Jiayin Qi

4 Collective aggregation and the influence mechanisms

There is no doubt that collective power plays a key role in every economic phenomenon, political decision, or social transformation. One of the best selling book published in 1897, The Crowd [1] (Gustave Le Bon, 1841–1931) further provoked people's interest in seeking an in-depth understanding of groups, especially group behavior. As the great master of media Marshall Mcluhan (1911–1980) commented, media is a hidden factor that shapes our history and society, and because online social networks enable numerous individuals to gather via the internet, they have become a new force in promoting social evolution [2]. Collective intelligence and group polarization[1] are the two extreme ways in which a society is influenced by collective aggregation. On one hand, online social networks allow users to contribute their ideas to the shaping of collective intelligence; on the other hand, they lead to a loss of users' self-judgment during group interactions, resulting in a tendency of identical irrationality in group behaviors.

The aim of this chapter is to explore collective aggregation and the mechanisms that influence it from the perspectives of collective intelligence and group polarization. The contents of this chapter are significant concerning how collective intelligence is formed through online social networks and how the advantages of group polarization can be exploited in online social networks while avoiding its disadvantages.

This chapter is organized as follows: Section 4.1 defines the concept of a group in a social network from different perspectives and provides unified definitions used throughout the book. Sections 4.2 and 4.3 expound upon the mechanisms through which collective intelligence and group polarization are generated. First, developments in current researches are discussed based on concepts and relevant theories, generation conditions, and the major factors that influence collective intelligence and group polarization; second, analytical models for the two types of group behaviors are further explained. Finally, Section 4.4 provides a brief summary of this chapter.

---

1 Briefly, collective intelligence is a group behavior where in many individuals generate problem-solving ability superior to individuals through mechanisms such as competition and cooperation, differentiation and integration, and feedback and selection. Group polarization refers to the effect of discussions among group members on individual members' opinions or decisions in group decision-making situations, leading to behavioral consistency within groups.

https://doi.org/10.1515/9783110599411-004

4.1 Introduction

A group is a cross-disciplinary concept, and different researchers from different disciplines have defined it from different perspectives.

Definition 8-1: David W. McMillan (1917–1998), a well-known professor of psychology at Harvard University, defined a group as a feeling [3]; that is, the connection, membership, and shared beliefs among group members where members meet their needs through organization. A group should contain four elements: membership, influence, integration, and fulfillment of needs and shared emotional connection. From the perspective of psychology, a group should provide its members with a sense of belonging; individuals can influence the decision-making process of their group, and their needs can be satisfied by the group. This definition also emphasizes the common emotional ties within a group; namely, members share the same history, location, and hobbies, which mark the boundary that separates a group from outside. Psychological researchers mainly analyze the psychological feelings of individuals within a group and define a group from the perspective of individual psychology.

Definition 8-2: In the field of sociology, the concept of a group is a popular topic. In 1981, Marvin E. Shaw [4] defined a group as "two or more persons who are interacting with one another in such a manner that each person influences and is influenced by each other person," where interactions among the members of the group must occur. He also believed that the distinction between "a group" and "a crowd" lies in the influence among the members of the group, and because of phenomena such as "group facilitation" and "group polarization," a group is not simply an aggregation of individuals. This sociological definition also includes the mutual influence among the members of a group; further, from the viewpoint of group function, it emphasizes that a group is not an aggregation of individuals; certain phenomena such as group polarization increases the uncertainty of group decisions and performance.

Definition 8-3: Anthropologist Marcello Andrea Canuto [5] defined a group as a collection of individuals geographically adjacent to one another who have regular contact and interactions. The definition of a group in the field of anthropology is similar to that of sociology as they both indicate the presence of interaction among individuals within the group. However, the anthropological definition of a group emphasizes on the real geographical proximity of the members and their interaction with other group members.

The definition of a group in this book is comprehensive as it is based on the definitions from psychology, sociology, and anthropology, with an emphasis on information sharing, mutual influence, aggregation, and other characteristics of induviduals in a group. Therefore, in this book, a "group" is defined as a number of people who come together, either spontaneously or organizationally, by sharing information and working toward common goals where each member influences and is in turn influenced by other members.

A group in an online social network refers to a number of people who are motivated by common goals or interests, come together through online social networks, either spontaneously or organizationally for sharing information, where each member influences and is in turn influenced by others. It has the following characteristics:
1. Relying on social networks as the carrier.
2. Exchanging information as the purpose.
3. Free of geographical restrictions.

Members of a group in a social network influence one another by sharing information and interacting with other members through online social networks; therefore, a group in a social network is a virtual community. In 1998, Iain Pears noted that, although some online virtual communities are based geographically, most have no geographical restrictions, which is a distinct feature from the traditional concept of a group [6].

Because people can link with each other and share information on the internet, thousands of millions of independent internet users connect with each other and create numerous lively virtual communities with unified behaviors. Consequently, the Web 2.0 world is full of countless virtual groups with different sizes, various purposes, and dynamic variations. Information flows within these virtual communities and their viewpoints become a force driving individuals to quickly gather to form a virtual community. Hence, this chapter explores the phenomenon and the influence mechanism of collective aggregation in social networks from the perspective of information sharing.

Online social network, as a public platform where individuals come together and form group opinions, has undoubtedly become an effective catalyst for collective intelligence and group polarization due to its high levels of interaction, aggregation, and uncertainty. This chapter focuses on collective intelligence and group polarization in social networks and discusses the concepts, theoretical basis, generation, conditions, influencing factors, and analytical models concerning these two topics. It then anticipates the future prospects of this specific field of research.

4.2 Mechanisms engendering collective intelligence

4.2.1 Collective intelligence

Collective intelligence emerges from cooperation and competition among a number of individuals. We may say that research on collective intelligence is a long-term proposition in the field of collective behaviors, which covers the hierarchy from quark to bacteria, to plant, to animal, and to human society.

The concept of collective intelligence originated from biology, initially from the observations of entomologist William Morton Wheeler (1902–1981) [7]. In 1911, William Morton Wheeler found that ants behaved like an animal cell and seemed to have a collective mind, which he referred to as a larger creature, namely, the aggregation of ants seems to create a "super-organism." In 2010, Howard Bloom described the evolution of swarm intelligence in his book and noted that swarm intelligence started to play a role since the origin of life. Notably, this biological definition emphasizes that the aggregation of individuals makes the group more powerful.

In sociology, Émile Durkheim (1982) considered that a society group has higher intelligence than its members in terms of time and space [8]. GeorgePór, a pioneer in collective intelligence research, defined collective intelligence as "the capacity of human communities to evolve towards higher order complexity and harmony, through such innovation mechanisms as differentiation and intergration, competition and collaboration." Sociologists borrowed the concept of swarm intelligence from biology, applied it to human society, calling it collective intelligence. However, this sociological definition describes collective intelligence as a capacity of human communities, rather than a biological phenomenon, which emphasizes that collective intelligence is derived from the initiative and motility of group members.

To understand this connotation of collective intelligence, we have to describe the basic features of collective intelligence systems. Martijn C. Schut (2010) concluded that previous studies have summarized five characteristics of a collective intelligence system [9]:

(1) Integrity and locality. If a collective intelligence system is divided into two levels, the individual level comprises individuals comprising the system, which is the locality feature of the system; the overall level takes the entire system on a whole, which is the integrity feature of the system.

(2) Randomness. A complex system typically has some random characteristics, which allows it system to enter a self-organized critical state. Such a critical state enables the system to be at the edge of chaos: disordered on the one hand but structured and ordered on the other.

(3) Emergence. The simplest description of emergence is that "the whole is greater than the sum of its parts," which is especially true in the case of a collective intelligence system.

(4) Redundancy. This characteristic refers to the fact that the same knowledge may be embodied in a series of different positions in a system, and can be either concrete knowledge such as interaction rules or information *per se*. That is to say, a large number of individuals may follow the same rules if we view it from a simple dimension; however, such rules or information may not apply to all individuals within the system if we examine it from a more complex viewpoint.

(5) Robustness. Similar to redundancy, the robustness of a system can resist system failures. If one rule appears more than once in a system, even if an individual misses the rule, other individuals in the system can follow the rule.

Based on the definitions and theories mentioned above, we define collective intelligence in this book as the capacity of a group of individuals to fulfill tasks that separate individuals may find difficult to conquer through innovation mechanisms such as competition and cooperation, differentiation and integration, and feedback and selection.

Online social networks provide a more efficient platform through which collective intelligence is realized. In this new era, new technologies on which collective intelligence relies have played a role in increasing the efficiency of knowledge sharing on the internet, which has significantly sped up the flow of global culture and knowledge. Further, collective intelligence in social networks not only increases the amount of information but also plays an important role in improving and maintaining the quality of such information.

4.2.2 Self-determination theory and collective intelligence

Self-determination theory, a theory concerning the motivational process of human self-determination, was proposed by an American psychologist Edward Desi in the 1980s. The theory suggests that self-determination potentially drives people to choose the behaviors that are both in line with their own personal interest and conducive to their individual developments; thus, self-determination is the main component of intrinsic motivation behind human behavior [10]. According to the self-determination theory, human behavior is mainly driven by three needs: autonomy, competence, and interpersonal relatedness.

The need for autonomy is the core driving force of human behavior. In brief, an individual is the physical abstraction of an actual system or the functional unit of the system. Individuals can take certain autonomous actions to meet the desired goals in a certain environment, and can perceive the environment and adapt themselves to changes in the environment. Since their advent, social networks have become the infrastructure for the self-organization of individuals, where they can independently select or post content and exhibit more independence and autonomy. Therefore, the need for autonomy is more intense in social networks.

Competence refers to the underlying personal characteristic that can distinguish outstanding achievers from mediocre individuals in a certain workplace, organization, or culture. It can be the motivation, character, self-image, attitudes, values, expertise, cognitive skills, behavioral skills, or any other qualities of a person that can be reliably measured or quantified, and that can serve to significantly distinguish excellence from average. Although individuals in social networks are equal, competence can differentiate them according to their performances of content contribution. For instance, opinion leaders and forum hosts may be distinguished from ordinary internet users. However, as individuals always attempt to distinguish themselves from others through certain performance indicators, the need for competence still exists among internet users.

In sociology, interpersonal relatedness is defined as a kind of social relationship that is established in the process of production and living activities in society, whereas psychologists define it as the direct psychological connection between people established during communication. In daily life, interpersonal relatedness often refers to general interactions between people, including those in familial relationships, social relationships, alumni (classmate) relationships, teacher–student relationships, and employment relationships, such as those between colleagues and supervisors. In the world of social networks, people do not communicate face to face any more. Although the need for interpersonal relatedness may be diminished in such a context, the need for a sense of belonging still induces people to seek their own group on the internet, which is the reason why online communities, forums, and interest groups exist. Moreover, the need for a sense of belonging is associated with intrinsic motivation. Self-determinism theory assumes that interpersonal relatedness engenders a kind of dynamic force. When an individual has a sense of security and belonging in an environment, he/she will have greater intrinsic motivation. Therefore, the need for interpersonal relatedness is still very important on the internet.

With self-determination theory, we can better analyze the intrinsic motivation behind users' behavior of contributing to collective intelligence and quantify the degree of their contributions. In contributing to collective intelligence, individuals' needs for self-determination and competence are fully met, however, it may not be the case in a traditional production organization. In online communities, there is no hierarchy or task allocation and participants choose tasks entirely based on their own interests and needs. Meanwhile, collective intelligence is a process through which participants work out a solution to a problem by gathering wisdom from all participants, which relies on cooperation among group participants. The participants can discuss problems through online communication, interactive discussion, etc., which further promotes interaction and communication between participants, fosters the motivation for exchanges, and satisfies participants' need for interpersonal relatedness.

In the Web 2.0 environment, the greater openness and decentralized environment of social platforms allows participants to obtain their desired information and publish their views, regardless of time and geographical restrictions. The impetus to aggregation in a network community is participants' shared interest, which increases the their motivation for participation.

Therefore, social networks sufficiently meet participants' needs for self-determination, competence, and interpersonal relatedness, providing a favorable environment for the generation of collective intelligence.

4.2.3 Conditions engendering collective intelligence

In May 1968, an American nuclear submarine called "Scorpion" suddenly disappeared in the North Atlantic and no one could determine where it sank. The U.S. Navy searched for several months to no avail. At that time, a man named Craven organized experts, including mathematicians, submarine experts, and fishing specialists, to analyze the possible location of the submarine. Instead of organizing a group discussion, which is the conventional method, he required them to analyze the possible location and performed a comprehensive analysis of the preliminary results. The final results turned out to be different from any individual results. Surprisingly, the submarine was found 22 yards away from the final analysis results.

This story is from the book "The Wisdom of Crowds" [11] by James Surowiecki. In his work, he stated that, under the right circumstances, collective wisdom could be very surprising; it is generally superior to the judgment made by the person with the highest IQ alone. However, on no account can we ignore Tom Hayes's explanation (2010) about the prerequisites for the sentence "the right condition:" independence, diversification, and dispersion [12]. According to Ames Surowiecki, "if we can gather together people from different industries, different areas, with different knowledge backgrounds, they have the ability to make the right decisions on major issues is superior to a couple of so-called elites."

In 2006, Don Tapscott and Anthony D. Williams summarized three guidelines to produce extensive group collaboration and ultimately engender powerful collective intelligence: foster a goal of collaboration, guide individuals to contribute efforts independently, and integrate independent contributions [13]. Tom Hayes (2010) further showed that, if a group has a very high degree of homogeneity, their output will lack diversity [12]. Bede Miller also noted that only when all members make decisions independently and bear responsibility for their actions can they collectively light up the light of wisdom. If members follow each other blindly, the group will produce foolish outcomes. In 2010, Thomas W. Malone stated that, for a wise collective, regardless of whether it is a collective of ants or lawyers, its members must be independent and bear responsibility [14].

This book argues that there are four necessary conditions for generating collective intelligence:

First, there must be specific goals for collaboration.

Second, individuals in a group must have the ability to think independently; that is, they must have independence. Indeed, the independence of individuals is a more important factor in collective intelligence than intelligence at the individual level as it ensures that each individual will not be negatively affected by others, can think independently, tap into and stimulate their maximum potential, and can contribute accurate and creative ideas.

Third, individuals within a group must be diverse, heterogeneous, and dispersed. Diversity of ideas is a prerequisite for ensuring adequate information. Thus, the group should try to attract people with different knowledge backgrounds and rich experience, and guide and encourage each person to form unique, complementary insights that can be integrated to stimulate greater collective potentials. Dispersion and decentralization allows respect for individual differences and personality such that every opinion can get the attention of the group. By exploiting users' unique perspectives, the group can establish a more comprehensive and accurate understanding of the problem.

Fourth, a mechanism is required to eventually concentrate the decentralized intelligence to collect individual views and create group-level decision-making intelligence. The collection mechanism is not simple addition or averaging but rather the comprehensive consideration of various factors. It is the optimal decision made on the basis of listening to the views of the group members.

It is true that a group can produce intelligence but it does not always produce high-quality collective intelligence. One of the factors affecting the quality of collective intelligence is the size of the group. Furthermore, individuals' speculation and judement may comprise both real information and errors. James Surowiecki noted that, if the error can be stripped away, then the remainder is the real information. If a sufficiently large group comprising individuals from various industries who are not influenced by one another, makes a forecast or estimation with respect to a problem and if the result is then averaged, the error made by each individual will be offset by the mean value. However, it is worth noting that sufficient information is a prerequisite for offsetting the error. For example, if a group of children without any experience in the stock market are engaged to predict market trends, the result will most likely be erroneous even if all the above conditions are met.

4.2.4 Factors influencing group intelligence

How much intelligence a group can produce is quite uncertain, for it is subject to many factors. These factors include the size of the group, heterogeneity of the group members, the systems of participation and withdrawal of the group members, communication channels between the group members, mode of organizational management, and the special role of conflicts.

1. Group size

In 2012, Sinan Aral and Dylan Walker [15] demonstrated that group size is one of the most important factors that affect group intelligence and that groups with a limited size may not generate group intelligence.

Some scholars believe that group size is positively related to group intelligence. For instance, German sociologist Georg Simmel (Georg Simmel, 1858–1918) [16] argued that small groups could not achieve scientific group decision-making and that a group's ability to solve problems increases with the size of group. Stenfan

Krause and Brent Gallupe's experiment also showed that larger group size leads to group decision making of higher quality. Moreover, Ioanna Lykourentzou [17] and Wu-Chih Hu [18] believed that group size is an important factor in group collaboration and large-scale social networking activities, and that larger groups can attract more members and lead to greater collaboration.

However, neither Western nor domestic researchers have quantified the specific sizes of groups. According to the definition of group size in social statistics, groups of large size should contain no fewer than 2000 individuals. Furthermore, group size should be quantified in units of one hundred or one hundred thousand if information exchange, communication, and statistical techniques are taken into account.

2. Heterogeneity of group members

Heterogeneity is a positive factor in group intelligence. A famous biological behavior scientist Thomas D. Seeley [19] believed that diversity of views is of great value for groups, and that groups with more diverse characteristics are more adept at solving problems.

Thomas D. Seeley [19] wrote in his book "The Wisdom of the Hive" that diversity in a swarm of bees allows the swarm to find nectar sources more efficiently, and that such efficiency depends on the colony-specific division of labor in the hive and the collaboration of bee species. Scott E. Page [20] held the opinion that diversity in the view of group members is very valuable for helping groups solve problems. Everett Stiles [21] found that the process of achieving group intelligence is the process of collective creation conducted by a group of individuals that have different motives and goals. Indeed, diversity in a group can guarantee independent ideas, increase the number of creative ideas, and enrich the type of creative ideas.

While group member heterogeneity has a positive impact on group intelligence, it is worth noting that the diversity of group members still relies on the amount of information which each individual possesses; otherwise, the diversity of group members will have no effect on group intelligence.

3. Participation and withdrawal of group members

In addition to studying the characteristics of the main group body, De Liddo et al. [22] also found that the quality of group intelligence is closely related to the participation system of a group. De Liddo [23] stated that group intelligence can be roughly divided into two forms: unconscious and conscious. In social media networks, the views, ratings, reviews, and purchase records of users and the social networks established therefrom constitute the unconscious group intelligence. In contrast, group intelligence consciously deployed and produced by a group which hold the goal of collaboration is the conscious group intelligence. Comparatively, the quality and level of unconscious group intelligence is lower than that of conscious group intelligence. From another perspective, when solving problems such as urban planning and climate change, conscious participation is essential for achieving high-level group intelligence through high-level awareness. Therefore, the participation system of group members has a certain impact on group intelligence (Dai Yang, 2014).

Due to the effect of "The Spiral Of Silence" in the knowledge economy [24], lowered threshold for withdrawal from groups makes it possible for individuals holding objections to withdraw or be removed from the group, which accelerates group polarization and has a serious negative impact on group intelligence. Since the proposition of the threshold theory by Granovetter, researches on the relationship between withdrawal mechanisms and group intelligence have flourished. Given a lower threshold for withdrawal, rational individuals are more likely to withdraw from a group; the members who remain in the group are those who have a higher threshold for withdrawal. In such a case, the homogeneity of the group increases while the diversity decreases. Consequently, the withdrawal of group members impacts group intelligence.

4. Communication channels between group members

In 1996, Mohamed et al. suggested that modern information and communication technologies would enable instant information exchange among group members, promoting the generation and communication of groupthink, which has a positive impact on group intelligence [25].

Interaction and information sharing among individuals is the key to achieve group intelligence. The popularity of the internet, especially the generation and application of Web 2.0 technology, has injected new vitality into group intelligence. Indeed, such convenient technologies allow users to instantaneously interact through the internet, without programming skills, and enable them to directly participate in the sharing and creation of content. As stated by John Smith in 2005, the extensive applications of the internet and communication technology in human production and life again stimulated people's awareness of group intelligence. In 1999, Pierre Levy also stressed that network technology had human-friendly effect on human beings. Such effect arises from the collision of all kinds of views on the internet, which engenders group intelligence and verifies the contribution of each individual.

Numerous scholars have suggested that the formation of group intelligence is a dynamic interactive multi-stage process, and that information exchange and communication technologies play a pivotal role in this process. Thus, new interaction channels between the individuals of a group will have a positive impact on group intelligence.

5. Mode of organizational management

The mode of organizational management plays an extremely important role in group cohesion. Cartwright and Dorwin [26] stated that group cohesion can promote group members to act for the sake of the whole group to the greatest extent possible, fostering autonomy of individuals. The impact on group intelligence of group cohesion mainly depends on its influence on group decision-making. However, improper manifestations of group cohesion will have an adverse impact on group intelligence.

When other manifestations of groupthink (such as command-style leadership) arise, too much cohesion can lead to degraded group decision making [27]. For example, centralized organizational management can promote group polarization, shorten the decision time, and negatively affect group intelligence [28].

As the above studies have shown, the mode of organizational management has certain influences on group intelligence.

6. Special role of conflicts

Rather than affecting the quality of group decisions, appropriate conflicts play a positive role in forming group intelligence [29] in most cases.

Liu (2011) suggested that, to prevent groupthink from restricting the decision-making process, a reasonable conflict must be created in the group. This type of conflicts does not refer to interpersonal conflicts, rather, it is a "brainstorming" method designed to avoid generating the bandwagon effect during group decision making. If conflict occurs in a harmonious atmosphere, and if a decision is made by people belonging to different professional backgrounds and with different thinking styles, a higher level of participation and cooperation can be expected in discussions, more likely to ultimately leading to a good decision. This approach fosters clear-mindedness in group decision making and prevents the decision-making process from becoming irrational. Therefore, under certain circumstances, conflict can have a positive effect on group intelligence.

4.2.5 Analytical models of collective intelligence

1. Model of collective intelligence based on Bayesian theory

In real life, we are forced to make decisions while facing risks and uncertainties. The horse racing problem provides a good example. Gamblers often choose their horses based on their judgment of the possibility of each horse winning the game. A betting market, such as that for a sporting event like horse racing, provides a typical scenario where individual behaviors aggregate into collective intelligence. It should be noted that investors are often attracted by investments with high profitability.

Consider an event in which ten horses participate in a horse racing as a simple example. If this is the only information available for us to make a wager, then we can do nothing but select a horse randomly; the possibility of winning in such a case is only 0.10. Such an approach will certainly lead to losing the bet. However, this is a problem that can be solved with Bayesian logic [30]. As each horse has participated in this event several times, they all have a racing history. If horse no. 1 is sure to win whenever it participates in a game, while horse no. 2 is sure to lose whenever it participates in a game, then we have a real and well-documented basis for a bet: wager money on horse no. 1 rather than on horse no. 2. Such information helps us to better predict the winning horse rather than simply choosing one from the ten horses randomly. The process of analyzing these factors is the Bayesian process.

Modeling based on Bayesian theory is probabilistic reasoning. That is, it is a method to perform reasoning and decision-making tasks when all conditions, except the probabilities of occurrence, are uncertain. Take stock forecasting for instance: we calculate the posterior probability of the same stock price using a Bayesian estimation formula with different observations in different periods on the basis of knowledge of prior information of the stock price; then, we can make a reasonable estimation of the trends in the fluctuation of the stock price.

Taking stock price forecasting as an example, we introduce these basic procedures for investigating collective intelligence based on Bayesian theory, which include the following steps.

(1) Build a research model on the basis of a reference review of relevant research results on collective intelligence and Bayesian theory. Bayesian predictive models are established mainly based on the judgment of prior information and sample-based information. Prior information refers to the non-sample information based on experience and historical data; it is a random variable with respect to the required unknown parameter θ. In contrast, sample information refers to the information regarding the unknown parameter θ which is obtained from a sample derived from the total. To forecast, prior information is combined with the posterior information to obtain the posterior distribution of parameter θ.

For example, Yuqiu Sun and Shengtao Chen (2003)[2] proposed a model based on the Bayesian decision-making methhld to predict stock prices. They divided the stock prices into k intervals, denoted as $E_1 \ldots E_k$, and the probability that a predicted object would fall into the interval E_i was denoted as p_i. They treated the event that the stock prices fall into a certain interval as an n-fold Bernoulli experiment and assumed that the prior distribution of p_i obeys an incomplete β distribution. They then acquired the density function of p_i, and were able to obtain the sample density function because the conditional distribution of the sample with respect to parameter p_i obeys a binomial distribution [31].

Combining both methods, we are able to obtain a joint distribution of the samples and parameters (predicted value), and therefore, determine the posterior distribution of p_i. Further, according to Bayesian estimation theory, in the condition of square loss, the Bayesian estimation of p_i becomes the mean of the posterior distribution, and the final Bayesian estimation formula can be obtained.

(2) Obtain quantitative data required for model validation based on the results of previous studies regarding the issue of collective intelligence. By establishing a

2 For more information, refer to the following paper: Yuqiu Sun, Shengtao Chen, Bayes decision method applied in the stock price forecasting. Guangdong Polytec1hnic Normal University, 2003, (4): 78–80.

model, we can obtain the Bayesian estimation formula. However, to carry out specific forecasts, we have to collect real sample data. For example, in the model of Yuqiu Sun and Shengtao Chen (2003) for forecasting stock prices, the authors obtained, through data collection, the closing price of stock No. 000029 in the Shenzhen stock market from February 1, 2002 to April 5, 2002, where the values were 5.38, 5.60, 5.59, 5.28, 5.42, 5.41, 5.95, 6.21, 6.33, 6.26, 6.64, 6.86, 7.55, 8.31, 9.14, 9.76, 9.64, 9.92, 9.74, 10.30, 9.66, 10.63, 11.00, 10.92, 10.77, 10.24, 10.32, 10.78, 10.99, 10.55, 10.31, 10.73, 11.07, 10.51, 10.41, and 10.35.

(3) Conduct statistic classification of the collected data and carry out further processing and computation. Plugging the sample data into the Bayesian formula, we can determine the probability distribution of the predicted values obtained after collecting prior information and sample information. First, Yuqiu Sun and Shengtao Chen (2003) classified and analyzed statistical information in the original data and divided it into different groups based on their states. In the following example, the data is divided into seven groups, and the number of observations falling in each group is counted. Then, the multilayer prior density of each state is calculated. The results from the above steps are shown in Table 4.1.

Table 4.1: Outcomes of the Bayesian model calculation.

i	Ei	Range of states	Number of observations under state Ei	$\hat{P}_i$				
				$C=2$	$C=3$	$C=4$	$C=5$	$C=6$
1	E1	<6.00	7	0.14909	0.14856	0.14803	0.14752	0.14702
2	E2	[6.00,7.00)	5	0.10144	0.10110	0.10077	0.10045	0.10012
3	E3	[7.00,8.00)	1	0.01520	0.01517	0.01515	0.01512	0.01509
4	E4	[8.00,9.00)	1	0.01520	0.01517	0.01515	0.01512	0.01509
5	E5	[9.00,10.00)	6	0.12504	0.12461	0.12418	0.12376	0.12335
6	E6	[10.00,11.00)	14	0.32589	0.32459	0.32337	0.32250	0.32124
7	E7	≥11.00	2	0.03477	0.03468	0.03460	0.03451	0.03443

(4) Draw conclusions based on the statistical results. As shown by Yuqiu Sun and Shengtao Chen (2003), to analyze the distribution of predict values, we can judge their future states by finding the maximum probability with which they fall into an interval. The authors predicated that the stock price on April 8, 2002 would be in the interval of [10.00,11.00), and indeed, the price of the stock on April 8, 2002 was 10.35, indicating that the prediction is accurate. As can be seen from the above examples, it is feasible to use a Bayesian model to predict stock prices; moreover, this method can not only predict stock price trends but also accurately forecast the scope of the fluctuation of stock prices.

2. Collective ntelligence model based on Ant Colony algorithm

Ants are highly social creatures that live in communities and forage for food collectively. In the process of finding food, each ant forages alone but "remembers" and tracks the trails of foraging by releasing pheromones. Once it finds food on one of the trails, other ants will aggregate to this path, increasing the amount of pheromones on the path. They can also distinguish the different distances of the paths, choosing the nearest. At the same time, they notify another ants by means of the amount of pheromone on this path. This phenomenon reflects a kind of swarm intelligence and collective wisdom (Figure 4.1).

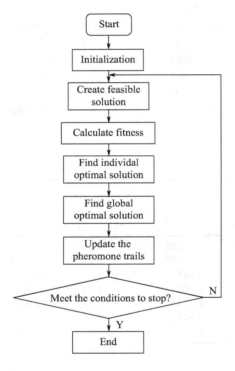

Figure 4.1: Problem solving flow chart based on Ant Colony Algorithm.

In 1959, Pierre-Paul Grassé initially proposed the Stigmergy theory to explain the behaviors of termites building their nests, as identified in the research on Ant Colony Algorithm. In 2000, Marco Dorigo et al. published a review on Ant Colony Algorithm in *Science* [32, 33], which pushed this research field into the international academic frontier. An Ant Colony Algorithm (ACA) is a probabilistic algorithm that finds the optimal path on a map, as shown in Figure 4.1. The basic algorithm is as follows.

Algorithm 8.1

Step 1: Set the parameters and initialize pheromone trails.
Step 2: Create m feasible solutions.
Step 3: Calculate the fitness of each ant.
Step 4: Find the best position of every ant (the optimal solution).
Step 5: Find the best position on a global level (the optimal solution).
Step 6: Update the pheromone trails.
Step 7: Decide whether the termination conditions are met; if so, go to the end.
Iterate or go back to Step 3.

For example, in the TSP (Travelling Salesman Problem) which is classically solved by ACA, to simulate the behaviors of real ants, the initial parameters are set as follows[3]: m represents the number of ants in the colony; n represents the number of cities; d_{ij} represents the distance between city i and city j; $r_{ij}(t)$ represents the intensity of the pheromone trails along edge (i, j) at time t; η_{ij} represents the visibility of edge (i, j); in the ACA, η_{ij} usually equals the reciprocal of the distance between city i and city j (i.e., $\eta_{ij} = 1/d_{ij}$); $\Delta\tau_{ij}^k$ denotes the amount of pheromone per unit of the trail length that ant k left on edge (i, j); and p_{ij}^k represents the probability of ant k transferring to city j, the city that the ant has not yet visited [34].

Assuming that the amount of information on each path is the same and set $r_{ij}(0)=C$ (C is a constant), each ant independently chooses the next city on the path according to the retained information. At time t, the probability of ant k transferring from city i to city j, namely, p_{ij}^k , is as follows:

$$
p_{ij}^k = \begin{cases} \dfrac{\tau_{ij}^\alpha \cdot \eta_{ij}^\beta}{\displaystyle\sum_{s \in \text{allowed}_k} \tau_{is}^\alpha \cdot \eta_{is}^\beta}, & j \in \text{allowed}_k \\ 0, & \text{otherwise} \end{cases} \tag{4.1}
$$

α indicates the significance of the amount of information that ants accumulate during movement; β indicates the significance of the heuristic information that influences an ant's choice of the path in movement. Further, allowed $k = \{0,1,2, \ldots, n\text{-}1\}$ tabu$_k$ represents all the cities that ant k is allowed to select in the next step, where tabu$_k$ denotes the cities to which ant k has currently traveled. When all n cities have been included in tabu$_k$, ant k will complete one cycle and the path of ant k becomes a solution to the problem. When all ants have completed one cycle, the information in each path will be adjusted according to Equations (4.2) and (4.3):

---

3 For more information, please refer to the following paper: Yanling Wang, Longshu Li, Zhe Hu, Collective Intelligence Optimization Algorithm, *Computer Technology and Development*, 2008, 18 (8): 114–117.

$$\tau_{ij}(t+n) = (1-\rho) \cdot \tau_{ij}(t) + \Delta\tau_{ij}, \ \rho \in (0,1) \tag{4.2}$$

$$\Delta\tau_{ij}(t) = \sum_{k=1}^{m} \Delta\tau_{ij}^{k}(t) \tag{4.3}$$

ρ represents the evaporation coefficient of the information on the path; 1-ρ denotes the retention coefficient of the information; $\Delta\tau_{ij}$ represents increment in the information on path ij in this cycle. If ant k has never been to path ij, then the value of $\Delta\tau_{ij}$ will be zero; otherwise it will be Q/L_k (where Q is a constant and L_k denotes the total length of the path that ant k has travelled in this cycle).

The ACA based on the TSP proposed by Marco Dorigo in 1997 is also a good example of applying the algorithm to collective intelligence. In the TSP, a salesman must find the shortest possible route to visit many cities once given a group of cities and the distances among them. The ACA for solving the TSP uses a virtual "ant" that explores different routes and leaves virtual "pheromones" that may gradually disappear over time, indicating the characteristic signal that a salesman left on a path. Based on the principle that "the higher the amount of pheromone is, the shorter the route," the best route can be determined. By simulating an ant colony's search for food, we effectively solve the problem of increased complexity of traveling salesmen when the number of cities increases.

3. Model of collective intelligence based on particle swarm optimization

Particle Swarm Optimization (PSO) is an evolutionary computation technique developed by James F. Kennedy [35] and Russell C. Eberhart in 1995, derived from the simulation of a simplified social model. The technique was originally intended to graphically simulate the beautiful and unpredictable movements of birds and was derived from the artificial life and evolutionary computation theories. By observing the social behavior of animals, scholars found that information sharing in a community can lead to the acquisition of greater benefits during evolution. PSO has been applied in numerous applications, including neural network training, medical analysis, and robotic applications.

Yang et al. [36] stated in a review of PSO that, when practical problems are solved using PSO, the solution to the problem corresponds to the position of a bird in the search space where birds are called "particles" or "subjects." Each particle has its own position and speed (depending on the direction and distance of its flight), and an adaptation value is determined by the optimal function. Every particle memorizes and follows the current optimal particle, searching in the solution space. Further, each iteration of the process is not completely random: if a better solution can be found, it will become the basis for exploring the next solution.

Given that PSO involves a group of random particles (requiring a stochastic solution), the particles update themselves by tracking two "extreme values:" the best solution that can be found by the particle itself called the individual extreme point (where P represents its position); and the best solution that can be found so far in the entire community or in a portion of the group. In the global version of PSO, the entire community is considered, and is called the global extreme point (where G represents its location). In contrast, in the local version of PSO, a portion of the group rather than the entire community is considered neighbors of the particles; thus, the best solution among all the neighbors is called the local extreme point (where L represents its position). After finding the two best solutions, the particles update their velocities and positions according to the relevant formula. The information of particle i can be expressed with a D-dimensional vector, where the position is $X_i=(x_{i1}, x_{i2}, ..., x_{iD})_T$, and the velocity is $V_i=(v_{i1}, v_{i2}, ..., v_{iD})_T$; other vectors remain similar.

The basic procedures in PSO can be described as follows:

(1) Initialize the particles: position X_i^0 and speed V_i^0 of the initial search point are usually generated randomly within the allowable scope; the P coordinates of each particle are set to its current position, and the corresponding individual extreme value (the fitness value of the individual extreme point) is calculated. The global extreme point (the fitness value of the global extreme point) is the optimal individual extreme point; the serial particle number of the optimal value is recorded, and G is set as the current position of the optimal particle. Russell C. Eberhart and Xiaohui Hu (1999) proposed an analytical model for tremor behavior based on PSO following relevant theories and previous findings [37]. In initialization phase, they set 30 particles and their current positions; then, they set the maximum tremor rate as the initial search point and its speed.

(2) Evaluate the particles: this step mainly involves calculating the fitness values of the particles to update the individual extreme values and global extreme values. Russell C. Eberhart and Xiaohui Hu (1999) referenced previous studies on tremor behaviors to evaluate each particle's behavior and calculate the fitness values of the particles. If the value for a particle is superior to the current individual extreme value, then this value is set as the position of this particle and the individual extreme value is updated. If the best value among all the particles' individual extreme values is superior to the current global extreme value, then this value is set as the position of the particle; then, the serial number of the particle is recorded, and the global extreme value is updated.

(3) Update the particles: update the speed and position of each particle with the updating equation. According to the previous evaluation of particles' tremor behavior, certain rules are adopted to update the particles. For example, in the study on tremor behaviors based on PSO, Russell C. Eberhart and Xiaohui Hu (1999) updated the particles by regulating the weight of each layer of the neural network based on the tremor behavior.

(4) Verify whether the termination conditions are met: if the number of current iterations reaches the preset maximum number (or if the minimum number of

false requests is met), then the iteration is stopped and the optimal solution is identified; otherwise, step 2 is repeated. For example, in this case, the initial damping weight of 0.9 decreases to 0.4 after 2000 iterations; thus, the iteration is stopped, and the optimal solution becomes the output. Russell C. Eberhart and Xiaohui Hu (1999) found that the neural network model based on the PSO algorithm can effectively distinguish between normal people and tremor patients. In the above-mentioned application, this method can be used to make quick, accurate diagnoses. Further, in the diagnosis of diseases, such as breast cancer and heart disease, a PSO-trained neural network can also achieve a higher diagnostic success rate, demonstrating the merits of PSO in generating collective intelligence.

4.2.6 Simulation of collective intelligence in social networks[4]

1. Wikipedia

Wikipedia wherein entries are created by internet users through their collective participation is a typical case where collective wisdom is generated through the participation, editing, interaction of the public; therefore, it provides high-quality data resources for studying collective intelligence. Collective intelligence advocates such concepts as basic openness, equivalence, sharing, and global operation. First, in terms of openness, there are 282 different language editions of Wikipedia; as of January 2013, the total number of registered users exceeded 32 million, and the total number of edits exceeded 1.2 billion. Both users and entries on Wikipedia are increasing. Wikipedia users are diverse, independent, decentralized, scattered, and widely distributed. Second, in terms of equivalence, Wikipedia abandoned the hierarchical model to encourage users' self-organized production and development. In general, Wikipedia users are given the autonomy to edit any entries, while professional editors are responsible to eliminate maliciously damaged entries and accounts. These measures serve to improve user's preferences and increase the quality of entries. Third, in terms of sharing, Wikipedia's sharing feature guarantees increase in participants and the generation of UGC, while improving user's preferences for generating and sharing UGC. Finally, in terms of global operation, with people from all over the world participating in the collaboration, such a broad distribution range also constitutes an advantageous condition to ensure enormous number of participants.

---

4 This section is based on the following papers: Shiyu Du, Jiayin Qi. Modeling and Simulation on Collective Intelligence in Future Internet - A Study of Wikipedia [J]. Information Technology Journal, 2013, 12 (20): 5531–5535. Bo Huang, Shiyu Du, Jiayin Qi, Research of Collective Intelligence in the Future Internet Based on Wikipedia Entry Classification [J], Jourinal of Computer Applications, 2013, 30: 48–49.; reference link: http://pan.baidu.com/s/1bnrgs0J.

To collect data for this study,[5] on one hand, we selected the time-series data of the numbers of both users and entries, the number of edits, users' demographic data, and other related data spanning from January 2001 to December 2011 provided on the open platform of Wikipedia; on the other hand, on the Chinese Wikipedia, we selected the new item "entry score" as the indicator of UGC quality, comprising four components: credibility, objectivity, completeness, and readability. The total score of each part is 5 points, and the sum of the four parts (20 points) is the final score of an entry. Table 4.2 shows an example of the obtained data. In addition, entries on Wikipedia are divided into 11 categories: culture and art, people, geography, social and social sciences, history and events, natural and physical sciences, technology and applied science, religion and belief, health, mathematics and logic, and philosophy. Due to the huge number of sample entries, it is important to select an appropriate sampling method. In terms of overall distribution, the number of edits of the sampled entries conforms to power law distribution. If an ordinary, random sampling method is used, it will probably result in a large number of entries with the number of edits of 1 or even 0; these results with respect to the number of edits are not significantly different from each other and cannot reflect the impact of the number of edits on the quality of entries. Therefore, a stratified sampling method is adopted: first, samples are stratified according to the number of edits, followed by pro rate sampling from each level. It is possible that the higher the number of edits that the entries in a level have, the higher sampling ratio the level is given. Thus, entries are distributed into different hierarchies based on the number of edits, and then simple random sampling is conducted from these entries in each hierarchy to obtain entry samples with a capacity of 105. Table 4.2 shows some examples of the 105 samples.

Table 4.2: Examples of sample data for entry scoring.

Number of edits	Entry Name	Entry Score
1698	Hong Kong Disneyland	15.3
1684	Zhejiang Province	16.2
1653	Detective Conan	15.5
409	Photorespiration	15.5

2. Modeling collective intelligence in social networks

Based on the above discussion, the hypotheses and assumptions presented in this model are as follows:

Hypothesis 1: as a present entry is edited and modified by internet users based on the existing knowledge and quality of the entry, the more frequently an entry is edited or modified, the higher the quality of the entry.

Hypothesis 2: the diversity of users is directly related to the diversity of UGC produced by them; the more diversified the users are, the more diversified the entries in the network.

Assumption: provided that the above hypotheses are well supported, the larger the user size, the higher the overall quality, the total number, and the variety of UGC; the higher the level of collective intelligence, the more users will be attracted to participate in group collaboration.

Based on the multi-agent modeling method, the specific composition of the collective intelligence model based on Wikipedia in this study is as follows.

The agent layer: because Wikipedia users participate in the generation and editing of entries in a self-organizing manner and on an equal footing, we assume that each agent has the same attributes, and multiple homologous agents are abstracted into one agent class defined as *InternetUser*.

The individual agent attribute model layer: this layer comprises four parts: inner states, sensors, effects, and environment.

- Internal states: User-Attributes=(intxPos,yPos,double IUknowledgeLevel, intIUvariety), where "intxPos" and "yPos" represent user's location in the network; "double IUknowledgeLevel" represents the educational level of an agent; "intIUvariety" denotes user category. As 11 categories of entries are defined in Wikipedia, 11 different UGC classes are also defined correspondingly.
- Sensors: defined as "viewUGC()" in this model.
- Effects: defined as "generateUGC()" and "editUGC()" in this model.
- Environment: comprises three output variables in this model to show the representation of collective intelligence: UGCquality (the quality of entries), generateUGCacc (the quantity of entries), and calculateVar (the variety of entries).

The MAS layer: according to real data on Wikipedia, three behavior rules and four data rules are defined as follows:

Behavior Rule 1: a viewed entry, if user interaction (agent overlapping) or if the entry quality is greater than 16.

if ((IUSpace.getObjectAtX$Y (xPos,yPos)!=null)||internetEnv.UGCquality >16) {viewUGC ();}

Behavior Rule 2: an editable entry, if the entry quality is less than 20.

public void viewUGC (){generateUGC(); if (internetEnv. UGCquality<20) {edit UGC();}}

Behavior Rule 3: an agent can choose to move in one of the eight directions around it at the rate of once every second; overlap may occur during movement.

xPos + = Globals.env.uniformIntRand.getIntegerWithMin$withMax(-1, 1);

yPos + = Globals.env.uniformIntRand.getIntegerWithMin$withMax(-1, 1);

xPos = (xPos + modelswarm.worldX) % modelswarm.worldX;

yPos = (yPos + modelswarm.worldY) % modelswarm.worldY;

Data Rule 1 is shown in Table 4.3.

Table 4.3: Fitting functions for changes in agent number.

Time Period	Fitting Equation	Parameters	Goodness of Fit
2001.1~2005.11	number of agents = $\alpha \times exp(\beta \times t)$	$\alpha = 0.3023, \beta = 0.2016$	0.9981
2006.1~2007.1	number of agents = $\alpha t + \beta$	$\alpha = 39.82, \beta = -1082$	0.9974
2007.3~2011.11	number of agents = $(\alpha - 0.3 \cdot t) \cdot t + \beta$	$\alpha = 67.94, \beta = -1708$	0.9996

Data Rule 2 is shown in Table 4.4.

Table 4.4: Fitting functions for numbers of new UGC.

Time Period	Fitting Equation	Parameters	Goodness of Fit
2001.1~2007.1	number of new entries = $\alpha \times (no. of par.^\beta) + \gamma$	$\alpha = 26990, \beta = 0.417, \gamma = 16330$	0.9493
2007.3~2011.11	no specific fitting function in this period during which data fluctuated between 7000 and 10000		

Data Rule 3 is shown in Table 4.5.

Table 4.5: Fitting functions for number of edits.

Time Period	Fitting Equation	Parameters	Goodness of Fit
2001.1~2005.1	number of edits = $\alpha \times t^\beta + \gamma$	$\alpha = 2.118, \beta = 0.4201, \gamma = 2.889$	0.9288
2005.3~2011.11	number of edits = $\alpha \times t^\beta + \gamma$	$\alpha = 1.139, \beta = 0.4653, \gamma = 7.39$	0.9993

Data Rule 4 is shown in Table 4.6.

Table 4.6: UGC quality fitting functions.

Fitting Equation	Parameters	Goodness of Fit
UGC quality = $(\alpha \times x^3 + \beta \times x^2 + \gamma \times x + \lambda)/(x + \mu)$	$\alpha = -4.96e{-}008$, $\beta = 0.0008735$, $\gamma = 14.02$, $\lambda = 245.9$, $\mu = 29.8$	95% confidence interval

3. Model simulation and results demonstration

On the Swarm platform, with the above fitting functions being the behavior rules of agents, the relationship between the size of a group and the quantity, quality, and variety of entries is achieved through the simulation results of the model.

Because the changes in internet users are divided into three stages, three simulation points (25s, 35s, 45s) are selected from the three stages to reflect the corresponding changes in the results. As shown in Figures 4.2, 4.3, and 4.4, when the simulation time is 25 s, the number of agents is 47000, the cumulative number of UGC is 90510, and the overall UGC quality is 14.89. When the simulation time is 35s, the number of agents is 312000, the total number of generated UGC is 287089, and the overall UGC quality is 15.66. When the simulation time is 45 s, the number of agents is 742000, the total number of generated UGC is 2122030, and the overall UGC quality is 16.20. At the same time, as shown in Figure 4.5, we can tell from the outputs of Java Eclipse command lines that, when the simulation time is 15 s, the entry varieties 2, 3, 7, 8, 10, and 11 (Wikipedia has 11 entry categories) do not exist; when the simulation time is 25 s, the entry varieties 10 and 11 do not exist; and when the simulation time is 35 s, all the entry varieties exist. The quantity, quality, and variety of visible entries all increase with the increase in group size.

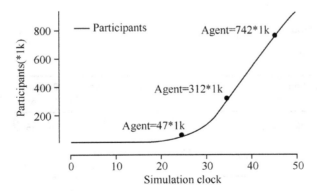

Figure 4.2: Agent quantity change trend chart.

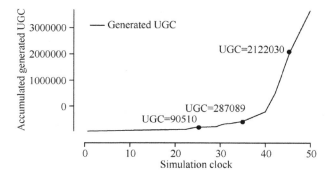

Figure 4.3: UGC quantity change trend chart.

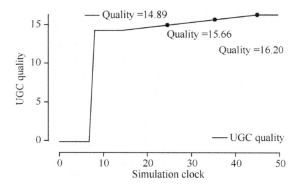

Figure 4.4: UGC quality change trend chart.

4. Collective intelligence simulation taking into account entry classification

To further explain how group participation forms a relationship with editing of entires and professional knowledge, it is necessary to explore whether collective intelligence is equivalent to knowledge. On the basis of the above research results, this study intends to classify the 105 sample entries by "knowledge" or "information." According to the knowledge-oriented view of information, information is the raw material of knowledge, whereas knowledge is the abstracted product of information processing. As shown in Table 4.7, the entries "Hong Kong Disneyland" and "Detective Conan" are classified into the "information" category because such entries have relatively low threshold of editing, which are inclined to information transmission; the entries "Zhejiang Province" and "photorespiration" are classified as "knowledge" entries because these entries have significantly higher threshold of editing, requiring professional knowledge of geography, history, biology, and other

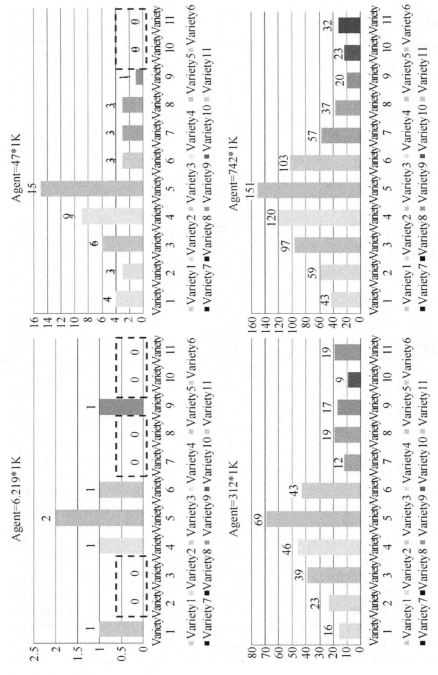

Figure 4.5: Entry variety in groups of different scales.

disciplines, which are refined information products. Fifty-nine out of the 105 sample entries fall into the knowledge category and 46 in the information category.

Consider the above two types of entries as the fitting of the number of edits and the score of entries to achieve the relevant fitting equation, as shown in Table 4.8.

Table 4.7: Reclassifying entries into information and (knowledge).

Number of Edits	Entry Name	Total Score	Category
1698	Hong Kong Disneyland	15.3	Information
1684	Zhejiang Province	16.2	Knowledge
1653	Detective Conan	15.5	Information
409	Photorespiration	15.5	Knowledge

Table 4.8: Fitting results in the condition of entry sample classification.

Fitting function:	$f(x) = (p_1 \cdot x^3 + p_2 \cdot x^2 + p_3 \cdot x + p_4)/(x + q_1)$
	Parameter estimation (95% confidence interval)
	$p1 = -1.268e{-}008(-3.398e{-}007, 3.145e{-}007)$
	$p2 = 0.0002874(-0.001616, 0.002191)$
	$p3 = 14.8\ (12.03, 17.57),\ p4 = 615.9\ (-2468, 3700)$
	$q1 = 65.62\ (-209.3, 340.6)$
	Fit Goodness Index SSE: 92.33
	R-square: 0.3606, Adjusted R-square: 0.3132, RMSE: 1.308

Fitting function:	$(x) = p_1 \cdot x^3 + p_2 \cdot x^2 + p_3 \cdot x + p_4$
Information	Parameter estimation (95% confidence interval)
	$p1 = -6.737e{-}011(-4.453e{-}010, 3.106e{-}010)$
	$p2 = 5.803e{-}007(-1.637e{-}006, 2.798e{-}006)$
	$p3 = -0.000142\ (-0.003909, 0.003625)$
	$p4 = 13.94\ (12.06, 15.83)$
	Fit Goodness Index SSE: 73.9
	R-square: 0.47, Adjusted R-square: 0.4322, RMSE: 1.326

Visualize the above-mentioned equation with MATLAB or other such mapping tools to generate graphs showing the relationships between the quality of entries, either in the knowledge or the information category, with the number of edits, as shown in Figure 4.6.

It can be seen from Figure 4.6 that the quality of both knowledge entries and information entries improves with the increase in the number of edits. The difference between the two types lies in the fact that, as shown in Figure 4.6 (a), the quality of

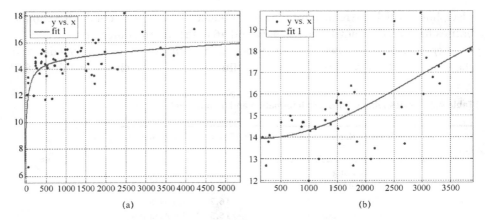

Figure 4.6: Relationship between quality of entries and number of edits (knowledgeentries/information entries).

knowledge entries improves slowly and the goodness of fit is relatively low ($R = 0.3606$). In contrast, as shown in Figure 4.6 (b), the quality of information entries improves fast and the goodness of fit is relatively high ($R=0.47$). Therefore, such a difference shows that the result obtained from information entries is more convincing than knowledge entries in supporting the conclusion that "the increase of the number of edits and that of the group size will lead to the increase of the quality of entries." In addition, the increase in group size exerts greater impact on the quality improvement of information entries than on that of knowledge entries.

Therefore, we can explain the relationship between group participation and the formation of professional knowledge as: the role of group participation in the formation of collective intelligence is more significantly reflected in the information level, whereas the formation of professional knowledge might require the intervention of expert wisdom.

5. Result analysis

This model studies the influence of group size on collective intelligence based on the generation of collective intelligence. Through the collection and research of actual data on Wikipedia, we came to the following conclusions:

(1) Group size plays a decisive role in forming collective intelligence in the internet. In this study, we found that the larger the group size is, the higher the total number, the overall quality, and the variety of UGC. The higher the level of collective intelligence, the more users will be attracted to participate in group collaboration. When the population size reaches 400,000, the number of UGC begins to increase exponentially, UGC quality begins to exceed 16, UGC variety reaches its maximum value, and group collaboration begins to generate collective intelligence. In addition, the quality of entries also increases with the increase in

group size. Finally, the role of group participation in the formation of collective intelligence is more significantly reflected in the information level, whereas the formation of professional knowledge might require the intervention of expert wisdom.

(2) In particular, this study explores the nature of collective intelligence and finds that information entries are more likely to be positively influenced by the growth of group size than knowledge entries, indicating that the collective intelligence formed on the basis of group participation inclines toward the transmission of information rather than the production of knowledge. Knowledge formation may require the participation of experts. This conclusion may remind people of the results of the comparison between collective intelligence and individual intelligence published by Woolley et al. in "Science" in 2010, which showed that, as far as information-based applications like video games are concerned, where the ultimate victory is achieved by converging group provided experience, such as game strategies, paths, and equipment, in these cases, collective intelligence is significantly superior to individual intelligence. In contrast, in knowledge-based disciplines, such as architectural design, collective intelligence is not significant any more, where the ultimate goal is achieved mainly through individual expertise. Naturally, this is because the information needed for playing video games is evidently less professional than the knowledge or information needed for architectural design.

This study attempts to explore how humans can increase their collective wisdom; that is, human beings can improve their intelligence through large-scale interactions; however, intelligence achieved in this manner is more significantly embodied in the information level. Regarding intelligence achieved in the knowledge level, expert intervention is required. In addition, after the group size exceeds a certain value, the growth rate of entry quality becomes modest, indicating that, even though collective intelligence still exists, a group size of billions class is required to push the entry quality to the level of 20. Such a situation is, on one hand, because sampled data is rated by users, which is more or less subjective, as users barely give an all-round full-score evaluation on an entry. On the other hand, it also shows the limitations of group intelligence itself; that is, it is difficult for group intelligence to approach the "truth" in the future due to a lack of expert participation.

4.3 Mechanisms engendering group polarization

4.3.1 Group polarization

Group polarization was first proposed by James Arthur Finch Stoner at the Massachusetts Institute of Technology in 1961 [38]. Through an empirical study, he found that, in a scenario of group decision-making, individual opinions or decisions tend to produce uniform results owing to the discussions among group members. As a sociological concept, group polarization has a certain connection with "herd behavior" (the bandwagon effect) in psychological and financial markets researches and with "information cascades" in informatics.

Herd behavior in psychology, according to the definition of Scharfstein in 1990 [39], refers to the phenomenon in which investors go against the Bayesian posterior distribution of rational rules by merely following others in their actions while ignoring their own private information. Being widely applied in financial analysis, the herd effect describes a kind of financial investment behavior wherein investors ignore private information and choose to follow the crowd. This effect highlights that individuals are very likely to lose themselves in a group as they tend to trust the information that is generally held by other members in the group losing the ability to judge the value of the information.

According to information science research, an information cascade occurs when people observe others' actions and then engage themselves in the same actions, without any marking of their own personal information. In many cases, people are subject to the influences of others in some aspects such as as views, shopping, political stance, activities, or technologies that people use [40]. Information cascades show the influence of information on individuals. When individuals observe the behavior of other individuals in the group, they tend to hide their private information and exhibit "herd behavior."

As a sociological term, an information cascade is often defined as a social phenomenon where decisions within a group are likely to be more extreme than individual decisions made separately because of group influence. Researches in psychology and information science have examined the phenomenon of population polarization by focusing on individuals processing external information, whereas researches in sociology focused on the influenced of the group on individuals, i.e., in sociological researches, group polarization is taken as a group decision-making behavior rather than individual decision-making behavior.

Gensheng Wang (2012) proposed a scientific classification of group polarization phenomena by categorizing them into four categories.

1. Unipolar aggregation in which the views become completely uniform in the evolution process, namely, information cascade appears.
2. Bipolar fragmentation in which users form two completely opposite views in the process of interaction, where the power of the two poles may be asymmetric but more stable.
3. Multipolar fragmentation in which users form many different but stable views in the process of interaction.
4. Zero-polar dilution in which a view or attitude was suddenly lost for some reason in the process of interaction.

With respect to the four categories of group polarization phenomena, unipolar aggregation is usually associated with an unfavorable trend, in which a public crisis event tends to arise. Bipolar fragmentation satisfies the trend of an event where discussion leads in a positive direction, which pushes the group polarization toward the levels of multipolar fragmentation and zero-polar dilution. Because unipolar aggregation and bipolar fragmentation are more common, whereas multipolar fragmentation and zero-polar dilution represent special cases in the evolution process, this book focuses on unipolar aggregation and bipolar fragmentation.

In summary, this book defines group polarization as a phenomenon in which individuals imitate behavior of other instead of behaving based on their own information under certain conditions, which causes individuals in a group to hold the same view; such behaviors can be marked by either unipolar aggregation or bipolar fragmentation.

In recent years, the internet and online social media have gradually become a context for observing the phenomena of group polarization. When a group of individuals begin to hold the same view of a topic and produce similar dialogues, group polarization can be observed. This book defines group polarization in a social network as a phenomenon in which individuals imitate behavior of others instead of behaving based on their own information within the context of a social network under certain conditions, which causes individuals in group to hold the same view. Such behaviors can be marked by either unipolar aggregation or bipolar fragmentation.

4.3.2 Social comparison theory and group polarization

Many theories have been proposed to explain group polarization. Among them, the most classic and comprehensible theory is the social comparison theory. In 1954, Leon Festinger, an American social psychologist, proposed social comparison theory, suggesting that in the absence of objective evaluation each individual evaluates himself or herself through comparison with others, eventually leading to convergent behavior in the group [41]. Festinger suggested that social comparison theory explains why people imitate models in media; one of the reasons is to enhance individuals' self-confidence which becomes a reasonable basis for self-perfection.

After Festinger proposed the social comparison theory, many new theories have been expounded and improved researches on social comparison. For example, Mackie et al. pointed out that in the theory proposed by Festinger [42-45], "social comparison mainly involves the comparison with those who are similar to themselves" was not comprehensive. In social comparison in interpersonal communication, on one hand, people make similar people the object of comparison to confirm that they are similar to others; on the other hand, they compare themselves with different people to confirm their own abilities from the opposite side to improve their self-evaluation and develop their own social behavior, which serves as the auxiliary social comparison. A wise man would combine the two aspects of social comparison to improve his/her self-evaluation. Therefore, in 1979, Tajfel Henri and John Turner proposed three stages of evolution in social comparison wherein individuals evaluated both ego and alter ego. The three stages of the social comparison theory are: self-categorization, social identity, and social comparison [46].

Self-categorization refers to the process of establishing a psychological relationship between the individual and the group. Then, the individual can psychologically become a member of the group and form relationships with other members of the same genus. The central element of the cognitive process of self-categorization is depersonalization. In brief, depersonalization refers to the phenomenon in which people deliberately maintain a distance from others who belong to different types of groups and even have an attitude of indifference and hostility. Social identity is the process through which an individual is judged to be a member of a particular group through subjective perception, forming the in-group and out-group. The final stage is social comparison where small groups begin to form owing to the increased homogeneity in the two groups. That is, the extreme views of the groups become intensified, leading to group polarization. Hence, social comparison theory explains the mechanism through which group polarization occurs. The theoretical formation process is shown in Figure 4.7.

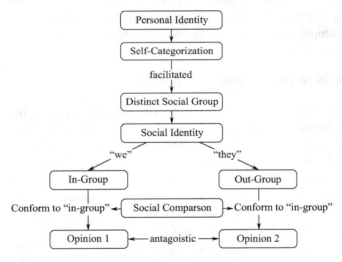

Figure 4.7: The evolution of social comparison theory.

4.3.3 Conditions engendering group polarization

Tom Hayes described the following cases in his book "No Size Fits All." In December 2007, a research on MovieLens, an online film review community, shows that when a user knows about the behavioral mode of other people, he tends to intentionally behave in conformity with the norm of the group, resulting in identified behavior. In the study, the researchers merely sent users a message about the average usage level of users on the site. After sending the message, the monthly comments from low active users increased by 530%, while the monthly comments from highly active users decreased by 62%. That is to say, all users changed their behaviors to make it closer to the median value of the group.

This case highlights the view of Burns, one of the researchers who developed cognitive therapy: when a group exerts some pressure on its members, the advantages of group thinking disappear. This phenomenon is also known as the information cascade effect. The core value of the effect is that people tend to naturally abandon their capacity of independent thinking and follow the practice of others when the collectively identified authenticity exceeds a certain critical value.

An information cascade forms in the following four stages: (1) A triggering event emerges. (2) An idea is proposed by someone who is believed to be trustworthy. (3) The rest of the people notice this idea and believe that agreeing with this idea and giving up their own independent thought is in their best interests. (4) The more people think that this idea is correct, the more people and new information receivers will also think that it is true.

In the book "Science and Practice," Robert B. Cialdini, the world's leading expert of influence research, noted that the more people think a certain viewpoint is correct, the more correct that viewpoint becomes [47]. Moreover, he proposed that social certification is particularly influential in two cases. First, when people face uncertainty (i.e., when they do not have sufficient information and do not know the truth), they tend to observe other people's practices and views and think that their behavior is correct. Second, to be identified with others, people tend to follow and imitate the practices of people with whom they have higher homogeneity. Further, Owen Janis proposed five important characteristics of a homogeneous group: limitation of discussions among group members, superiority of majority-supported views, neglecting of minority's views, repellency against external views, and convergence of group views. These results trigger further exploration into the mechanisms which result in group polarization.

Domestic scholars have also conducted relevant research on the conditions that engender group polarization. For example, Bo Shi (2010) noted that there are three necessary conditions for the generation of group polarization: the emergence of an event, network filtering, and group collaboration [48]. In contrast to real society, a network provides a natural environment for systematic information filtering, which makes it easier for network groups to develop internal homogeneity and intra-group heterogeneity. Further, group cooperation is determined by the nature and characteristics of the network group. Individuals in the group through the mechanism of group consciousness experience an essential subconscious psychological change, losing their self-consciousness and converging toward the view of the group.

Based on the above description, we can conclude that there are four conditions that engender group polarization: first, there must be a triggering event. Second, individuals within the group know about the choices of others. Third, there is a lack of group information. Fourth, there is a certain level of homogeneity in the group.

Through collaborative filtering, people choose to follow the views of others without thinking independently and believe that this is their best choice.

4.3.4 Factors that influence the formation of group polarization

The factors that influence the formation of group polarization can be viewed from three dimensions: subject, group, and information.

1. Subject dimension
While discussing "group classification," Bon suggested that, when individuals are members of a group, their group psychology differs from their individual psychology and their ability of individual thinking is influenced by this difference. Thus, when an individual is no longer independent, the phenomenon of group polarization is very likely to arise. Social identity theory holds that, when individuals identify themselves with a group, their will consciously conforms their own attitude to the group recognized by them. American political scientist Zallcr examined how individuals in a group are exposed to information, how they receive information, and how they form a public opinion. Chinese scholar Xinzhou Xie (2004) stated that, if an individual's ability of independent thinking is strong enough, he/she will be more tolerant to other independent views instead of blindly following them [49]. Thus, individuals' degree of independence has a very important influence on group polarization.

Furthermore, Cass R. Sunstein (2002) believes that, according to the "first possession theory" and "the first impression theory," all individuals subconsciously have their own self standards. First possessed opinions or first impressions often play a dominant role in their minds, and it is not easy for people to change their viewpoints in front of different opinions [50]. Thus, individuals' initial views influence the change in their subsequent views.

In summary, we can conclude from the subject dimension that the following factors affect population polarization: the degree of independence and initial opinions of individuals.

2. Group dimension
Le Bon Gustave, a French scholar, stated that individual's intelligence and his personality are both weakened in collective psychology. Heterogeneity is swallowed by homogeneity, and the quality of unconsciousness has the upper hand. Further, Cialdini stated that people tend to follow and imitate other people whose behaviors are similar to their own. Related researches have shown that group pressure on an individual is greater in a group where an individual is active than that in a group where the individual is completely unfamiliar. Moreover, at the group level, group polarization is more likely to arise in a group of acquaintances rather than in a group of strangers. Further, Morris Charles (2000) showed that, when a cascade

encounters a high-density cluster (if each node has at neighbors at a proportion of N that also belong to the node set, then this node set is called a cluster with a density of P), it will stop, and this is the only reason why cascading stops [51]. Thus, high homogeneity within the group is required for population polarization to arise.

From the perspective of economics and finance, Harrison Hong (2005) found that fund managers are vulnerable to the influence of fund managers in both the same city and other cities; that is, the herd effect exhibits when fund managers select stocks [52]. Accordingly, intensive interaction among people is a prerequisite for the generation of group polarization. Further, Yang et al. (2009) found that the duration of interactions and the size of the group had a significant impact on the emergence of herd behavior, which follows certain rules. Thus, the interaction duration and the group size are factors that influence group polarization [53]. We can then conclude that the interaction frequency (the density of the group) is related to the effect of group polarization.

The theory of Duncan J. Watts and Sheridan Dodds Peter (2007) provokes more thoughts [54]. Researchers found that large-scale cascade formation is driven not by opinion leaders but by key individuals who first show polarization. Of course, opinion leaders may also be such key individuals. Thus, group polarization is triggered by both opinion leaders and individuals in the group who first show polarization.

In summary, we can draw the conclusion from the group dimension that the following factors influence group polarization: group homogeneity, group density, and the initially influenced groups.

3. Information dimension

Haewoon Kwak and other related researchers have found that groups tend to share two types of information [55]: the first type is the primary disseminated information and the second type is information that requires a second though before dissemination. The speeds with which different types of information is diffused are different. For example, for information on events (usually explosive news or headlines), the speed of diffusion within the group is very fast, as it requires little analysis from the part of the group members. In contrast, the discussion-type information (which usually carries a viewpoint) is diffused more slowly because it requires group discussion and review.

Group polarization is a process in which information is rapidly diffused and communicated; thus, the nature of information is very important. G. Thomas (1973) and other studies have found that sensitive topics (such as government, public policy, law, war, and violent behavior) are more likely to give rise to group polarization; thus, the sensitivity of information is a factor that influences group polarization. Zhang et al. (2012) defined two types of inner dynamism related to a sudden public crisis event: the sensitivity of the event and the public nature of the event [56]. The sensitivity of the event is the basis for the formation of inner dynamism. The sensitivity of a topic indicates that, after a crisis event occurs, it is highly possible that online public opinions will explode when certain topics are concerned. After the event, because of certain factors, the attention of internet users, media, government, and other organizations on the event will increase, which will generate a considerable amount of information on the event consequently. As the information on the event gradually increases, online public opinions will form. The public nature of an event refers to the degree of its threat to the social value system. If the public nature of an event is greater, the event will pose a greater threat to the social system. When the public crisis occurs, individuals in the public will naturally consider whether such an event will affect them, and the more the public believes that similar events will affect them, the more likely social panic will arise, and the more likely population polarization will occur. Further, Li Ke (2005) proposed that the fuzzy degree of information is an important factor in whether individuals follow the views of others. If the ambiguity of information is high, the accuracy and reliability of the information received by individuals will be very low, and the usefulness of the information will not be guaranteed. In such a case, individuals will be less likely to be convinced of a particular viewpoint.

In summary, we can conclude from the information dimension that the following factors influence group polarization: information sensitivity, information publicity, and information ambiguity.

4.3.5 Main models of group polarization analysis

1. Herd behavior model based on game theory and principal-agent theory

In real life, many activities require coordination between related people. For instance, the premise of normal bank operation is that the creditors of a bank trust that the bank is able to operate normally and reliably. Based on such a belief, they will not withdraw money from the bank at the same time. In this case, they are taking a "concerted action." However, this trust-based "concerted action" is very fragile. Once some actors receive error messages (e.g., rumors, accidental impacts) that may make them lose faith in the action, a coordinated global collapse may occur.

In 1992, Abhijit V. Banerjee proposed a herd behavior model based on game theory and principal-agent theory. The model which is mainly used to predict economic behavior in fund and stock markets explains this phenomenon well [57]. In the herd behavior model, investors' herd behavior is consistent with the rule of maximum utility and is considered irrational behavior in the presence of factors such as "group pressure." Herd behavior models can be classified into two types: sequence and nonsequence models.

The herd behavior model proposed by Abhijit V. Banerjee belongs to the sequence type; in this model, each decision maker observes a previous decision maker's movement when making decisions. Such behavior is rational because the previous decision maker may send important signals. The decision-making process of an individual is shown in Figure 4.8.

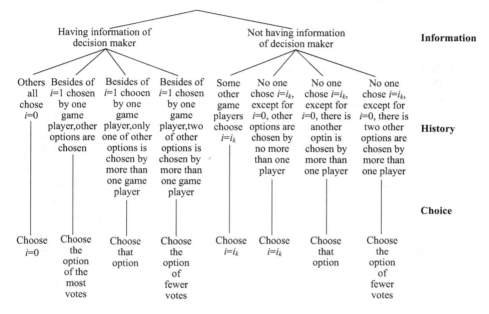

Figure 4.8: Decision-making process of decision maker k (Banerjee, 1992).

(1) An insider is defined as a participant of a match or a game who has the decision-making power. Therefore, any participants who take part in the decision-making process are defined as insiders in the model of Abhijit V. Banerjee.
(2) Definition of game strategy: each participant in a game has to choose a practical and integrated action program which is not for a certain stage but rather for guiding the overall action. Such a program is a strategy of an insider. For instance, in the model of Abhijit V. Banerjee, the game strategy is defined as follows: with A and B (A and B represent any two different actions that exert different effects on the actors) as any of the two elements in a set of options for this group of actors, assuming that at the beginning N-1 out of N actors received the signal indicating that A is superior to B; however, the only one that received the opposite message which prefers B over A ranks first in the sequence of action, obviously, the first person will choose B according to the signal he/she received.

The second person, after observing the action of the first person, knows that the signal received by the first person is that B is superior to A; however, his own signal reads that A is superior to B. Under the premise that everyone is assumed to have signals of the same quality, the second person will abandon his private signal and choose B based on the prior probability action. Thus, the action of the second person does not provide new information for the next person in the sequence.

The situation for the third person is the same as that for the second person who will make the same choice.

As the sequence proceeds, everyone will choose B instead of A even though the gathered information shows that A should be superior to B. Therefore, a herd effect arises.

If the second person always acts according to his own signal, the third person would know that the second person prefers signal A rather than signal B, and he would obviously choose A. The rest may be deduced by analogy, and the final result is that N-1 people except the first person will choose A over B, which reflects the best choice shown by the gathered information. Because the second person abandoned his private signal to take part in the herd, a negative externality affects the rest of the people in the group. If the second person makes his decision according to his private signal, his action will provide information to the rest of people in the group. This action rule that each person in the sequence makes choices based on his own signal rather than the previous person's choice will lead the next person to act the same. In this way, the result will be different from the previous result. This type of externality is called a herd externality.

(3) Definition of gain and loss in a game: the final result of a game shows the gain and loss of a game player. Each person has his or her own result in a game—either a gain or a loss. The results depend not only on an individual's strategy but also on a set of strategies selected by all other individuals in the game. For example, in this herd behavior model, Abhijit V Banerjee assumes that a group of N actors have the same VNM[6] utility functions that is risk neutral, with a target of utility maximization, when there are at least two people who have not received the right signal, the probability that the nth decision maker will receive the right signal is $1 - (1 - \alpha\beta)^{n-1} - (n-1)(1 - \alpha\beta)^{n-2}\alpha\beta$, where α is the probability of obtaining a real signal of investment profit and β is the probability that all individuals failed making the right choice. For any arbitrarily small value $\varepsilon > 0$, when $n(\varepsilon)$ is sufficiently large, the probability will be at least 1-ε, and the minimum value for the external utility function will be $z[N-n(\varepsilon)](1-\varepsilon)/N$, where N is the size of the group, z is the individual's physical return on investment (see the article "A simple model of herd behavior" for more information). It's specially worth noting that when N is sufficiently large, the external utility function will approach $N(1-\varepsilon)$. On the opposite side, if the decision maker receives the right signal, the probability of the right choice being made in herd behavior model is $\Pi \equiv [1 - a(1 - \beta)]^{-1}(1 - a)(1 - \beta)$, and the maximum value of the external utility function is $zN[1-\Pi]$.

---

6 VNM utility function theory is a framework for analysis established by Von Neurmann and Morgenstem in 1950s on the basis of the axiomatic hypothesis by using logical and mathematical tools under uncertain conditions of rational actors.

(4) Explain the equilibrium of the game process, and analyze the results of a game. Each game player will have a result. Equilibrium means balance, and in economics, equilibrium indicates that a related variable tends to be stable. According to the analysis of Banerjee, the characteristics of the decision made in this model are as follows: when the group is sufficiently large, the equilibrium state action is inefficient, if measured with prior probability. This explains why herd behavior is irrational. In this case, the actor has independent information, and the group is sufficiently large; thus, there always be circumstances for an individual to make the right decision. However, because the externality of herd behavior has positive feedback, the equilibrium state action is unstable in some stages of a game. The signals sent by preceding decision makers determine the formation of first group; based on this law, every individual takes part in the group action eventually.

Abhijit V Banerjee's research shows that an individual decision maker who makes decisions based on the previous actor's information seems irrational, but such behavior is rational for the individual because the previous actor may have important information that the decision maker does not know. However, following this rule may result in the Pareto inefficient equilibrium of the group behavior [58].

2. Group consistency model Based on information cascades

The herd behavior model proposed by Abhijit V Banerjee et al. can soundly explain the consistency of group behavior, but the spillover effect caused by different shocks and the way of sudden events causing the group behavior was not considered. In this regard, in 1992, Bikhchandani, Hiershleifer and Welch introduced the concept of an information cascade, which is one of the most important keywords in research on group behavior. The information cascade model, which is called the BHW model, was later applied in financial market analysis. The basic principle of the information cascade model is that after observing previous investors' decisions, observers decide that it is a rational and optimal choice to disregard their own private information and follow the decisions of other investors. Thus, an information cascade arises.

The following steps are used in research on behavioral consistency within groups based on information cascades.

(1) Define variables for the effectiveness of decision making according to the application scenarios and risk preference; then, refine and summarize the investment behavior of decision makers. According to the information cascade model developed by Bikhchandani et al., the investors are risk neutral. We take investments in the stock market as an example. The investors have to decide whether or not to invest in a particular stock in turns in accordance with the order of exogenous decisions. Investment result $v \in V = \{-1, 1\}$ is randomly decided before the start of the first stage, and remains unchanged in the later stage. Good investment results are denoted as $v = 1$, and bad investment results are denoted as $v = -1$. We assume that the

investment results take the value $v = 1$ with the probability $\mu_1 = 1/2$. The investment results are revealed after all investors have made decisions.

(2) Variational definition for the private signal obtained by decision maker, the investment decision, and the investment history observed previously based on the process of information acquisition. For instance, in the information cascade model, before making an investment decision, every investor can receive a private signal that reveals the investment results. Investors' private signals with the given investment results are independently distributed. The signal of investor i is $s_i \in S = \{-1, 1\}$. Good signals are denoted as $s = 1$, while bad signals are denoted as $s = -1$. The accuracy of the private signal refers to the probability that the signal is correct with the given investment results. Except for private signals, each investor can also observe the investment decisions made by previous investors. Therefore, the information set of investor i contains his private signals and all previous investors' investment history $h_i = (a_1, a_2, \ldots, a_{t-1})$. In addition, the public faith μ_i of stage i can be treated as the probability that the investment results are good, given the investment history h_i. This variable is computed as $\mu_i = p(v = 1/h_i)$. In this model, each investor chooses an investment decision that is $a_i \in A = \{0, 1\}$ in discrete sets. If $a_i = 1$, the investment decision is positive, whereas if $a_i = 0$, the decision is negative.

(3) After defining investors' returns and results, establish a model of the relationship between decision-making behavior and investment returns in combination with the process of information acquisition. Then, calculate the expected value of investors' returns according to the relevant information and signal probability. We assume that investors do not have an initial endowment. The return of investor i depends on his investment decision and investment result:

$$\mu_i(a_i, v) = \left\{ \begin{array}{l} 0, a_i = 0 \\ v, a_i = 1 \end{array} \right\} \tag{4.4}$$

In uncertain circumstances, the return of an investor is the expected value of $\mu_i(a_i, v)$ under the information set:

$$E\mu_i(a_i, v/h_i, s_i) = \left\{ \begin{array}{ll} 0, & a_i = 0 \\ E(v/h_i, s_i), & a_i = 1 \end{array} \right\} \tag{4.5}$$

In this equation, $E(v/h_i, s_i) = p(v = 1/h_i, s_i) \times 1 + p(v = -1/h_i, s_i) \times (-1)$. For instance, when an investor i decides to invest; namely $a_i = 1$, his expected return will be $E(v/h_i, s_i) = 0.7 + 0.3 \times (-1) = 0.4$ if the probability μ_i of good signal s_i received by investor i is 0.7, whereas that of the bad signal is 0.3.

Investor i is included in this sequence decision model. The structure of the model and Bayesian rationality is public information. After observing other investors' decisions, each investor updates his investment faith in the investment results by applying the Bayesian rule and makes his investment decision.

(4) Analyze the process of obtaining information and the model results. With such an analysis, we can discuss the behavioral tendency and consistency of group decision-making based on the information cascade model and explain the causes of information cascades. The analysis of the above model shows that all the subsequent investors choose to invest when the number of the investors who choose to invest is greater than the number of investors who do not choose to invest by two or more. In such a case, the information cascade and herd behavior related to investment occurs. When the number of the investors who choose not to invest is greater than the number of investors who choose to invest by two or more, all the investors that follow choose not to invest. Thus, the information cascade and herd behavior related to giving up investment occurs. Otherwise, whether an information cascade occurs depends not only on the number of good and bad signals received by the preceding investors but also on the order of the received signals. Moreover, the information cascade is path dependent, specific and variable. In the conditions that new information is present, the accuracy of private signals improves, or the investment results change, the existing information cascade is likely to stop or change.

(5) Further analyze and discuss the polarizing effects of group decision-making and information cascades according to existing results of information cascade research. Then, using the actual problem, explain the root causes of information cascades. Bikhchandani et al. noted that an information cascade could be either positive or negative; that is, all individuals may accept or refuse a particular action. For example, a group of young people facing the decision to try drugs may have a strong motivation to try drugs if their friends are trying them; by contrast, young people may avoid drugs if their friends refuse to try them.

According to the relevant rules regarding decision making, the probabilities of forming positive information cascade, zero information cascade, and negative information cascade are expressed as follows respectively:

$$\frac{1-(p-p^2)^{n/2}}{2}, (p-p^2)^{n/2}, \frac{1-(p-p^2)^{n/2}}{2} \tag{4.6}$$

In this formula, p represents the accuracy of private signals mentioned above, and n denotes the number of initial decision makers. When $n=2$, the probabilities of forming positive information cascade, zero information cascade, and negative information cascade can be shown as follows respectively:

$$\frac{1-p+p^2}{2}, p-p^2, \frac{1-p+p^2}{2} \tag{4.7}$$

As shown in formula (4.7), when probability p approximates 1/2, the information cascade is delayed, and the signal provides no information. When p departs from 1/2, the noise in the signal increases; in other words, people will more clear about whether or not to adopt a signal or an action. Furthermore, we can conclude from the above formula that the probability of zero information cascade occurring expo-nentially decreases as the value of n increases. For instance, for a signal, if $p = 1/2+\varepsilon$ and if ε is assumed to be arbitrarily small, the probability of zero information cascade occurring is less than 0.1 even when n is set to 10.

Therefore, the probability of an information cascade occurring varies with changes in p and n, as shown in Figure 4.9.

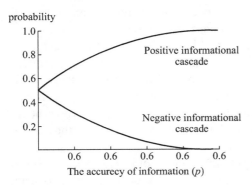

Figure 4.9: The probabilities of positive and negative information cascades occurring.

The BHW model explains not only why people demonstrate uniform behaviors but also why the behavioral convergence may be idiosyncratic and fragile (i.e., eventually there will be multiple equilibria that are unstable). This model is thus one of the most important developments in research on herd behavior. Within the BHW model, we argue that the following four kinds of mechanisms may lead to uniform behavior within a group: sanctions on deviants, positive payoff externalities, conformity preference, and communication. It explains why social behavior is of historical dependence in the former 3 mechanisms, and we can see from the last one that if communication is costless and reliable, group convergence behavior is likely to occur.

In conclusion, the important contribution of the BHW model is that it dynami-cally imitates information cascades in the process of decision making. Furthermore, the problem of effectively disclosing information to the public is discussed based on this model.[7] People tend to have greater belief in the government when information is more accurate. Objective and adequate communication about markets and related institutions helps to prevent a coordinated collapse of the system and to influence public behavior. To perfect the information disclosure system, the government should strengthen information disclosure, increase the openness of the market in

---

7 The integrity and sufficiency of information disclosure are necessary and sufficient conditions for the effectiveness of stock markets; further, the integrity and sufficiency of information disclosure are objective requirements for not only listed companies but also market regulation.

order to ensure that timely, complete and accurate information can be provided, and that the release of information can help investors to form rational expectations.

3. Simulation of Herd behavior in group decision-making based on cellular automata

In traditional modeling methods, complex and classical mathematical formulas always need to be established. Considering the constantly emerging complications and problems related to human behavior, it is difficult to use mathematical symbols to describe human behavior in many realistic problems. In the fields of computer science and artificial intelligence, simulation has attracted people's attention as an experimental method to explore the inherent nature of human behavior. There are currently mainly the following microscopic simulation models that obtain macroscopic results based on micro mechanisms through the simulation of individual behaviors and interactions: the multi Agent model, the seepage flow model, the critical value model and cellular automata etc.

A cellular automaton is a discrete mathematical model of time and space. This model was proposed by Von Neumann and his partners for the simulation of self-replicating biological system in the 1950s. Structurally, a cellular automaton is a Quintet, consisting of five basic parts: a cellular automaton, cellular space, neighbors, cellular automata state set and evolution rules. The main content of using applied cellular automata to build simulation models for actual systems is to complete the establishment and construction of the above mentioned five components by using cellular automata. The last two of the five components, the cellular automata state set and the evolution rules, are of utmost importance.

The simulation of herd behavior in group decision making based on cellular automata developed by Shan-lin Yang et al. in 2009 revealed the effect of pseudo herd behavior[8] on group decision making. The simulation results show that conformity preference, the number of group interactions and group size exert significant influences on three kinds of herd behaviors, and such influences follow certain rules.

The process of simulating herd behavior in group decision-making based on cellular automata comprises the following steps.

(1) First, clearly define the concepts in the research question, and propose hypotheses of the model based on scenarios. For example, in this model, Shan-lin Yang (2009) defined the concept of herd behavior and divided group behavior into three categories: "real herd behavior"; "pseudo herd behavior" and "real non-herd behavior"; "pseudo non-herd behavior". Based on the prerequisites of herd behaviors, two hypotheses are put forward.

---

[8] Many decision makers have similar information sets, therefore, they make similar decisions, which are, however, not recognizable to the market; these decision makers are mistaken for taking a herb behavior, and such a behavior is called "pseudo-herb behavior".

Hypothesis 1: The decision making of other decision makers in the group is observable.

Hypothesis 2: All decisions are made in a sequence rather than at the same time.

(2) Based on the research hypothesis, and combined with the cellular automata model of five basic components, the cellular automata, cellular space, neighbors, cellular automata state sets and evolution rules are expounded, so as to complete the construction of the model. The two most important components among others: the cellular automata state set and the evolution rules, are defined.

For example, the evolution model and the quintet structure of cellular automata constructed by Shan-lin Yang et al. (2009) is as follows:

$$A = (d, Ld, N, S, F) \tag{4.8}$$

Where, A is the model for evolution; d represents the cellular automata; Ld represents cellular space, which is a network system composed of all individuals in the decision making group, denoted by an $n{\times}n$ square cellular space; each cellular automaton in the square grid indicates a decision maker; the distances between cellular automata are not geographic distances; rather, they can be taken as professional distances, or decision resources owned by other cellular automata, or the availability of the information set; N represents neighbors; S represents cellular automata state set; F represents the evolution rules. The cellular automata state set and the evolution rules are particularly expounded.

There are two types of cellular automata state sets: the mother state set S_m and the derivative state set S_c, the mother state set $S_m = S_1{\times}S_2$. In this equation, S_1 denotes the conformity preference, including the "follow-the-fashion" type (δ_{11}), the environmental adaption type (δ_{12}) and the independent action type (δ_{13}). That is, $S_1 = (\delta_{11}, \delta_{12}, \delta_{13})$. Further, S_2 is the decision making resources owned by the central cellular automaton; namely, the unit amount of information. In the derivative state set $S_c = S_3{\times}S_4{\times}S_5$, S_3 denotes a true solution of a cellular automaton at a certain moment, S_4 denotes the final solution selected by a cellular automaton at a certain moment, S_5 denotes denotes the real herd behavior of a cellular automaton at a certain moment, including "real herd behavior"; "pseudo herd behavior" and "real non-herd behavior"; "pseudo non-herd behavior".

Regarding the evolution rules, usually the state at time $t+1$ is influenced by the state of the neighbor cell, the self state and control variables at moment t, as represented in the following equations:

$$S_r^{t+1} = F(S_r^t, S_{rL}^t; R) \tag{4.9}$$

$$S_{rL}^t = (S_{rL(1)}^t, \ldots, S_{rL(k)}^t) \tag{4.10}$$

$$S \in S_1 \times S_2 \times S_3 \times S_4 \times S_5, \ t = 0, 1, 2, \ldots \tag{4.11}$$

Further, the evolution rules of the four states of the central cellular automaton, S_2, S_3, S_4, S_5, are expounded. Due to space limitation, we will not go into details about the specific analysis process.[9]

(3) When the model is established, carry out simulation on a relevant simulation platform (such as, Visual Basic, MATLAB, Swarm, etc.) through program design and implementation.[10] For example, Shan-lin Yang et al. (2009) used the Visual Basic 6.0 development tool in a Windows environment to implement the simulation model. The analog input parameters include the size of the grid, group conformity preference ratio, cell size, type of neighbors, alternative sets and initial decision resources. The number of conformity preferences is set to reflect three kinds of conformity bias proportional to the group. At the same time, the neighbor type for this simulation region is set as Von Neumann, and the rules of information distribution is set to determine the owning amount of initial information. For example, in this paper, the supporting weights of 200 information elements for five backup solutions are calculated in the model, to achieve the weights of five backup solutions for decision targets {0.2104, 0.1894, 0.2104, 0.1894, 0.2062}. Thus, it is concluded from the calculation result that solution 1 is the optimal solution.

(4) Change the input parameters, and observe the changes of the output results, and then simulate and analyze the herd behavior under different conditions, to get the relevant conclusions of the simulation of herd behavior evolution. Yang Shanlin et al. (2009) carried out the simulation of herd behavior through the experiments of two cellular automata. They simulated and analyzed herd behaviors under different conformity preferences and different group sizes respectively. For example, the authors made three sets of experiments by changing the times of conformity preferences of input parameters $y = \{1,0,0\}$, $y = \{0,0,1\}$ and $y = \{0.25, 0.5, 0.25\}$. With different interaction times, they achieved the ratios of "false conglomerates" and "not uncommon" in the output parameters respectively, and then conducted descriptive statistical analysis to obtain the trend of the change in the size of the pseudo herd behavior ratio and the number of interactions required to reach the optimal decision.

(5) After the general simulation of the model, the universal conclusion of herd behavior in group decision-making is drawn, to solve the problems such as the factors influencing the formation of group polarization behaviors in reality. For example, after the change and simulation of parameters in the model, Yang Shanlin et al. (2009) obtained the following conclusions: when the herd behavior

---

9 For the full contents, refer to the following paper: Shan-lin Yang, Ke-yu Zhu, Chao Fu, et al. Simulation of the Group Decision Herd Behavior based on Cellular Automata [J]. Journal of Engineering System Theory and Practice, 2009(9): 115–124.
10 The related learning code is available on the website[EB/OL] http://pan.baidu.com/s/1dD3n285.

appears to be fully acting in the group, the final evolutionary result of the group decision is very sensitive to the initial state; when the herd behavior appears in part of the group participants only, what influences the interaction convergence speed of the group is more than just conformity preference; the increase of the group size also significant influences the convergence speed of the group. That is to say, the bigger the group is, the slower the decision make process is. In the evolution of decision-making in groups that exhibit fully and partially herd behaviors, evident rules can be observed between the pseudo herd behavior and the change in group size.

It is possible to carry out modeling and simulation in studies of human group behavior by means of computer simulation, and thus to discover the main causes and laws of group polarization behavior, which is an important method that deserves attention and exploration in related studies.

4.3.6 Simulation of group polarization in social networks without the influence of social network structure

Based on the above factors that influence group polarization, this part is aimed to construct a multi-agent based model of group polarization in social networks; in addition, with the duration of group polarization (the time period required for 80% of Internet users to reach polarization) and the percentage of group polarization (the percentage of Internet users holding different views after group polarization) as the two representation factors of group polarization performance, the following three scientific questions are investigated:

1. How group polarization on the Internet is affected by these factors?
2. Which one of the factors exerts greater impact on the behavior of group polarization?
3. With all the above factors taken into account, what is the threshold level at which a group polarization behavior arises?

1. Model hypotheses
The relevant hypotheses presented in this model are as follows.

Hypothesis 1: This model is built based on a specific media system; that is, the impact of such factors as media and network structure on group polarization behaviors is temporarily ignored.

Hypothesis 2: Based on the relevant theories and mechanisms about the generation of group polarization, we assume that when the group pressure perceived by individuals exceeds a certain threshold, the individuals will follow the group opinions without seeking to process their private information, due to the fact that individuals believe that such a behavior is to their best benefits.

2. The formation of group polarization

In this model, we divide the process of group polarization formation into three stages, which are the latency period, the emergence period and the formation period, as shown in Figure 4.10.

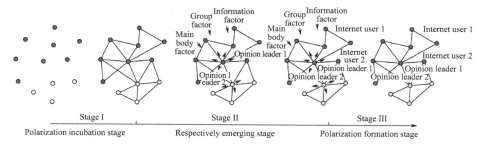

Figure 4.10: The process of polarization formation.

Stage I, Latency: since the advent of the Web 2.0 era, self-organising Internet users have become the major force of forming networks and enormous user-generated contents (UGC) have been created. If some UGC involve highly sensitive and public events, which are also explicitly described, they are most likely to initiate group discussions and attract attentions across the Internet.

At first, Internet users are taken as varied and isolated points. Individuals in the same group sharing the same interests are marked with the same color. When they start to follow an event, individual Internet users will interact and discuss with each other; two individuals in interaction or discussion will be connected with edges. This process is the initial stage of group polarization.

Stage II, Emergence: a certain individual with high perceived benefits (for example, an opinion leader) notices the event and posts their personal views on the Internet; at the same time, another individual of the same status (for example, another opinion leader) may post an opposing view on the Internet. At this point, under the guidance of the nonlinear coupling theory, the subject, the group and the topic factors will synthetically affect the influence of other individuals on the judgement of viewpoints. Therefore, when observing the views of the above two individuals, other individuals will choose a point of view to follow under the influence of the polarization effect.

As the polarization progress progresses and more users start to follow a point of view, more and more individuals will believe in the validity of this view; thus, group polarization begins to form gradually. This process is the emergence stage of group polarization.

Stages III, Formation: As can be seen from Figure 4.10, at stage II, Internet user 1 has not interacted with any opinion leaders, so he always maintains his original opinion. In the third stage, however, because his neighbors follow the opinion of opinion leader 1, under the influence of others, user 1 adaptively aligns his opinion with that of opinion leader 1. As for Internet user 2, we can observe that he is connected to both opinion leader 1 and opinion leader 2, but he is in the same interest group as opinion leader 1 (the two are more homogeneous); therefore, he is more likely to follow the views of opinion leader 1.

Finally, the views in the system gradually reach a stable equilibrium state: polarization takes shape at both ends. At this point, the group polarization is finally formed. This is the third stage of the overall process.

3. Construction of a model of group polarization in social networks
In this part, group polarization in social networks is modelled as follows. It is also a multi-agent based modelling method.

Agent Layer: two heterogeneous agent categories are set up, which are respectively defined as InternetUser and OpinionLeader.

Individual agent characteristics model layer:
Internal status:
1. Individual independence, defined as variable "Ind_thinking(I_e) $\in (1, 5)$".
2. Group diversity, defined as variable "Group_var(G_k) $\in (1, 5)$".
3. Ratio of the views from different opinion leaders, defined as variables "OLopinion1" and "OLopinion2".
4. Perceived benefits, defined as variable "Percep_benefit".
5. Information sensitivity, defined as variable "Topic_Sensi(T_s) $\in (1, 5)$".
6. Information publicness, defined as variable "Topic_Pub(T_p) $\in 1, 5)$".
7. Information ambiguity, defined as variable "Topic_Ambi(T_a) $\in (1, 5)$".

Perceptron: defined in this model as the interaction between users and viewing UGC: interact() and viewUGC().
Effector: defined in this model as changing one's own opinion: opinionChange().
Environment: in this model, two output variables are included to reflect the characterization of group polarization, which are the Polarization Time and the Polarization Percentage.

MAS layer: the relevant rules of group polarization in social networks are constructed based on the model of Michael W. Macy and other classic Hopfield network models.

$$P_{\text{acc}} = \frac{\sum_{i=1}^{N-1} I_0 D_0}{N - 1} \tag{4.12}$$

Where $N = \rho \cdot A$ is the number of Internet users in the system, ρ is the density of the population, and A is the area of the simulation area. When faced with two different views, if an Internet user adopts point 1, then $I_0 = -1$, if an Internet user adopts point 2, then $I_0 = +1$. D_0 represents the number of internet users who shift from their point of view to point 1 or point 2. P_{acc} is the group pressure on an individual user from an individual with who the former has an interaction with, when he or she adopts or rejects a certain point of view.

$$\text{Percep\_benefit} = \frac{V_s}{1 + e^{-P_{acc} \cdot \text{Co\_Factor}}} + (1 - V_s) \cdot P_{ex} \tag{4.13}$$

$$\text{Co\_Factor} = \frac{T_s \cdot T_p}{\lambda \cdot I_e \cdot G_k \cdot T_a} \tag{4.14}$$

In the above equation, $V_s \in [0, 1]$ is the parameter that regulates an individual's perceived press ratio from either inside or outside the system. Co_Factor is the comprehensive influencing factors of the group polarization effect, including the subject factor, the group factor and all variables of information factors, which ranges from 0 to 1.The higher value of Co_Factor, the more significant the group polarization effect, where λ is the adjustment parameter and P_{ex} is the perceived press outside the system.. Here, we set a threshold value $\pi_{\text{threshols}} = 0.7 + \beta\chi$, where β is an regulation parameter and χ is a random value at $(-0.5, 0.5)$. When Percep_benefit $> \pi_{\text{threshold}}$, individual Internet users will change their point of view to view 1 or view 2; otherwise, their maintain their views unchanged.

4. Model simulation and results
According to the the above equation, we assume that $V_s = 1$ and that all the perceived press is from within the system; namely, all the information transmissions are from the same medium, coinciding with hypothesis 1. At the same time, we set parameters λ and β to 25 and 0.5, and the simulation time is in seconds, to achieve ideal simulation results.

Table 4.9 shows the parameters in two extreme cases of group polarization, where Case 1 reflects the easiest setting to produce group polarization, and Case 2 reflects the most difficult setting to produce group polarization. The corresponding simulation results in both cases are shown in Figures 4.11 and 4.12 below.[11]

Figure 4.11 shows that the value of group diversity is 1, indicating that all Internet users belong to the same group, as represented by squares of the same brightness. In the initial stage, each Internet user holds his or her own point of view. After the opinion leaders disseminate their views in the network (represented by squares of two different brightnesses), the Internet users are affected by a combination of

---

11 Reference link: http://pan.baidu.com/s/1dDh8M2l.

Table 4.9: Simulation of two extreme cases of group polarization.

	Individual Independence	Group Diversity	Information Sensitivity	Public Nature of the Information	Information Ambiguity
Case 1	1	1	5	5	1
Case 2	5	5	1	1	5

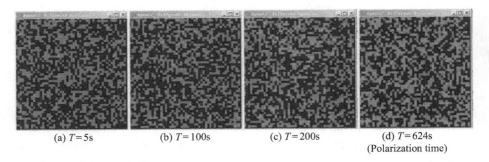

    (a) T=5s   (b) T=100s   (c) T=200s   (d) T=624s
                                                          (Polarization time)

Figure 4.11: Simulation result from Case 1.

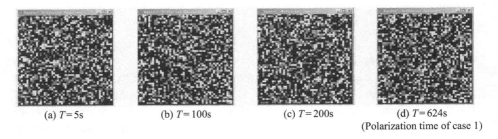

    (a) T=5s   (b) T=100s   (c) T=200s   (d) T=624s
                                                           (Polarization time of case 1)

Figure 4.12: Simulation result from Case 2.

factors, and they choose to follow other people's point of view (represented by squares shifting from the initial brightness to the other two brightnesses, as shown in Figure 4.11). Finally, when 80 percent of Internet users have changed their views to form two extremes (indicated by squares in the other two brightnesses), group polarization arises.

Figure 4.12 shows that the group diversity of Internet users is 5 (represented by five kinds of brightness), similar to the evolution of Case 1; however, obviously we can see that only a few individuals change their views over time in Case 2. When the polarization time in Case 1 (T=624s) is reached, polarization does not arise in Case 2 (the brightness indicating Internet users' views remain unchanged). Therefore, this model can effectively simulate the evolution of group polarization.

Then, we changed the value of each influencing factor (individual independence, group diversity, population density, information sensitivity, information publicness, information ambiguity), and we observed the effect of such changes on group polarization. Furthermore, we ranked the influencing factors based on the extent to which each of them influences group polarization, and achieved the following result: group diversity > information ambiguity > individual independence > information sensitivity > information publicness. Finally, we determined the threshold at which all the influencing factors can synthetically influence group polarization. When Co_Factorgt0.2, despite the differences in the time and the percentage of group polarization in different cases, polarization will eventually occur. By contrast, when Co_Factor ≤ 0.2, group polarization basically does not occur. This conclusion proves the critical influence of the integrated influencing factors on sudden events in the system, especially on group polarization. You may refer to the original text for more in-depth and comprehensive information.[12]

4.3.7 Simulation of group polarization in social networks with the influence of social network structure[13]

In the previous section, we did not consider the influence of network structure on group polarization; in this section, we will elaborate on the important influence and significance of the social network structure.

This section first presents an improved local-world evolving model and a group polarization model, and then theoretically describes the impact of social network structure on group polarization. For the empirical study, the social relations between members of a laboratory were examined to verify the correctness of the models, and proposed the rules in which social network structure influences group polarization. Computer simulation methods were used to demonstrate that different platforms have difference influences on information diffusion from the perspectives of topic networks and real networks respectively. Finally, the following issues were investigated:
1. How does the social network structure influence group polarization?
2. Do different social network platforms influence group polarization differently?
3. For different scenarios, which social network platforms are best suited for diffusing information and reducing group polarization. By answering this question, we can further explore the function mechanisms of the network structure and social media, develop better information diffusion strategies, and improve the effectiveness of information diffusion, which is of certain reference value for improving online business models in social networks and mining the potential application values.

---

12 Refer to the following article: Shiyu Du, Jiayin Qi. Multi-agent Modeling and Simulation on Group Polarization Behavior in Web 2.0 [J]. Journal of Networks, 2014.
13 Refer to the following article: Shiyu Du, Jiayin Qi. Study on the Influence of Social Network Structure on the Polarization of Group Opinions [J]. Journal of Information Systems, 2014.

1. Improved local-world evolving mode

Based on the improved local-world evolving model, this part of the research is aimed to construct an evolving undirected scale-free network model (EUSN model) and an evolving directed scale-free network model (EDSN model). The EUSN model is mainly applied to typical undirected online social networks, such as Renren and Facebook; friends' relations in this kind of networks are bi-directional. By contrast, the EDSN model is mainly used to simulate typical directed online social networks, such as Sina Weibo and Twitter; friends' relations in this kind of networks are unidirectional. These two models describe the evolution of an online local world in a nonlinear way, and more accurately describe the structural characteristics and evolution of online social network platforms.

The optimum selection probability of the EUSN model is shown in equation (4.15), where $P(i)$ is the probability of a certain node i with a node degree of $k(i)$ being connected. By contrast, for the EUSN model, both indegree k_{i_in} and outdegree k_{i_out} of node i need to be considered, which is shown in equation (4.16) and equation (4.17).

$$P(i) = \frac{k_i^{1+0.5\log_{10}k_i}}{\sum_j k_j^{1+0.5\log_{10}k_j}} \tag{4.15}$$

$$P_{out}(i) = \frac{k_{i\_out}^{1+0.5\log_{10}k_{i\_out}}}{\sum_j k_{j\_out}^{1+0.5\log_{10}k_{j\_out}}} \tag{4.16}$$

$$P_{in}(i) = \frac{k_{i\_in}^{1+0.5\log_{10}k_{i\_in}}}{\sum_j k_{j\_in}^{1+0.5\log_{10}k_{j\_in}}} \tag{4.17}$$

The evolution process of this network includes the addition of new nodes and the generation and extinction of new links. Moreover, according to relevant theories, users prefer to establish contact with "closely related nodes"; therefore, the specific process is as follows.

1. Network initialization: the initial network is a random network with m_0 nodes and e_o edges, where the connectivity of each node is at least 1, so that the network has no isolated nodes.
2. Network evolution: in each time interval, $1/M$ of all the nodes are randomly selected as a local network, and the following process is repeated according to a certain probability.

The addition of new nodes: a new node is added to the selected local network with a probability of p_1, the new node is connected to m_1 nodes according to the optimum selection probability, and the member relationship matrix is updated.

New link generation mechanism I: m_2 new links are added to the network with a probability of p_2. A node is randomly selected within the network, and one of its neighbors' neighbors is selected as the opposing node, to establish a link. Repeat this action for m_2 times, and update the member relationship matrix.

New link generation mechanism II: m_0 new links are added to the network with a probability of p_3, and a node is randomly selected within the network. Then, for the EUSN model, the opposing node is selected among nodes in the local world according to equation (4.15), and a link is established between them, generating m_2 undirected links. For the EDSN model, a node is selected according to equation (4.16) as a follower, and a node from the local world is selected according to equation (4.17) as the followed, generating m_2 directed links.

Distinction of new links: one edge of the network is removed with probability p_4. If the removal of this edge causes an isolated node, then the links are rematched using the above steps. If the network becomes several unconnected small groups, then give up removing the link.

2. Group polarization model based on social network structure

To determine the perceived stress of every Internet user in the network, the PageRank algorithm is used to evaluate the priority for visiting the user (Lei, 2009). According to the member relationship matrix $A_{N \times N}$, the PageRank matrix $R_{1 \times N}$ of the nodes is generated. Moreover, based on social comparison theory, we know that the path distance between two nodes affects the level of "trust" between the members (Latan B., 1981). Therefore, the shortest path between nodes is assumed to be related to the level of perceived stress, and the shortest path matrix between two nodes is represented as $\{D_{ij}\}$.

According to classical theories on group polarization, a user's perceived press from the other nodes is directly proportional to the influence of the relevant nodes (indicated by PageRank value R_j) and inversely proportional to the shortest path between the nodes (indicated by the shortest path matrix $\{D_{ij}\}$). Thus, the representation of perceived stress is shown in equation (4.18), where I_{ij} represents the perceived stress applied by node j within the group influence matrix $I_{N \times N}$ on node i.

$$I_{ij} = R_j / D_{ij} \tag{4.18}$$

In the network, the perceived group stress P_i of each node, which represents the average value of pressure applied by all the members of the network, is evaluated by using equation (4.19), derived from the Hopfield network model. N is the number of nodes in the network, S_j is the opinion value of node j, and when node j holds a supporting, opposing or neutral attitude, $S_j = 1$, -1 or 0, which is captured in the group view matrix $S_{1 \times N}$.

$$P_i = \frac{\sum_{j=1}^{N} I_{ij} S_j}{N} \tag{4.19}$$

The final opinion of the group members depends not only on the overall group pressure but also on the initial point of view. Therefore, a change in point of view is also related to the value of $\beta \times S_i + (1 - \beta) \times P_i$. S_i is node i's initial point of view, while β is an adjustable parameter in the (0, 1) range, whose value is set to 0.5 in the simulation process.

3. The integrated model

The integrated model is a combination of the local-world evolving model and the group polarization model. As shown in Figure 4.13, it includes three stages of the simulation process.

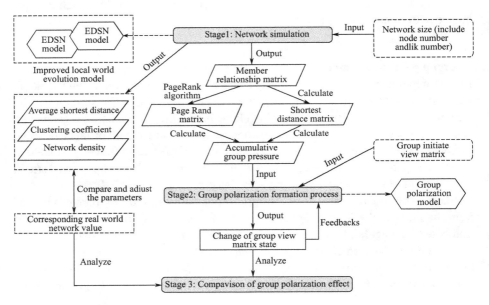

Figure 4.13: Model structure.

Stage 1: Network simulation

In this stage, first, the given number of nodes and the number of links of the real network is entered, the corresponding parameters are adjusted, and the corresponding artificial simulation network is obtained. Secondly, by comparing the structure parameters of the artificial simulation network and the real network, we can determine whether the artificial simulation network can describe the structure and information diffusion characteristics of the real network.

Stage 2: Process of group polarization formation

According to the group polarization model, threshold π_{thresh} is randomly set. When $\beta \times S_i + (1 - \beta) \times P_i > \pi_{\text{thresh}}$, node i's view in the initial opinion matrix is updated to a value of 1, and when $\beta \times S_i + (1-\beta) \times P_i < -\pi_{\text{thresh}}$, node i's view is updated to a value of -1; otherwise, the value of node i's view remains unchanged. This process is repeated until a stable state of polarization is reached.

Stage 3: Comparison of the group polarization effects

Two indicators reveal the group polarization effect: time and quantity. Group polarization time refers to the length of time required for the dominant emotion in the group to reach 0.9. The proportion of group polarization refers to the proportion of each view of users after polarization has been reached on the same platform.

On a single platform, while holding the values of all the other variables constant, adjust the corresponding network structure parameters, to determine how the structure of the online social network influences the effect of group polarization. As for different online topic networks and real networks, by comparing the different polarization times and proportions of different platforms, we can analyze whether different social networks have different effects on group polarization, and which kind of social network platforms are most suitable for diffusing information and reducing group polarization in different application scenarios.

4. How changes in the structure parameters of a social network affect group polarization

In the study, we selected social network relationships between laboratory members (13 teachers and 108 postgraduates) as the empirical research objects, and then compared and analyzed the structures of four different social networks (Fetion, QQ, Renren, Sina Weibo) by using the social network analysis (SNS) method, thus to study the impact of social network structure on group polarization.

By comparing the outputs of phase I in the integrated model with the structure parameters of a real network (see Table 4.10), we found that the structure parameters of the artificial simulation network are basically consistent with those of the real network. Moreover, the degree distribution of the simulation network follows a power-law distribution, and it is in accordance with the small-world characteristics of online social networks. Therefore, that the ability of our model to simulate a real social network is verified.

After simulating the real social network, we further examined the general rule by which social network structure affects group polarization. Here, we chose to take changing the clustering coefficient in Weibo as an example of simulation. As shown in Figure 4.14, while maintaining other parameters unchanged, we increased the value of the clustering coefficient in Weibo by approximately 50% (the clustering coefficient is 0.2985 on the left side of Figure 4.14 and 0.4590 on the right side of Figure 4.14), we were able to determine the impact of this change on the time and ratio of polarization. When the polarization ratio (shown in Figure 4.14) reaches 0.9,

Table 4.10: Network structure parameters of online social network platforms.

	Renren		Feition		QQ		Sina Weibo	
	Simulation value	Real value	Simulation value	Real value	Simulation value	Real value	Simulation value	Real value
Number of nodes	121	121	121	121	121	121	121	121
Number of Links	2108	2099	3880	3879	1692	1677	1626	1623
Average degree of the network	17.4215	16.475	32.066	32.41	13.984	12.443	13.438	12.163
Network density	0.14518	0.1334	0.2672	0.2544	0.1165	0.0776	0.112	0.0996
Average shortest path	1.9573	1.928	1.7331	1.747	2.0497	2.21	3.0267	2.832
Clustering coefficient	0.44707	0.479	0.533	0.581	0.4254	0.47	0.1296	0.1995

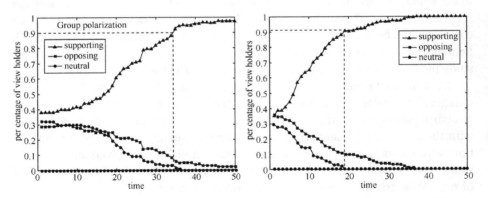

Figure 4.14: Comparison of group polarization times for different clustering coefficients based on Sina Weibo platform data.

the amount of time before polarization is reduced from 34 to 18. Moreover, as can be seen in Figure 4.15, for the same time steps, the polarization ratio is significantly improved with an increase in the clustering coefficient. Therefore, it can be concluded that if the other parameters are kept constant, increasing the clustering coefficient can promote the formation of polarization, as it shortens the time before polarization and increases the polarization ratio.

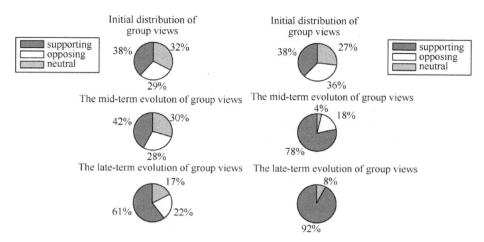

Figure 4.15: Comparison of the proportion of users showing group polarization for different clustering coefficients based on Sina Weibo platform data.

Moreover, we also simulated the clustering coefficient, network density and average shortest path for different platforms; however, owing to space limitations, we list only the relevant conclusions here.

(1) The greater the clustering coefficient, the larger the polarization effect.
(2) The greater the network density, the larger the polarization effect.
(3) A change in network density will cause a change in the average path length. The greater the network density and the shorter the average path length results are, the larger the polarization effect.

5. Comparison analysis of group polarization between different social network platforms

1) Network simulation of different platforms based on topic networks

To expand the scope of the study, we analyzed the similarities and differences in the effects of group polarization and information diffusion in different online topic networks. We first selected the typical case of "Fang Han incident" in 2012 as a study object and then collected data relevant to this case from RenRen and Sina Weibo, including event nodes, connections between nodes, each node's view on this event and other relevant data.

On the Renren platform, we searched the keyword "Han Fang" and obtained a popular blog with high numbers of views (116,232), shares (22,773) and comments (1039). Considering that the connection information about this user cannot be determined based on whether or not users have "read" or "forwarded" the information, we examined the comments to determine the connections between nodes, and we extract 165 nodes from top ranked comments by reading comments one by one to assess the relationships and emotions in the comments among these nodes. Following the data collection method for the Renren platform, we selected a popular blog from Sina Weibo's 63,251,307 microblogs on "Han vs. Fang" with high numbers of forwards (28,137) and comments (12,377), and we again extracted 165 nodes to determine the connections between these nodes.

By the adjusted model parameters, we construct two artificial topic networks respectively based on the two platforms, to obtain the graphs of group polarization effects, with which we compared the different effects of different social network platforms on group polarization regarding the same topic. Here, the same analysis method as above is used, as shown in Figure 4.16. We found that when the polarization ratio reaches 0.9, the time before polarization is 42 on Sina Weibo and 35 on Renren. Moreover, as shown in Figure 4.17, with the same time step, the polarization ratio of Sina Weibo is generally greater than that of Renren. The simulation results show that, if viewed from the effects of a particular topic, in the network structure of Sina Weibo is more conducive to the generation of group polarization. However, whether or not this conclusion is applicable to a real social network requires further study.

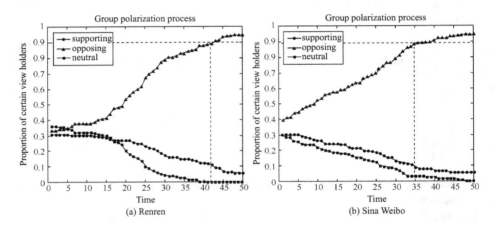

Figure 4.16: Comparison of group polarization times in Renren and Sina Weibo topic networks.

2) Network simulation based on different real network platforms

In this study, based on the relevant data about real networks in the reference (Fu et al., 2007; Jin Xin et al., 2012), the group polarization effects of different social network platforms are compared by adjusting the analog network parameters and simulating different real social network platforms described in the reference (see Figure 4.17).

Because of the large size of the real network data, we simplified the step 4 of network evolution (i.e., "the death of new links") in the model in order to improve the efficiency of the simulation. The real network simulation results based on Renren and Sina Weibo demonstrate that different online social network platforms can exert different group polarization effects. As Figure 4.18 shows, on the artificial network, the time before polarization for Sina Weibo is 36 when the group polarization ratio reaches 0.9; however, as time goes on, the proportion of users showing polarization

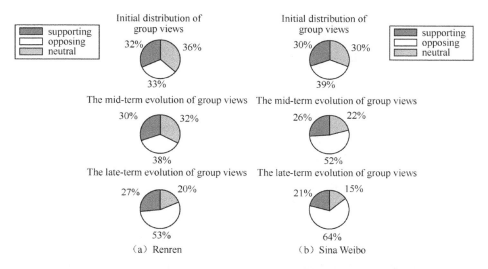

Figure 4.17: Comparison of group polarization ratios in Renren and Sina Weibo topic networks.

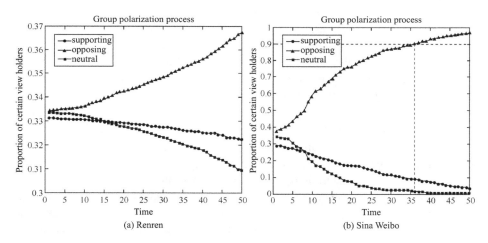

Figure 4.18: Comparison of group polarization time in Renren and Sina Weibo topic networks.

in Renren does not change substantially, with only an increase of 0.035 percentage points. Further, as Figure 4.19 shows, with the same time step, the polarization ratio of Sina Weibo is far greater than that of Renren, and the polarization phenomenon generally does not appear on the Renren platform. Hence, considering the overall network structure, we can conclude that it is difficult for group polarization to arise on the Renren platform, whereas the Sina Weibo network structure facilitates the spread and diffusion of information.

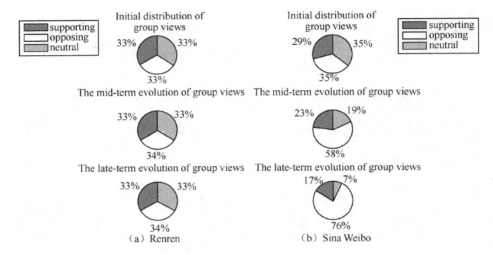

Figure 4.19: Comparison of group polarization ratios in Renren and Sina Weibo real networks.

3) Conclusion

This part of the study explores the impact of social network structure. We found that both clustering coefficient and network density have a positive effect on the formation of group polarization, while the average shortest path has a negative effect on it. These simulation results show that as far as the single-platform social network structure and groups are concerned, a compact and dense network structure fosters the formation of group polarization.

Regarding networks with intense communication, a social network platform based on instant messaging (such as the Fetion network in this study) engenders the most remarkable effect on information diffusion among the four categories of online interactive applications, and it is most conducive to the spread and diffusion of information. Regarding topic-based networks, microblog-type social network platforms (such as Sina Weibo in this study) and online social network platforms (such as Renren in this study) both show significant group polarization, with microblogging applications having the more significant effect. Overall, microblogging social network platforms (such as Sina Weibo in this study) show more significant group polarization, and online social network platforms (such as Renren in this study) generally show no polarization, due to the lack of topic guidance.

4.4 Summary

This chapter examined the mechanism of the two types of group behaviors, namely, collective intelligence and group polarization, to explain group aggregation and the mechanisms that influence it. With respect to group intelligence, we first described the specific concepts of group intelligence and the related theories, including self-determination theory. We then discussed the status quo of researches in this field from the perspectives of the conditions and factors that engender collective intelligence and group polarization, as well as analytical models that describe them. Finally, we concluded the results of our study, and elaborated on group polarization in the similar structure.

The evolution of human civilization was made possible by individuals acting in groups, with gathering in groups being the only feasible way to win wars. Because of the various mechanisms that influence group behavior, the organization and ideology of groups tend to be diversified. Although significant theoretical and practical achievements have been made in the research of group behavior, research concerning group intelligence and group polarization, especially those on the internet, is still a nascent field, allowing further investigation and development.

(1) The description of group intelligence is still considered to be in a "contending" state [59]. While most studies recognize the concept of "group intelligence," we cannot ignore some of the dialectical visions regarding this concept. For example, Charles Mackey scoffed at the idea that "a group knows everything;" he thought that group judgment was bound to be extreme. The global investment guru Bernard Baruch (Bernard Baruch, 1870–1965) even remarked that anybody considered as sensitive and rational become an idiot when they join a group. Group intelligence has a long history of development over human history. It is not the development of group intelligence that will inevitably lead to the development of a pluralistic society, however, the development of a pluralistic society promotes the development of group intelligence. However, most scholars now believe that a group is not merely a mob, rather, has its own mobilization, decisions, actions, and logic of risk aversion, which result in certain conditions that will generate group intelligence. As the ancient Chinese stated, "Three cobblers with their wits combined equal Zhuge Liang, the mastermind;" thus, perhaps group intelligence does exist, and can even play an increasingly important role in the future development of human society. For example, in studying the speakers and audiences of speech, Tinati et al. [60] demonstrated group intelligence in the application of "Online Citizen Science." Moreover, Diggle et al. [61] showed how group intelligence can help find a solution to the global scarcity of water. These are issues of great practical significance that are worth further exploration. In addition, our next research focus is the application of group intelligence to solve real-world problems.

(2) Regarding group polarization, if guided improperly, would undoubtedly have a negative impact on society, and the failure to take effective measures will lead to extreme behavior that can threaten the normal order. Although sufficient evidence demonstrates the prevalence of group polarization, the way polarization arises and its effects are still worth researching. For example, in a study of group polarization, Fishkin and Luskin found that group polarization did not arise in many groups even though they showed behavioral consistency. Similarly, not all groups polarize in the

same manner. Moreover, under certain conditions, strong group polarization can also have a very positive impact. For example, group polarization can consolidate a dominant ideology and prevent the social conflicts from breaking the "safety valve" (Song Jiageng, 2010). Companies may also be able to take advantage of group polarization in promoting their products and forming an invisible force. Other studies have showed that well-established groups are less likely to generate group polarization as the main purpose of these groups is to solve problems, and group members are well informed of the content of the probmes (Shi Bo, 2010). However, when a group is newly established or faced with new tasks, group polarization can have a more profound impact on the process of group decision making. In recent years, research on group polarization has continually progressed. For example, Muste Christopher et al. [62] redefined polarization as the differentiation and "culture war" of social groups. Further, Zhu et al. [63] studied the influence of polarization on the workshop decision making of businesses or companies. Clearly, how group polarization evolves, what effects it engenders, and how group polarization theory can be integrated with practical issues constitute the major research areas in the future.

References

[1]   Le Bon G: The crowd: A study of the popular mind. Macmillan, 1897.
[2]   McLuhan M: Understanding media: The extensions of man. MIT press, 1994.
[3]   McMillan DW, Chavis DM: Sense of community: A definition and theory. *J Community Psychol* 1986, 14:6–23.
[4]   Shaw ME: Group dynamics: The psychology of small group behavior. 1971.
[5]   Canuto MA, Yaeger J: The archaeology of communities: A new world perspective. Psychology Press, 2000.
[6]   Pears I: An instance of the fingerpost. Random House, 1998.
[7]   Wheeler WM: Ants collected in British Guiana by the expedition of the American Museum of Natural History during 1911. *Bull Am Museum Nat Hist* 1916, 35:1–14.
[8]   Durkheim E: Rules of sociological method. Simon and Schuster, 1982.
[9]   Schut MC: On model design for simulation of collective intelligence. *Inf Sci* 2010, 180:132–155.
[10]   Deci EL: Intrinsic motivation. New York: Plenum Publishing, 1975.
[11]   Surowiecki J: The wisdom of crowds. Random House LLC, 2005.
[12]   Hayes T, Malone MS: No size fits all: From mass marketing to mass handselling. Penguin, 2009.
[13]   Tapscott D, Williams AD: Wikinomics: How mass collaboration changes everything. Penguin, 2008.
[14]   Malone TW, Klein M: Harnessing collective intelligence to address global climate change. *Innovations* 2007, 2:15–26.
[15]   Sinan A, Walker D: Identifying influential and susceptible members of social networks. *Science* 2012, 337:337–341.
[16]   Simmel G: Sociological theory. 2008.
[17]   Lykourentzou I, Papadaki K, Vergados DJ, Polemi D, Loumos V: CorpWiki: A self-regulating wiki to promote corporate collective intelligence through expert peer matching. *Inf Sci* 2010, 180:18–38.
[18]   Hu WC: Deriving collective intelligence from reviews on the social Web using a supervised learning approach. *Exp Syst Appl* 2011, 38:13149–13157.

[19]   Seeley TD: The wisdom of the hive: The social physiology of honey bee colonies. Harvard University Press, 2009.

[20]   Page SE: The difference: How the power of diversity creates better groups, firms, schools, and societies (New Edition). Princeton University Press, 2008.

[21]   Stiles E, Cui X: Workings of collective intelligence within open source communities. Advances in Social Computing. Springer Berlin Heidelberg, 2010: 282–289.

[22]   De Liddo A, Buckingham SS: Cohere: A prototype for contested collective intelligence. 2010.

[23]   De Liddo A, Sándor Á, Buckingham SS: Contested collective intelligence: Rationale, technologies, and a human-machine annotation study. *Comput Support Comp W* 2012, 21:417–448.

[24]   Noelle-Neumann E: The spiral of silence: Public opinion–Our social skin. University of Chicago Press, 1993.

[25]   Mohamed AA, Wiebe FA: Toward a process theory of groupthink. *Small Gr Res* 1996, 27:416–430.

[26]   Cartwright D: The nature of group cohesiveness. *Group Dyn-Theor Res* 1968, 91:109.

[27]   Mullen B, Copper C: The relation between group cohesiveness and performance: An integration. *Psychol Bull* 1994, 115:210.

[28]   Liu H: The group decision in the menu. *Bus Rev* 2012, 4:106–108.

[29]   Hui W, Luo X: A study on the relationship between intellectual capital and different types os innovation. *East China Econ Manage* 2010, 1:109–114.

[30]   Harsanyi JC: Games with incomplete information played by "Bayesian" players, I-III part I. The basic model. *Manage Sci* 1967, 14:159–182.

[31]   Sun Y, Chen S: Bayesian method for forecast of stock. *J Guangdong Polytechnic Normal University* 2003, 4:78–80.

[32]   Bonabeau E, Dorigo M, Theraulaz G: Swarm intelligence: From natural to artificial systems. New York: Oxford University Press, 1999.

[33]   Dorigo M, Gambardella LM: Ant colony system: A cooperative learning approach to the traveling salesman problem. *IEEE T Evolut Comput* 1997, 1:53–66.

[34]   Wang Y, Li L, Hu Z: Swarm Intelligence Optimization Algorithm. *Comput Tech Dev* 2008, 18:114–117.

[35]   Kennedy JK, Eberhart RC: Swarm intelligence. Morgan Kaufmann, 2001.

[36]   Yang W, Li Q: Study of the variable load while estimating existing bridge structure. *Eng Sci* 2004, 6:87–94.

[37]   Eberhart RC, Hu X: Human tremor analysis using particle swarm optimization. Evolutionary Computation, 1999. CEC 99. Proceedings of the 1999 Congress on. IEEE, 1999, 3.

[38]   Stoner J, Finch A: A comparison of individual and group decisions involving risk. Massachusetts Institute of Technology, 1961.

[39]   Scharfstein DS, Stein JC: Herd behavior and investment. *Am Econ Rev* 1990, 465–479.

[40]   Bikhchandani S, Hirshleifer D, Welch I: A theory of fads, fashion, custom, and cultural change as informational cascades. *J Polit Econ* 1992, 992–1026.

[41]   Festinger L: A theory of social comparison processes. *Hum Relat* 1954, 7:117–140.

[42]   Mackie DM: Social identification effects in group polarization. *J Person Soc Psychol* 1986, 50:720.

[43]   Tajfel H. Experiments in intergroup discrimination. *Sci Am* 1970, 223:96–102.

[44]   Tajfel H, Billig MG, Bundy RP, Flament C: Social categorization and intergroup behaviour. *Eur J Soc Psychol* 1971, 1:149–178.

[45]   Van Swol LM: Extreme members and group polarization. *Soc Influence* 2009, 4:185–199.

[46]   Turner J, Brown RJ, Tajfel H: Social comparison and group interest in ingroup favouritism. *Eur J Soc Psychol* 1979, 9:187–204.

[47]   Cialdini RB: Influence: Science and practice. Boston, MA: Allyn and Bacon, 2001.

[48] Shi B: A study of the dynamic mechanism and coping strategies for group polarization of network public sentiment. *J Intell* 2010, 29:50–53.

[49] Xie X: Experiments of postulate of "Spiral of silence" on internet. *Mod Commun* 2004, 6:17–22.

[50] Sunstein CR: The law of group polarization. *J Polit Philos* 2002, 10:175–195.

[51] Morris CE, Tieu A, Dixon K: Seed coat dormancy in two species of Grevillea (Proteaceae). *Ann Botany* 2000, 86:771–775.

[52] Hong H, Kubik JD, Stein JC: Thy neighbor's portfolio: Word-of-mouth effects in the holdings and trades of money managers. *J Finance* 2005, 60:2801–2824.

[53] Yang S, Zhu K, Fu C, Lu G: Simulation of the group decision conformity based on cellular automata model. *Syst Eng Theory Pract* 2009, 9:115–124.

[54] Watts DJ, Dodds PS: Influentials, networks, and public opinion formation. *J Consum Res* 2007, 34:441–458.

[55] Kwak H, Lee C, Park H, Moon S: What is Twitter, a social network or a news media? In Proceedings of the 19th international conference on World wide web. ACM, 2010: 591–600.

[56] Zhang Y, Qi J, Fang B: Online public opinion risk warning based on Bayesian network modeling. *Lib Inf Serv* 2012, 56:76–81.

[57] Banerjee AV: A simple model of herd behavior. *Quart J Econ* 1992, 107:797–817.

[58] Chang M: Information cascade and coordination failure—A study of a theory based on network extemality. *J Beijing Tech Bus Univ* 2006, 21:93–99.

[59] Keen A: The Cult of the amateur: How blogs, MySpace, YouTube, and the rest of today's user-generated media are destroying our economy, our culture, and our values. Random House LLC, 2008.

[60] Tinati R, Simperl E, Luczak-Röesch M, Van Kleek M, Shadbolt N: Collective intelligence in citizen science–a study of performers and talkers. 2014.

[61] Diggle T: Water: How collective intelligence initiatives can address this challenge. *Foresight* 2013, 15:342–353.

[62] Muste CP: Reframing polarization: Social groups and "Culture Wars". *Polit Sci Polit* 2014, 47:432–442.

[63] Zhu DH: Group polarization on corporate boards: Theory and evidence on board decisions about acquisition premiums. *Strat Manage J* 2013, 34:800–822.

Index

https://doi.org/10.1515/9783110599411-005

www.ingramcontent.com/pod-product-compliance
Lightning Source LLC
Chambersburg PA
CBHW082118070326
40690CB00049B/3794